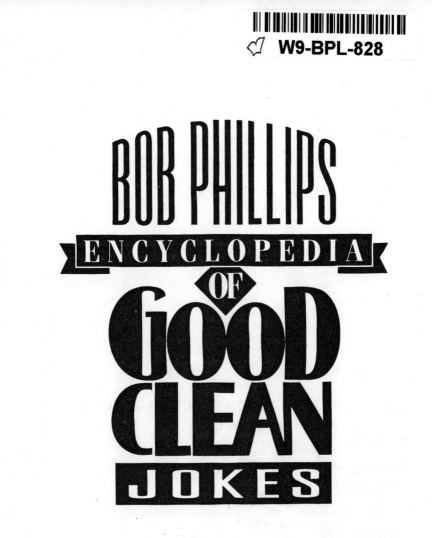

BOB PHILLIPS
ENCYCLOPEDIA
OF
GOOD
CLEAN
JOKES

HARVEST HOUSE PUBLISHERS
Eugene, Oregon 97402

BOB PHILLIPS' ENCYCLOPEDIA OF GOOD CLEAN JOKES

Copyright © 1992 Harvest House Publishers
Eugene, Oregon 97402

Library of Congress Cataloging-in-Publication Data

Phillips, Bob, 1940–
   [Encyclopedia of good clean jokes]
   Bob Phillips' encyclopedia of good clean jokes / Bob Phillips.
   ISBN 0-89081-947-5
   1. Wit and humor, American.   I. Title.
 PN6162.P457 1992
818'.5402—dc20   91-37782
                                                                              CIP

Printed in the United States of America.

                    00 01 02 03 04 05 / BC / 13 12 11 10 9

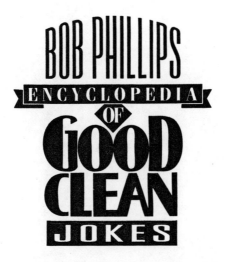

BOB PHILLIPS
ENCYCLOPEDIA
OF
GOOD
CLEAN
JOKES

───── ABOVE AVERAGE ─────

Wife: Scientists claim that the average person speaks 10,000 words a day.

Husband: Yes, dear, but remember, you are far above the average.

───── ABSENTMINDED ─────

I'm getting so absentminded that sometimes in the middle of a sentence I...

───── ABSURD ─────

Jack: Aren't some of the clothes women wear absurd?

Frank: Yes, and yet they look so appropriate on some of them.

───── ACCIDENT ─────

Policeman: How did this accident happen?

Motorist: My wife fell asleep in the backseat.

───── ACQUAINTANCE ─────

Jay: I understand you have a speaking acquaintance with her.

Bill: Merely a listening acquaintance.

───── ACTIVE ─────

Visitor: Pastor, how many of your members are active?

Pastor: They all are! Some are active for the Lord and the rest are active for the devil!

—————— ADAM AND EVE ——————

Q: What is that which Adam never saw or possessed, yet left two of for each of his children?
A: Parents.

Sunday school teacher: Can anyone tell me the story of Adam and Eve?
Little girl: First God created Adam. Then He looked at him and said, "I think I could do better if I tried again." So He created Eve.

"I found this dry leaf in this old Bible. Do you suppose it belonged to Adam and Eve?"

Q: How were Adam and Eve prevented from gambling?
A: Their paradise (pair-o-dice) was taken away from them.

Even Adam and Eve had their problems. One day Adam got angry.
"You've done it again, Eve," said Adam. "You put my shirt in the salad again."

Q: What nationality were Adam and Eve?
A: Soviet citizens, of course . . . nothing to wear, only an apple to eat, but living in paradise.

Adam and Eve had many advantages, but the principal one was that they escaped teething.

The only things Adam would recognize if he came back to earth are the jokes.

———————◆———————

Adam was rejected for Eden the apple.

———————◆———————

What a good thing Adam had. When he said something, he knew nobody had said it before.

———————◆———————

Adam may have had his troubles, but at least he didn't have to listen to Eve talking about the man she could have married.

———————◆———————

The first Adam-splitting gave us Eve, a force which ingenious men in all ages have never gotten under control.

———————◆———————

Eve was nigh Adam; Adam was naive.

———————◆———————

Eve: Adam, do you love me?
Adam: Who else?

———————◆———————

Conversation between Adam and Eve must have been difficult at times because they had nobody to talk about.

———————◆———————

Adam and Eve were the first bookkeepers; they invented the loose-leaf system.

———————◆———————

Adam and Eve lived thousands of years B.C.—before clothing.

———————◆———————

And here are Adam and Eve living together in paradise. You can tell it's paradise. Not once does Eve ask Adam to take out the garbage.

———◆———

You remember Eve, the first woman who ever said, "I haven't got a thing to wear" and meant it!

———◆———

Whatever other problems poor Adam may have faced, he at least never had to listen to Eve complain about other women having finer clothes than she.

———◆———

When Eve tried to get out of the Garden without him, Adam called up to the Commanding Officer, "Eve is absent without leaf!"

———◆———

The Bible begins with a man and a woman in a garden and it ends with the Revelation.

———◆———

Q: What is the first theatrical event the Bible mentions?
A: Eve's appearance for Adam's benefit.

———◆———

Q: Who was the fastest runner in the world?
A: Adam, because he was first in the human race.

———◆———

Q: What did Adam and Eve do when they were expelled from Eden?
A: They raised Cain.

———◆———

Q: At what time of day was Adam born?
A: A little before Eve.

———◆———

Q: Why had Eve no fear of the measels?
A: Because she'd Adam.

———◆———

Q: Why was Adam's first day the longest?
A: Because it had no Eve.

———————◆———————

Q: Who introduced the first walking stick?
A: Eve—when she presented Adam a little Cain.

———————◆———————

Q: Who was created first, Adam or Eve?
A: Eve. She was the first maid.

———————◆———————

When God performed the first marriage in the Garden of Eden, it was between Adam and Eve not Adam and Steve.

———————◆———————

The little rich girl came back from her first trip to Sunday school and told her mother, "Oh, Mummy! They read us the nicest story! All about a Mr. Adam and a Miss Eve and what a nice time they were having under an apple tree until a servant came along and disturbed them."

———————◆———————

Sam: My daddy has a sword of Washington and a hat of Lincoln.
Bill: My father has an Adam's apple.

———————◆———————

A Sunday school teacher asked Little Willie who the first man in the Bible was.
"Hoss," said Willie.
"Wrong," said the teacher. "It was Adam."
"Ah, shucks!" Willie replied. "I knew it was one of those Cartwrights."

———————◆———————

A Sunday school teacher asked her class to draw a picture illustrating a Bible story. One paper handed in contained a picture of a big car. An old man, with long whiskers flying in the breeze, was driving. A man and a woman were seated in the back of the car. Puzzled, the teacher asked little

Johnny to explain his drawing. "Why, that is God. He is driving Adam and Eve out of the Garden of Eden."

———◆———

The little girl reported at home what she had learned at Sunday school concerning the creation of Adam and Eve: "The teacher told us how God made the first man and the first woman. He made the man first. But the man was very lonely with nobody to talk to him. So God put the man to sleep. And while the man was asleep, God took out his brains and made a woman of them."

———◆———

Q: When was radio first mentioned in the Bible?
A: When the Lord took a rib from Adam and made a loudspeaker.

———◆———

Adam and Eve were naming the animals of the earth when along came a rhinoceros.
Adam: What shall we call this one?
Eve: Let's call it a rhinoceros.
Adam: Why?
Eve: Well, it looks more like a rhinoceros than anything we've named yet.

———◆———

Adam was created first—to give him a chance to say something.

——— ADOLESCENCE ———

The period in which the young suddenly feel a great responsibility about answering the telephone.

———◆———

A teenager who acts like a baby when you don't treat him like an adult.

——— ADVERTISING ———

Bill: Do you think your advertising has done any good?

Pete: Yes indeed. Why only the other day I advertised for a night watchman and that very night my store was robbed.

——— AFRICAN CHIEFTAIN ———

An African chieftain flew to the United States to visit the president. When he arrived at the airport a host of newsmen and television cameras met him. One of the reporters asked the chief if he had a comfortable flight.

The chief made a series of weird noises—"screech, scratch, honk, buzz, whistle, z-z-z-z-"—and then added in perfect English, "Yes, I had a very nice flight."

Another reporter asked, "Chief do you plan to visit the Washington Monument while you're in the area?"

The chief made the same noises—"screech, scratch, honk, buzz, whistle, z-z-z-z-z . . . yes, and I also plan to visit the White House and the Capitol Building."

"Where did you learn to speak such flawless English?" asked the next reporter. Again came the noises—"screech, scratch, honk, buzz, whistle, z-z-z-z-z," and the chief replied, "From the shortwave radio."

——— AGE ———

"Did you see how pleased Mrs. Smith looked when I told her she didn't look a day older than her daughter?"

"I didn't notice Mrs. Smith . . . I was too busy watching the expression on her daughter's face!"

In a hat shop a saleslady gushed: "That's the hat for you. It makes you look ten years younger."

"Then I don't want it," retorted the customer. "I certainly can't afford to put on ten years every time I take off my hat!"

———◆———

"I'm approaching the age of 30."
"From which direction?"

———◆———

When a woman tells you her age, it's all right to look surprised, but don't scowl.

Husband: Dear, do you remember John Williams? He was the student body president at our high school. I saw him today.

Wife: That was 35 years ago.

Husband: I know. In fact, he has gotten so bald and so fat he didn't even recognize me.

After a serious operation a lady was still in a coma. Her worried husband stood at the foot of her bed.

"Well," said the nurse reassuringly, "at least age is on her side."

"She's not so young," said the husband. "She's 45."

At this point the patient moved slightly, and quietly but firmly murmured, "Forty-four."

Clara: My husband says I look younger in this hat.

Sara: Oh, really? What is your age?

Clara: Thirty.

Sara: No, I mean without the hat!

You can tell how old you are by remembering when a family went for a Sunday drive and everyone got in the same car.

The best way to cure your wife of nervousness is to tell her it is caused by advancing age.

Several women appeared in court, each accusing the other of the trouble in the flat where they lived. The judge, with Solomon-like wisdom, called for orderly testimony. "I'll hear the oldest first," he decreed. The case closed for lack of evidence.

———— AGING ————

There are three ways to tell if you are getting old: first, a loss of memory; second...

———— AGNOSTIC ————

A person who says that he knows nothing about God, and when you agree with him, he becomes angry.

————◆————

Agnostic: If those Christians would stop building such large and fancy buildings and give the money to the poor, it would be more to their credit.
Christian: I've heard that remark before.
Agnostic: Indeed! And by whom, may I ask?
Christian: Judas Iscariot.

———— AIR-CONDITIONED ————

Why is it that a businessman will go from his air-conditioned house to his air-conditioned office in his air-conditioned car, then go to a health club and pay $50 an hour to sweat?

————◆————

"Our church should be air-conditioned," snapped Mrs. Smith. "It is unhealthy for people to sleep in a stuffy room."

———— AIRLINES ————

A good-sized man approached the airline ticket counter and asked for a reservation from Los Angeles to New York. The clerk knew that the plane was very full with baggage and passengers.

"How much do you weigh, sir?" asked the clerk.

"With or without clothes?" the passenger asked.

"Well," said the clerk, "how do you intend to travel?"

———◆———

Airline passenger to stewardess: I know this is the economy section, but showing the copilot's home movies is carrying it a bit too far.

———◆———

My airplane flight was so rough that the stewardesses poured the food directly into the sick sacks!

———◆———

He: Excuse me, stewardess. How high is this plane?

She: About 30,000 feet.

He: Oh, and how wide is it?

——— ALARM ———

An alarm clock is a small device used to wake up people who have no children.

——— ALLOWANCE ———

Son to father: About my allowance, Pop. It's fallen below the national average for teenagers.

———◆———

Bob: I want to marry your daughter.

Dad: How much money do you make?

Bob: Two hundred dollars a month.

Dad: Well, her allowance is $150 a month—and that'll make...

Bob: No, I've already figured that in.

——— AMATEURS ———

I have always been confused when I hear the phrase "professional women"—are there any amateurs?

——— AMEN ———

Little Billy knelt beside his bed and prayed, "Dear God, if You can find some way to put the vitamins in candy and ice cream instead of in spinach and cod liver oil, I would sure appreciate it. Amen."

We've been letting our six-year-old go to sleep listening to the radio, and I'm beginning to wonder if it's a good idea. Last night he said his prayers and wound up with, "And God bless Mommy and Daddy and Sister. Amen—and FM!"

The sermon went on and on and on in the heat of the church. At last the minister paused and asked, "What more, my friends, can I say?"
In the back of the church a voice offered earnestly, "Amen!"

——— AMERICAN ———

Immigration men are knowledgeable. They are pretty clever guys. This one fellow in particular has a little trick.
He asks: "What's your nationality?"
"American."
"American, huh? Do you know the words of 'The Star Spangled Banner'?"
"No, I don't."
"You're an American; go in."

——— ANCESTRY ———

The following conversation was overheard at a party attended by high society people:
"My ancestry goes all the way back to Alexander the Great," said one lady. She then turned to a second lady and said, "And how far does your family go back?"
"I don't know," was the reply. "All of our records were lost in the Flood."

———— ANGEL ————

Melba: The King of England struck one of my ancestors on the shoulder with the tip of his sword and made him a knight.

Pam: That's nothing! My grandfather was walking next to a new building when one of the carpenters dropped his hammer. It struck my grandfather on the head and made him an angel.

Did you hear about the dead angel? He died of harp failure.

A conscientious minister decided to get acquainted with a new family in his congregation and called on them one spring evening. After his knock on the door, a lilting voice from within called out, "Is that you, Angel?"

"No," replied the minister, "but I'm from the same department."

A girl whose father was a photographer was out fishing with her parents one afternoon when a sudden storm came up and there was a brilliant flash. "Look," she said, "the angels are taking pictures of us!"

———— ANGER ————

In our marriage we made a decision to never go to bed mad. We haven't had any sleep for three weeks.

Angry wife to husband: You can't even play a friendly little game of Rook . . . no, you always have to try to win.

A young girl who was writing a paper for school came to her father and asked, "Dad, what is the difference between anger and exasperation?"

The father replied, "It is mostly a matter of degree. Let me show you what I mean." With that the father went to the telephone and dialed a number at random. To the man who answered the phone, he said, "Hello, is Melvin there?" The man answered, "There is no one living here named Melvin. Why don't you learn to look up numbers before you dial them?"

"See," said the father to his daughter. "That man was not a bit happy with our call. He was probably very busy with something and we annoyed him. Now watch . . . " The father dialed the number again. "Hello, is Melvin there?" asked the father.

"Now look here!" came the heated reply. "You just called this number and I told you that there is no Melvin here! You've got a lot of nerve calling again!" The receiver slammed down hard.

The father turned to his daughter and said, "You see that was anger. Now I'll show you what exasperation means." He again dialed the same number, and when a violent voice roared, "Hello!" the father calmly said, "Hello, this is Melvin. Have there been any calls for me?"

——— ANSWER MAN ———

Q: What do you get if you cross a chicken with an elephant?
A: I don't know, but Colonel Sanders would have a lot of trouble trying to dip it into the batter.

———◆———

Q: If a man died in England who was born in China, reared in France, worked in South America, and married in Japan, what is he?
A: Dead.

———◆———

Q: Why did Humpty Dumpty have a great fall?
A: To make up for a terrible summer.

———◆———

Q: What's worse than a giraffe with a sore throat?
A: A hippopotamus with chapped lips.

———◆———

Q: A man who always remembers a woman's birthday but forgets her age is called what?
A: A smart man.

———◆———

Q: What is the best way to keep fish from smelling?
A: Cut off their noses.

———◆———

Q: What do you call a funeral where you smell your own flowers?
A: A wedding.

Q: What is the difference between the North Pole and the South Pole?
A: All the difference in the world.

Q: If a man crosses the ocean twice without taking a bath, what is he called?
A: A dirty double-crosser.

Q: What do you call a camel without a hump?
A: Humphrey.

Q: What do you get when you cross an elephant with a computer?
A: A 5,000 pound know-it-all!

Q: How do you make an elephant fly?
A: Well, first you take a grea-a-t big zipper...

Q: What is the difference between unlawful and illegal?
A: Illegal is a sick bird.

Q: What goes Ha, Ha, Ha, Ha, plop?
A: Someone who is laughing his head off.

Q: What do they call cabs lined up at the Dallas airport?
A: The yellow rows of taxis.

Q: What do they call six women with one luncheon check?
A: Chaos.

Q: What was the largest island before Australia was discovered?
A: Australia.

Q: What do you call a crazy man who lives at the mouth of the Amazon?
A: A Brazil nut.

Q: What is worse than raining cats and dogs?
A: Hailing taxis and buses.

Q: What is the difference between a rooster, Uncle Sam, and an old maid?
A: The rooster says, "Cock-a-doodle-doo"; Uncle Sam says, "Yankee-doodle-doo"; and an old maid says, "Any dude'll do."

Q: How many peas in a pint?
A: One.

Q: What kinds of animals can jump higher than the Statue of Liberty?
A: Any kind. The Statue of Liberty can't jump.

Q: Who was King Midas?
A: He was the Greek king who fixed chariot mufflers.

Q: Why did the priest giggle?
A: Mass hysteria.

———— ANTIDOTE ————

The medicine that kills dotes.

———— ANTIQUES ————

Being an antique dealer is a strange way to make a living. It's the only business where the grandparents buy something, the parents sell it, and the grandchildren buy it again.

———— ANTS ————

Teacher: Why were you so late for school?
Student: I had to say good-bye to my pets.
Teacher: But you were two hours late.
Student: I have a large ant farm.

———— APOSTLE PAUL ————

Q: When was the apostle Paul a baker?
A: When he went to Philippi.

———— APPLAUSE ————

Applause before a speech begins is *faith*.
Applause during a speech is *hope*.
Applause when the speech is over is *charity*.

———— ◆ ————

Friend: You received a tremendous ovation. In fact, they are still clapping. What did you say?
Speaker: I told them I would not go on with my speech until they quieted down.

———— APPLE ————

While visiting a friend who was in the hospital, I noticed several pretty nurses, each of whom was wearing a pin designed to look like an apple. I asked one nurse what the pin signified.

"Nothing," she said with a smile. "It's just to keep the doctors away."

——— **APRIL FOOL** ———

Joe: When were you born?
Moe: April 2.
Joe: I see. One day too late!

——— **APTITUDE TESTS** ———

An executive came home and slumped in his favorite chair with a discouraged look. His wife asked what was wrong.

"You know these aptitude tests we're giving at the office? Well, I took one today for fun. It's a good thing I own the company!"

——— **ARMAGEDDON** ———

Ad in newspaper:
ARMAGEDDON—THE EARTH'S LAST WAR—HOW AND WHERE IT WILL BE FOUGHT—At the First Baptist Church

——— **ARMY** ———

During an Army war game a commanding officer's jeep got stuck in the mud. The C.O. saw some men lounging nearby and asked them to help him get unstuck.

"Sorry, sir," said one of the loafers, "but we've been classified dead and the umpire said we couldn't contribute in any way."

The C.O. turned to his driver and said, "Go drag a couple of those dead bodies over here and throw them under the wheels to give us some traction."

Officer: Soldier, do you have change for a dollar?
Soldier: Sure, buddy.
Officer: That's no way to address an officer. Now, let's try that again. Soldier, do you have change for a dollar?
Soldier: No, sir!

——— ASTOUNDING ———

A man walking along the road saw an Indian lying with his ear to the ground. He went over and listened. The Indian said, "Large wheels, Ford pickup truck, green color, man driving with large police dog next to him, Colorado license plate and traveling about 75 miles per hour."

The man was astounded. "You mean you can tell all that just by listening with your ear to the ground?" he asked.

"Ear to the ground, nothing," said the Indian. "That truck just ran over me."

——— ATHEISM ———

Nobody talks so constantly about God as those who insist that there is no God.

An atheist is one point beyond the devil.

Some are atheists only in fair weather.

By night an atheist half believes in a God.

——— ATHEIST ———

How to wipe out an atheist: Serve him a meal and then ask him if he believes there is a cook.

Atheist: Do you honestly believe that Jonah spent three days and nights in the belly of a whale?
Preacher: I don't know, sir, but when I get to heaven I'll ask him.
Atheist: But suppose he isn't in heaven?
Preacher: Then you ask him!

One day a little girl was visiting Sunday school when her teacher asked her to which denomination her relatives belonged. "Is it Baptists, Lutherans, Presbyterians, Seventh-day Adventists, or Methodists?" asked the teacher.

The little girl replied, "I think they are six-day atheists."

An atheist is one who hopes the Lord will do nothing to disturb his disbelief.

—*Franklin P. Jones*

The chief fault with atheism is that it has no future.

An atheist is a man who has no invisible means of support.

Did you hear about the son of the atheists who asked his parents: "Do you think God knows we don't believe in Him?"

Atheists are really on the spot: They have to sing "Hmmmmmm bless America."

An atheist is a disbeliever who prefers to raise his children in a Christian community.

Sign on the tomb of an atheist: "Here lies an atheist, all dressed up and no place to go."

They have all sorts of new services today. Now they've got a dial-a-prayer service for atheists. You call a number and nobody answers.

Pity the poor atheist who feels grateful but has no one to thank.

———————◆———————

I once wanted to become an atheist but I gave up the idea. They have no holidays.

——— **ATTENDANCE** ———

"Does your husband attend church regularly?"
"Oh, yes. He hasn't missed an Easter Sunday since we were married."

——— **AUSTRALIA** ———

An American was knocked unconscious in a traffic accident in Australia. The ambulance took him to a local hospital. When he finally woke up he asked the nurse, "Was I brought here to die?"
"No," said the nurse, "you were brought in here yesterday."

B

——— **BABIES** ———

"I'm really worried."
"Why?"
"Well, my wife read *The Tale of Two Cities* and we had twins. Later she read *The Three Musketeers* and we had triplets. Now she is reading *Birth of a Nation*!"

——— **BABY** ———

An alimentary canal with a loud voice at one end and no responsibility at the other.

——— BACHELOR ———

Bachelor: One who's footloose and fiancee free.

——— BACHELOR GIRL ———

A girl who is still looking for a bachelor.

——— BACKSEAT ———

Wife: This traffic jam is terrible. What shall I do?
Husband: I don't know, but I'm sure if you climb into the backseat you can figure it out.

——— BACKSLIDING ———

A tramp knocked at a farmer's door and asked for some food.
"Are you a Christian?" asked the farmer.
"Of course," said the tramp. "Can't you tell? Just look at the knees of my pants. Don't they prove it?"
The farmer and his wife noticed the holes in the knees and promptly gave the man some food.
As the tramp turned to go the farmer asked, "By the way, what made those holes in the seat of your pants?"
"Backsliding," said the tramp.

——— BAD SITUATION ———

Talk about bad situations . . . just think about

- a screen door on a submarine
- a stowaway on a kamikaze plane
- a teenager who parks in a dark alley with his girl and his horn gets stuck
- a soup sandwich
- one who ejects from a helicopter
- a Hindu snake charmer with a deaf cobra

——— BALD ———

Ken: I find that split hair is a problem.

Bob: Yeah, you're right. Mine split about five years ago.

If a man is bald in front, he's a thinker. If he's bald in the back, he is a lover. If he's bald in front and back, he thinks he's a lover.

A bald man's retort: In the beginning God created all men bald; afterward he became ashamed of some and covered them up with hair.

What a wife said about her baldheaded husband: I love to run my fingers through his hair because I can make better time on the open road.

At a certain time of life a man's hair begins to grow inward. If it strikes gray matter it turns gray. If it doesn't strike anything it disappears.

——— BAPTISM ———

A Methodist and a Baptist were arguing the virtues of their baptisms. The Methodist said, "All right, if I take a man and lead him in the water to his ankles, is he baptized?"

"No," said the Baptist.

" 'Til just the top of his head is showing above the water, is he baptized?"

"No."

"All right, then," asserted the Methodist. "That's where we baptize them."

I don't mind going to a church service in a drive-in theater. But when they hold the baptisms in a car wash, that's going too far!

——— BAPTIST ———

Q: When you have 50 people, all of different opinions, what do you have?
A: A Baptist church.

"Baptist fellowship is heavenly."

"Yeah, heaven is the only place it will work."

———◆———

A Presbyterian minister was about to baptize a baby. Turning to the father, he inquired, "His name, please?"

"William Patrick Arthur Timothy John MacArthur."

The minister turned to his assistant and said, "A little more water, please."

———◆———

Several churches in the South decided to hold union services. The leader was a Baptist and proud of his denomination.

"How many Baptists are here?" he asked on the first night of the revival.

All except one little lady raised their hands.

"Lady, what are you?" asked the leader.

"I'm a Methodist," meekly replied the lady.

"Why are you a Methodist?" queried the leader.

"Well," replied the little old lady, "my grandparents were Methodists, my mother was a Methodist, and my late husband was a Methodist."

"Well," retorted the leader, "just supposing all your relatives had been morons, what would that have made you?"

"Oh, I see. A Baptist, I suppose," the lady replied meekly.

———◆———

Two men from the Far East were heard discussing the denominational difference between the Baptists, Methodists, and English Friends. One of them said to the other:

"They say these denominations have different beliefs. Just what is the difference between them?"

"Oh," said the other, "not much! Big washee, little washee, and no washee; that is all."

———◆———

Two ministers were discussing the question of how the Baptists originated.

First minister: That's easy. Anybody knows we Baptists got started with John the Baptist.

Second minister: You're wrong. The origin goes back a lot further than that. Don't you remember when Abraham and Lot were surveying the land of Canaan? They walked together for a long time, over the hills, across the streams, through the valleys. Then Abraham said to Lot, "All right, you go your way and I'll go mine." That's when the Baptist denomination got started.

——— BARBER ———

A brilliant conversationalist, who occasionally shaves and cuts hair.

"What happened to the other barber that used to be here?"

"Well, he is now in the home for the insane. His business was slow and one day he asked a customer if he wanted a shampoo and the customer said, 'No.' I guess that was the last straw. He took a razor and slashed the customer's throat. By the way, how about a shampoo today?"

"Sure, go ahead," said the customer.

Barber to a customer with a lot of grease on his hair: Do you want it cut or just an oil change?

Customer: Before you begin, I want you to know that I like the weather that we are having, I have no interest in baseball or football, I do not want to hear who won the prize fights, I am not interested in the latest newspaper scandals, and I don't want to discuss political issues. Now, go ahead with your work.

Barber: Okay. And if it won't offend you, sir, I will be able to do my work better and faster if you don't talk so much.

A man entered a barber shop and asked for a shave. After the shave, the barber said, "That will be ten cents, please."

"But," said the man, "your sign says $1.25 for a shave. How come only ten cents?"

The barber answered, "Once in awhile we get a guy that is all mouth and we only charge him a dime!"

I couldn't stand my boy's long hair any longer, so I dragged him to the barber shop with me and ordered, "Give him a crew cut." The barber did just that, and so help me, I found I'd been bringing up somebody else's son!

Did you hear about the rock and roll singer who wore a hearing aid for three years . . . then found out he only needed a haircut.

A man entered a barber shop and said, "I am tired of looking like everyone else! I want a change! Part my hair from ear to ear!"

"Are you sure?"

"Yes!" said the man.

The barber did as he was told and a satisfied customer left the shop.

Three hours passed and the man reentered the shop. "Put it back the way it was," he said.

"What's the matter?" said the barber. "Are you tired of being a nonconformist already?"

"No," he replied, "I'm tired of people whispering in my nose!"

A cute girl was giving a manicure to a man in the barber shop.

The man said, "How about a date later?"

She said, "I'm married."

"So call up your husband and tell him you're going to visit a girlfriend."

She said, "You tell him yourself—he's shaving you."

BASEBALL

Baseball is talked about a great deal in the Bible: . . . In the big inning . . . Eve stole first . . . Adam stole second . . . Gideon rattled the pitchers . . . Goliath was put out by David . . . Prodigal Son made a home run . . .

——— BEANS ———

They serve a balanced diet in the Army. Every bean weighs the same.

———◆———

Husband: Beans again!
Wife: I don't understand it. You liked beans on Monday, Tuesday, and Wednesday and now all of a sudden you don't like beans.

——— BEAUTY ———

"And when I was 16, the president of the United States presented me a beauty award."
"Really? I didn't think Lincoln bothered with that sort of thing!"

——— BEGGING ———

Housewife: Why should a big, strong man like you be out begging?
Beggar: Well, lady, it's the only profession I know in which the gentleman can address a beautiful woman like you without an introduction.

——— BEHAVIOR ———

The reason the way of the transgressor is hard is because it's so crowded.

——— BELCH ———

"Sir, how dare you belch before my wife!"
"Sorry, ol' pal. I didn't know it was her turn!"

——— BIBLE ———

Most people are bothered by those passages of Scripture they do not understand, but the passages that bother me are those I do understand.

—*Mark Twain*

———◆———

The Bible must be the Word of God to withstand such poor preaching through the years.

——— **BIBLE QUIZ** ———

Q: When were automobiles first mentioned in the Bible?
A: When Elijah went up on high.

Q: What simple affliction brought about the death of Samson?
A: Fallen arches.

Q: Who was the most successful physician in the Bible?
A: Job; he had the most patience (patients).

Q: Who was the best financier in the Bible?
A: Noah; he floated his stock while the whole world was in liquidation.

Q: Who was the straightest man in the Bible?
A: Joseph. Pharoah made a ruler out of him.

Q: Where is tennis mentioned in the Bible?
A: When Joseph served in Pharaoh's court.

Q: What animal took the most baggage into the ark?
A: The elephant. He took his trunk, while the fox and the rooster only took a brush and comb.

Q: What man in the Bible had no parents?
A: Joshua, the son of Nun.

Q: Who is the smallest man in the Bible?

A: Some people believe that it was Zacchaeus. Others believe it was Nehemiah (Ne-high-a-miah), or Bildad the Shuhite. But in reality it was Peter the disciple—he slept on his watch!

Q: When was baseball mentioned in the Bible?

A: When Rebecca walked to the well with the pitcher.

Q: Who is the first man mentioned in the Bible?

A: Chap 1.

Q: When was money first mentioned in the Bible?

A: When the dove brought the green back to the ark.

Ned: What instructions did Noah give his sons about fishing off the ark?

Fred: I don't know.

Ned: Go easy on the bait, boys. I only have two worms.

Joe: Was there any money on Noah's ark?

Moe: Yes, the duck took a bill, the frog took a green back, and the skunk took a scent.

Q: Why didn't they play cards on Noah's ark?

A: Because Noah sat on the deck.

Q: How did Jonah feel when the great fish swallowed him?

A: Down in the mouth.

Q: When is high financing first mentioned in the Bible?
A: When Pharoah's daughter took a little prophet (profit) from the bulrushes.

Q: When did Moses sleep with five people in one bed?
A: When he slept with his forefathers.

Teacher: Where was Solomon's temple?
Student: On the side of his head.

——— BIG JOHN ———

A very small, sickly looking man was hired as a bartender. The saloon owner gave him a word of warning: "Drop everything and run for your life if ever you hear that Big John is on his way to town."

The man worked several months without any problems. Then one day a cowhand rushed in shouting, "Big John is a-comin'," and knocked the small bartender on the floor in his hurry to get out. Before the bartender had a chance to recover, a giant of a man with a black bushy beard rode into the saloon, through the swinging doors, on the back of a buffalo, and using a rattlesnake for a whip. The man tore the doors off their hinges, knocked over tables, and flung the snake into the corner. He then took his massive fist and split the bar in half as he asked for a drink. The bartender nervously pushed a bottle at the man. He bit off the top of the bottle with his teeth and downed the contents in one gulp, and turned to leave. Seeing that he wasn't hurting anyone, the bartender asked the man if he would like another drink.

"I ain't got no time," the man roared. "Big John is a-comin' to town."

——— BIGAMY ———

The extreme penalty for bigamy is two mothers-in-law.

——— BILL ———

Virginia: When was your son born?

Beverly: In March. He came on the first of the month.
Virginia: Is that why you call him Bill?

———◆———

Wife: There is a man at the door who wants to see you about a bill you owe him. He wouldn't give his name.
Husband: What does he look like?
Wife: He looks like you had better pay him.

——— BIRD ———

"A little bird told me."
"It must have been a stool pigeon."

———◆———

A Californian was visiting his Texan cousin and while walking with the cousin across a barren section of land, saw a funny looking bird flop across the road in front of them. "What is it?" the Californian asked.
"It's a bird of paradise," replied his Texan cousin.
The Californian replied, "Long way from home, isn't he?"

——— BIRD LEGS ———

A young college student had stayed up all night studying for his zoology test the next day. As he entered the classroom, he saw ten stands with ten birds on them with a sack over each bird and only the legs showing. He sat right on the front row because he wanted to do the best job possible. The professor announced that the test would be to look at each of the birds' legs and give the common name, habitat, genus, species, etc.

The student looked at each of the birds' legs. They all looked the same to him. He began to get upset. He had stayed up all night studying and now had to identify birds by their legs. The more he thought about it the madder he got. Finally, he could stand it no longer. He went up to the professor's desk and said, "What a stupid test! How could anyone tell the difference between birds by looking at their legs?" With that the student threw his test on the professor's desk and walked to the door.

The professor was surprised. The class was so big that he didn't know every student's name, so as the student reached the door the professor called, "Mister, what's your name!"

The enraged student pulled up his pant legs and said, "You guess, buddy! You guess!"

─── BIRTH CONTROL ───

"Do you know what the best birth control method in the world is?"
"No."
"That's it."

─── BIRTHDAY ───

Husband to wife: How do you expect me to remember your birthday when you never look any older?

━━━━━━◆━━━━━━

Do not put any candles on my birthday cake—I don't want to make light of my age.

━━━━━━◆━━━━━━

Today is the fifth anniversary of my wife's thirty-ninth birthday.

─── BITTER ───

"I have a bitter taste in my mouth."
"Been biting your tongue?"

─── BLABBERMOUTH ───

Postlude—
    To guests he is the gracious host,
    To children three he is "the most,"
    To loving wife the perfect mate,
    To fellow workers he's "just great!"
    How *sad* then that a humble friend
    Upon his promise can't depend,
    From east to west, from north to south,
    His name? You guessed it! *Blabbermouth!*

─── BLAME ───

He wrecked his car, he lost his job, and yet throughout his life, he took his troubles like a man—he blamed them on his wife!

━━━━━━◆━━━━━━

To err is human; to blame it on the other guy is even more human

——— BLINDNESS ———

During church services an attractive young widow leaned too far over the balcony and fell, but her dress caught on a chandelier and held her suspended in midair. The minister, of course, immediately noticed the woman's predicament and called out to his congregation: "The first person who looks up there is in danger of being punished with blindness."

One old fellow in the congregation whispered to the man next to him, "I think I'll risk one eye."

——— BLONDE ———

"What happened to that dopey blonde your husband used to run around with?"

"I dyed my hair!"

——— BLUNDER ———

Mark Twain was once asked the difference between a mistake and a blunder. He explained it this way: "If you walk into a restaurant and walk out with someone's silk umbrella and leave your own cotton one, that is a mistake. But if you pick up someone's cotton umbrella and leave your own silk one, that's a blunder."

——— BOAST ———

Bob was very tired of his friend Ken, who was always name-dropping.

"If you're such a big shot, why don't you go over to the phone, call the White House, and get the president on the line?"

"Okay," said Ken. He punched in a number and in a few seconds someone answered the phone. Ken handed the phone to Bob.

"Hello, this is the president," said the familiar voice on the other end.

Bob thought it was a trick. "Okay, that was impressive," said Bob. "But if you are really such a hotshot, why don't you call Buckingham Palace and let me talk with the queen?"

Ken went back to the phone and punched in a number and handed the receiver to Bob.

"Hello," came a distinctive voice. "This is the queen of England speaking."

Bob was very impressed, but still very suspicious. "All right, you happen to know the president and the queen. But if you're really a big deal, you'll get the pope on the phone."

"I'll do better than that," said Ken. Ken took Bob to the airport and they boarded a plane to the Vatican. There Ken disappeared, leaving Bob to mill about with the crowd in St. Peter's Square.

Suddenly the crowd became silent. Bob followed everyone's gaze to the balcony, where Ken and the pope stood side by side.

Before Bob could recover from his amazement, a man standing beside him poked him in the ribs.

With a heavily accented voice the man asked, "Who's that up there on the balcony with Ken?"

——— BOOB TUBE ———

Joe: Did you know there are 60 million TV sets in our country and only 45 million bathtubs?

Moe: No, I didn't, but what does that prove?

Joe: Just that there are 15 million dirty people watching TV.

———◆———

When an old TV star's show was canceled by the powers that be, a fan asked him, "Do you answer personally the hundreds of letters that come in every day demanding that your program be renewed?" He answered disarmingly, "Goodness, no! I scarcely have time to write them!"

———◆———

Nowadays a good conversationalist is anyone who can talk louder than the hi-fi or TV.

———◆———

A lot of old TV programs are going off the air and new ones are replacing them. But how can you tell?

———◆———

The longest word in the English language is the one that follows, "And now a word from our sponsor."

——— BOOING ———

Two speakers were on the same program. One of them did an outstanding job of delivery. The other speaker was boring. The boring speaker was overheard saying, "Poor Dr. Wilson, he's having it pretty rough. He spoke before I did and he didn't go over at all. In fact, the crowd didn't like him—they booed and hissed the poor fellow right off the stage. He was so bad that right in the middle of my speech, they started booing him again!"

—— BOOKS ——

A bank robber held up a bank. "Give me all your money."
"Here, take the books, too. I'm short $10,000."

—— BORE ——

A person who has nothing to say and says it.

One who opens his mouth and puts his feats in.

A tired minister was at home resting. But through the window he saw a woman approaching his door. She was one of those too-talkative people and he was not anxious to talk with her. He said to his wife, "I'll just duck upstairs and wait until she goes away."

An hour passed. He tiptoed to the stair landing and listened. Not a sound. He was very pleased so he started down calling loudly to his wife, "Well, my dear, did you get rid of that old bore at last?"

The next moment he heard the voice of the same woman caller, and she couldn't possibly have missed hearing him. Two steps down, he saw them both staring up at him. It seemed truly a crisis moment.

The quick-thinking minister's wife answered, "Yes, dear, she went away over an hour ago. But Mrs. Jones has come to call in the meantime and I'm sure you'll be glad to greet her."

She: Whenever some bore at a party asks me what I do for a living, I say I'm a juggler with a circus.

He: And what do you do for a living?

She: I'm a juggler with a circus!

"Well, I must be going."

"Don't let me keep you if you really must be going," said his bored host.

"Yes, I really must go. But, really, I did enjoy our little visit. Do you know, when I came in here I had a headache but now I have lost it entirely."

"Oh, it isn't lost," was the patient reply. "I've got it now."

Young man: Yes, I know a great deal about baseball and football. I was also the captain of our basketball team. I drive race cars and motorcycles. I can swim and dance and I'm sure that you would have a great time going out on a date with me. I am a good conversationalist.

Young lady: Do you have a group photograph of yourself?

Bore: I shot this lion in Africa. It was a case of him or me.

Bored: Well, the lion certainly makes a better rug.

BORED

After a long, dry sermon, the minister announced that he wished to meet with the church board following the close of the service. The first man to arrive was a stranger.

"You misunderstood my announcement. This is a meeting of the board," said the minister.

"I know," said the man, "but if there is anyone here more bored than I am, I'd like to meet him."

BOSS

The one who is early when you are late and late when you are early.

The thing mother allows father to think that he is.

BOUQUETS

First Actor: What's the matter with the leading lady?

Second Actor: She only got nine bouquets of flowers tonight.

First Actor: Good heavens! Isn't that enough?
Second Actor: Nope, she paid for ten.

——— **BOWLING** ———

Did you hear the one about the ministers who formed a bowling team?
Called themselves the Holy Rollers.

——— **BOXING** ———

Boxing coach: You did a terrible job out there. If I were as big as you, I
would be heavyweight champion of the world.
Boxer: Why don't you become the lightweight champion?

——— **BOY MEETS FATHER** ———

"Young man," said the angry father from the head of the stairs, "didn't
I hear the clock strike four when you brought my daughter in?"

"You did," admitted the boyfriend. "It was going to strike eleven, but I
grabbed it and held the gong so it wouldn't disturb you."

The father muttered, "Doggone! Why didn't I think of that one in my
courting days!"

She: You finally asked Daddy for my hand in marriage. What did he
say?
He: Not a word. He just fell on my neck and sobbed.

———◆———

Father: Sue, what are you doing out there?
Sue: I'm looking at the moon.
Father: Well, tell the moon to go home. It's half-past eleven.

———◆———

Boy: I'd like to marry your daughter.
Father: Have you seen my wife yet?
Boy: I have ... but I prefer your daughter.

——— BOY MEETS GIRL ———

One girl to another: There's never a dull moment when you're out with Wilbur—it lasts the whole evening.

On a lonely, moonlit country road as the car engine coughed and the car came to a halt, the following conversation took place:
"That's funny," said the young man. "I wonder what that knocking was?"
"Well, I can tell you one thing for sure," the girl answered icily. "It wasn't opportunity."

A modest girl never pursues a man, nor does a mousetrap pursue a mouse.

Boy to girl: Filet mignon? It's pickled goat's liver. Why?

Boy: Please whisper those three little words that will make me walk on air.
Girl: Go hang yourself.

One of the unmarried girls who works in a busy office arrived early the other morning and began passing out cigars and candy, both tied with blue ribbons. When asked what the occasion was, she proudly displayed a diamond solitaire on her third finger, left hand, and announced, "It's a boy . . . six feet tall and 187 pounds."

Boy: I'm afraid we'll have to stop here; the engine's getting pretty warm.
Girl: You men are such hypocrites; you always say the engine.

She: You remind me of Don Juan.
He (flattered): Tell me just how.
She: Well, for one thing, he's been dead for years.

Girl: You remind me of an ocean.
Boy: You mean wild...restless...and romantic?
Girl: No, you just make me sick.

He: If you would give me your phone number I would give you a call.
She: It's in the book.
He: Good, what is your name?
She: It's in the book, too.

After a Dutch-treat-on-everything date, the girl responded to her escort who brought her home, "Since we've gone Dutch on everything else, you can just kiss yourself goodnight!"

"If you refuse to marry me I will die," said the young romantic. And, sure enough, 50 years later he died.

———◆———

Girl: Would you like to take a walk?
Boy: I'd love to.
Girl: Well, don't let me detain you.

———◆———

Conceited: I can tell just by looking into a girl's eyes exactly how she feels about me.
Girl: Gee, that must be embarrassing for you.

———◆———

Boy: You look prettier every minute. Do you know what that is a sign of?
Girl: Yes, you are about to run out of gas.

———◆———

"When I went out with Fred, I had to slap his face five times."
"Was he that fresh?"
"No! I thought he was dead!"

Girl: The man I marry must be brave as a lion, but not forward; handsome as Apollo, but not conceited; wise as Solomon, but meek as a lamb; a man who is kind to every woman, but loves only me.
Boy: How lucky we met!

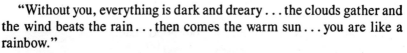

"Without you, everything is dark and dreary . . . the clouds gather and the wind beats the rain . . . then comes the warm sun . . . you are like a rainbow."
"Is this a proposal or a weather report?"

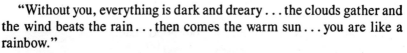

Joe: What's so unusual about your girlfriend?
Moe: She chews on her nails.
Joe: Lots of girls chew on their nails.
Moe: Toenails?

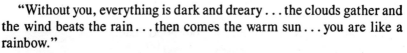

"Why does my sweetheart always close her eyes when I kiss her?"
"Look in the mirror and you'll know."

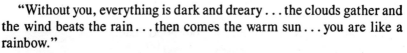

John: You must marry me . . . I love you, there can be no other . . .
Mary: But, John, I don't love you . . . you must find some other woman . . . some beautiful woman . . .
John: But I don't want a beautiful woman . . . I want you.

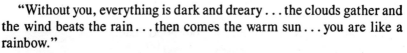

Boy: You know, sweetheart, since I met you, I can't eat . . . I can't sleep . . . I can't drink.
Girl: Why not?
Boy: I'm broke.

"My girlfriend takes advantage of me."
"What do you mean?"
"I invited her out to dinner and she asked me if she could bring a date!"

After a blind date a fellow said to his friend, "After I got home last night, I felt a lump in my throat."
"You really like her, huh?"
"No, she's a karate expert."

Boy: Will you marry me?
Girl: No, but I'll always admire your good taste.

"Do you have the book *Man, Master of Women*?" a young man asked the lady librarian.
"Fiction counter to your left," the librarian replied.

Boy (with one hand cupped over the other): If you can guess what I have in my hand, I'll take you out tonight.
Girl: An elephant!
Boy: Nope! But that's close enough. I'll pick you up at 7:30.

Boy: Ah, look at the cow and the calf rubbing noses in the pasture. That sight makes me want to do the same.
Girl: Well, go ahead . . . it's your cow.

Girl: Do you think you could be happy with a girl like me?
Boy: Perhaps, if she isn't too much like you.

"How come you go steady with Eloise?"
"She's different from other girls."

"How so?"
"She's the only girl who will go with me."

———————◆———————

He: Oh, my dear, how can I leave you?
She: By train, plane, or taxi!

———————◆———————

Boy: Gladys, do you love me?
Girl: Yeah.
Boy: Would you be willing to live on my income?
Girl: Yes, if you'll get another for yourself.

———————◆———————

Boy: Darling, I've lost all my money. I haven't a cent in the world.
Girl: That won't make any difference, dear. I'll love you just as much—
even if I never see you again.

———————◆———————

Girl: Do you love me?
Boy: Yes, dear.
Girl: Would you die for me?
Boy: No . . . mine is an undying love.

———————◆———————

John: Don't you think I'm rather good-looking?
Judy: In a way.
John: What kind of way?
Judy: Away off.

———————◆———————

Bill: That girl in the red dress isn't very smart.
Phil: I know. She hasn't paid any attention to me, either.

———————◆———————

Boy: What would I have to give you for one little kiss?
Girl: Chloroform!

———————◆———————

Harry: My girlfriend has a huge lower lip, but I don't mind.

Gary: You don't?
Harry: No, her upper lip covers it!

She: Look at my engagement ring.
Chi-Chi: That's a lovely ring. It's nice to know you're not marrying a spendthrift.

Boy: Boy, if I had a nickel for every girl I'd kissed...
Girl: You'd be able to buy a pack of gum!

———— BRAIN FOOD ————

Student: I hear that fish is brain food.
Roommate: Yeah, I eat it all the time.
Student: Well, there goes another theory.

———— BRAINS ————

Don: She's a bright girl...she has brains enough for two.
Art: Then she's just the girl for you.

"How long can a man live without brains?"
"I don't know. How old are you?"

———— BRAT ————

A child who acts like your own but belongs to someone else.

———— BREATH ————

"Oh, I can't catch my breath."
"With your breath you should be thankful!"

Husband: This report says that every time I breathe, three Chinese die!
Wife: That doesn't surprise me!

——— **BRICK** ———

Patient: My feet are always cold.
Doctor: Well, all you have to do is go to bed and have a brick at your feet.
Patient: I tried that.
Doctor: Did you get the brick hot?
Patient: Get it hot? It took me all night just to get it warm.

——— **BRIDAL** ———

A harness for a man.

——— **BRUSH YOUR TEETH** ———

Teacher: Why don't you brush your teeth? I can see what you had for breakfast this morning.
Student: What did I have?
Teacher: Eggs!
Student: You're wrong! That was yesterday!

——— **BULLETIN BOARD** ———

In front of church: "You are not too bad to come in. You are not too good to stay out."

——— **BUMS** ———

Two bums were discussing the reasons they became bums.
"I'm the fellow who never listened to anybody," said the first bum.
"Shake, partner," said the second bum. "I'm the man who followed everybody's advice."

——— **BURNT OFFERINGS** ———

Teacher: In our lesson today we have talked about the burnt offerings offered in the Old Testament. Why don't we have burnt offerings today?
Student: On account of air pollution.

——— **BUTCHER** ———

The customer wanted to buy a chicken and the butcher had only one in stock. He weighed it and said, "A beauty. That will be $1.25, lady."

"Oh, that's not quite large enough," said the customer. The butcher put the chicken back in the refrigerator, rolled it around on the ice several times, then put it back on the scales again.

"This one is $1.85," he said, adding his thumb for good weight.

"Oh, that's fine!" said the customer. "I'll take both of them."

—— C.P.N. ——

Myrlene: He's a C.P.N.
Sharon: You mean C.P.A: Certified Public Accountant.
Myrlene: No, C.P.N. Constant Pain in the Neck.

—— CAIN ——

Heckler: Who was Cain's wife?
Preacher: I respect any seeker of knowledge, but I want to warn you, young man, don't risk being lost to salvation by too much inquiring after other men's wives.

—— CAMEL'S BACK ——

Guest: What on earth do you put in your mattresses?
Innkeeper: The finest straw, sir.
Guest: Now I know where the straw that broke the camel's back came from.

—— CAMP LETTERS ——

Dear Mom and Dad,
    The camp director is making everyone write home.

Tammy
Camp Itchagooy
Hideaway Village, Washington

Dear Mr. and Mrs. Phillips:

Your daughter Lisa is having a terrific time at camp. Everyone on the staff thinks she is great. She is very popular with everyone in her cabin. We just wanted you to know how much we appreciate having her at Camp Itchagooy. You can be very proud of her.

Most sincerely,
David Ferriera
Director

R.E. Phillips
2972 East Willson Ave.
Willacke, Washington

Dear Mr. Ferriera:

My wife and I were very excited and pleased to learn that Lisa was having a fun time at camp. Being popular is very important. We are most proud of Lisa.

We have a daughter at Camp Itchagooy, too. Her name is Christy. It would be very nice of you to let us know how she is doing.

Warmly yours,
R.E. Phillips, Father

—— CANNIBAL ——

A cannibal chief had captured a man near his camp and said to the man, "What is your profession?" The man replied, "I was editor of my company paper." "Good," smiled the cannibal chief. "Tomorrow you will be editor-in-chief."

———◆———

A resourceful missionary fell into the hands of a band of cannibals. "Going to eat me, I take it," said the missionary. "You wouldn't like me." He took out his pocketknife, sliced a piece from the calf of his leg, and handed it to the chief. "Try it and see for yourself," he urged. The chief took one bite, grunted, and spat. The missionary remained on the island 50 years. He had a cork leg.

———— CAPTAIN ————

A young man made a great deal of money in real estate. He decided to buy himself a small yacht. He then bought the proper clothes and decked himself out in the regalia of a captain.

His first visitor on board his new yacht was his grandmother. He took her on a tour of the boat. In the process, the grandson pointed to his cap with crossed anchors on it and said, "This signifies that I am a captain."

The grandmother made no comment.

"You don't seem very impressed," said the young man.

"If you want me to be impressed, I'll be impressed," said his grandmother. "To yourself, you're a captain. To me, you're maybe a captain. But to captains, you're no captain."

———— CAR ————

Fifteen-year-old Fred: Dad, the Bible says that if you don't let me have the car, you hate me.

Dad: Where does it say that?

Son: Proverbs 13:24: He that spareth the 'rod hateth his son.

———— CAR SICKNESS ————

The feeling you get every month when the payment is due.

———— CAREER ————

Father pacing floor with a wailing baby in his arms as his wife lies snug in bed: Nobody ever asks me how I manage to combine marriage and a career.

———— CARP ————

Did you hear about the fellow who went carp fishing? As he was about to throw his first cast, his wallet fell out of his pocket into the lake. A carp grabbed the wallet and started to swim away with it. Suddenly, another carp ate the carp that had eaten the wallet. Then, yet another, even larger carp came along and swallowed the carp that ate the carp that devoured the wallet.

And that's how carp-to-carp walleting began.

——— CARPET LAYER ———

There's a story going the rounds that involves a carpet layer who had worked all day installing wall-to-wall carpeting. When he noticed a lump under the carpet in the middle of the living room, he felt his shirt pocket for his cigarettes—they were gone. He was not about to take up the carpet, so he went outside for a two-by-four. Tamping down the cigarettes with it would be easy. Once the lump was smoothed, the man gathered up his tools and carried them to the truck. Then two things happened simultaneously. He saw his cigarettes on the seat of the truck, and over his shoulder he heard the voice of the woman to whom the carpet belonged. "Have you seen anything of my parakeet?" she asked plaintively.

——— CAT ———

"Hello, police department? I've lost my cat and . . . "

"Sorry, sir, that's not a job for the police, we're too busy . . . "

"But you don't understand . . . this is a very intelligent cat. He's almost human. He can practically talk."

"Well, you'd better hang up, sir. He may be trying to phone you right now."

——— CAT FOOD ———

A butcher was waiting on one woman when a second woman ran into the shop. "Quick," the second woman said to the butcher, "give me a pound of cat food, will you?" Then she turned to the woman who had been ahead of her at the counter. "I hope you don't mind my butting in ahead of you," she said.

"No," said the first woman, "not if you're that hungry."

——— CEMETERY PLOT ———

"What did you give your wife for Christmas last year?"

"A cemetery plot!"

"What are you going to give her this year?"

"Nothing, she didn't use last year's gift!"

——— CHANDELIER ———

During a business meeting in a small mountain church, one of the deacons said, "Pastor, I think we need a chandelier for the church."

"No," replied another deacon. "I'm against it."

"Why don't you think we need a chandelier, brother deacon?" asked the pastor.

"Well, first, nobody in the church can spell it; second, nobody in the church can play it; and, third, what this church needs, above all else, is mo' light!"

——— CHICKEN ———

Q: Which came first, the chicken or the egg?

A: The chicken, of course, God couldn't lay an egg.

———◆———

Did you hear about the count who sold the king's crown? They tried and tried to make him confess but he would not. Finally, they said, "We will chop off your head if you don't tell us." He would not tell them so they took him to the chopping block. They told him that he would have one more chance but he did not take it. As the head chopper started down with the axe, the count said, "All right, I'll tell you." It was too late . . . his head went rolling to the ground.

Moral: Don't hatchet your counts before they chicken.

——— CHICKEN CHOW MEIN ———

"I was a kamikaze flier during the war," said a Japanese man who was named Chow Mein.

"How could that be? That was a suicide squad."

"Oh, they called me Chicken Chow Mein."

——— CHILDREN ———

"Darling," scolded the mother, "you shouldn't always keep everything for yourself. I have told you before that you should let your brother play with your toys half of the time."

"I've been doing it. I take the sled going downhill, and he takes it going up."

———◆———

An old Chinaman was eating too much rice, especially since he was too frail to work. Because the grandfather had become a burden, the father of the home, his son, determined to get rid of him. He put him in a wheelbarrow, then started up the mountain. The little eight-year-old grandson went along. He was full of questions. His father explained that the grandfather was old and useless and the only thing they could do was to take him up the mountain and leave him to die. Then the grandson had a bright idea. "I'm glad you brought me along, Father, because when you're old, I'll know where to take you."

Little Susan was mother's helper. She helped set the table when company was due for dinner. Presently everything was on, the guest came in, and everyone sat down. Then Mother noticed something missing. "Susan," she said, "You didn't put a knife and fork at Mr. Larson's place."

"I thought he wouldn't need them," explained Susan. "Daddy said he always eats like a horse."

Mother: Eat your spinach. Think of the thousands of starving children who would love some spinach like this.

Billy: Name two.

Mother: Suzie, what have you been doing this morning while I was working in the kitchen?

Suzie: I was playing postman.

Mother: How could you play postman when you don't have any letters?

Suzie: I was looking through your trunk in the garage and found a packet of letters tied with a nice ribbon, and I posted one in everyone's mailbox on the block.

CHILDREN OF ISRAEL

"Daddy, I want to ask you a question," said little Bobby after his first day in Sunday school.

"Yes, Bobby, what is it?"

"The teacher was reading the Bible to us—all about the children of Israel building the temple, the children of Israel crossing the Red Sea, the children of Israel making sacrifices. Didn't the grown-ups do anything?"

——— CHRISTMAS ———

I love Christmas. I receive a lot of wonderful presents I can't wait to exchange.

A famous writer once sent Christmas cards containing nothing but 25 letters of the alphabet. When some of his friends admitted that they had failed to understand his message, he pointed to the card and said, "Look! No L!"

There's nothing like the Christmas season to put a little bounce in your checks.

A little boy excited about his part in the Christmas play came home and said:
"I got a part in the Christmas play!"
"What part?" asked his mother.
"I'm one of the three wise guys!" was the reply.

——— CHURCH ———

I don't want to say it was a cold church, but the ushers were using ice skates.

"If absence makes the heart grow fonder," said a minister, "a lot of folks must love our church."

We have had no additions to our church but we had some blessed subtractions.

"Why don't you come to my church this next Sunday?"
"Because I belong to another abomination."

A member of the church came to the pastor and said, "Pastor, my six brethren are all asleep, and I alone have remained awake to worship God."

The pastor replied, "You had better been asleep yourself if your worship of God consists of accusations against your brethren."

A certain congregation was about to erect a new church edifice. The building committee, in consecutive meetings, passed the fellowship resolutions:
   1. We shall build a new church.
   2. The new building is to be located on the site of the old one.
   3. The material in the old building is to be used in the new one.
   4. We shall continue to use the old building until the new one is completed.

A church is a place where you encounter nodding acquaintances.

On one corner of a very small town were three churches, all of different denominations. One Sunday morning a passerby heard the first church singing, "Will There Be Any Stars in My Crown?" The next church was singing, "No, Not One." And the third church was singing, "Oh, That Will Be Glory for Me."

Church member: I don't know what we will do when you are gone, pastor.
Pastor: Oh, the church will soon get a better man than I am.
Church member: That's what they always say, but they keep getting worse and worse.

A church is a place where you encounter nodding acquaintances.

Pastor: Mrs. Smith, I really appreciate your devotion. You are present at all services.
Mrs. Smith: Yes, it is such a relief after a long, hard week of work. I just love to come to church, sit down on the soft cushions, and not think about anything for an hour.

A visiting pastor at a country church asked one of the farmers if he could use his barn to get away where it was quiet and study for his message. After several hours of study, the pastor left the barn for a walk. When he came back he discovered that the cow had eaten all of his sermon notes. The next day the farmer complained to the pastor that his cow had gone dry.

Deacon Johnson seemed to always fall asleep during the sermon on Sunday morning. His wife grew very tired of his behavior and she decided to deal with the embarrassing situation. The next Sunday when her husband fell asleep, she quietly removed some Limburger cheese from her purse and carefully passed it beneath his nose. Whereupon Deacon Johnson was heard to murmur, "No, Helen, no —don't kiss me now."

A millionaire who'd been bad all of his life was nearing the end of his time on earth and wanted to wipe the slate clean. To make amends for his evil ways, he donated a lot of money to a local church and had a meeting with the minister to discuss the possibility of getting into heaven.

Since the man had spent most of his life being evil, the minister couldn't really assure him he'd get into heaven, but he didn't want to disappoint the man and lose a big donation. Being diplomatic, the minister sized up the millionaire's chances like this:

"Mr. Jones, when it comes to riding on the heavenly railroad, think of yourself as a standby passenger."

A misprint in the church bulletin read: Our minister is leaving the church this Sunday. Will you please send in a small donation? The congregation wants to give him a little momentum.

Pastor: Yes, I know Mrs. Martin. She has been a corpse in our church for over 30 years.

A man had been shopping around for a church home when he stopped in one church just in time to hear the pastor say, "We have left undone those things which we ought to have done and we have done those things which we ought not to have done."

The man dropped into a pew and sighed with relief, "I've found my crowd at last."

A businessman happened to be staying in a hotel where a group of ministers was holding a conference. The next morning was very cold and as the businessman approached the dining room, he noticed the ministers gathered around a blazing log fire in the dining area. He was freezing and tried to get close to the fire but the ministers blocked the way. The businessman sat for a few minutes shivering in the cold. Suddenly he shouted, "Last night I dreamed I was in hell."

"Really?" said one of the ministers. "What was it like?"

The businessman replied, "Not much different than right here. I couldn't get near the fire for all the ministers were in the way.

I spoke in one church that was so small that when I took a bow I hit my head on the back pew.

The chief trouble with the church is that you and I are in it.

Wife: Did you see that hat Mrs. Jones wore to church?
Husband: No.
Wife: Did you see the new dress Mrs. Smith had on?
Husband: No!
Wife: A lot of good it does you to go to church!

You can always tell a church that isn't doing well. The Cadillac they raffle off is used.

58

A church is an organization supported by the husbands of its members.

———◆———

Some go to church to take a walk;
Some go there to laugh and talk;
Some go there to meet a friend;
Some go there their time to spend;
Some go there to meet a lover;
Some go there a fault to cover;
Some go there for speculation;
Some go there for observation;
Some go there to doze and nod;
The wise go there to worship.

———◆———

One Sunday as a farmer was getting in his hay crop his minister stopped by. The pastor asked the farmer if he had been to church. "To tell the truth, I would rather sit on the hay load and think about the church than sit in the church and think about hay."

———◆———

An usher went up to a man with his hat on in church and asked him to remove it. "Thank goodness," said the man. "I thought that would do it. I've attended this church for months, and you are the first person who has spoken to me."

———◆———

Jack: Do you know Pete Wilson?
Mack: I sure do. We slept in the same church pew for over 15 years.

——— CHURCH ATTENDERS ———

Dictionary of Church Attenders:
Pillars—worship regularly, giving time and money.
Leaners—use the church for funerals, baptisms, and marriages.
Specials—help and give occasionally for something that appeals to them.

Annuals—dress up for Easter and come for Christmas programs.

Sponges—take all blessing and benefits, even the sacraments, but never give out anything themselves.

Scrappers—take offense and criticize.

———◆———

Some church members who say "Our Father" on Sunday go around the rest of the week acting like orphans.

———◆———

Every church has, in addition to the brakeman, a construction and wrecking crew. To which do you belong? One of them for sure.

———◆———

Every church has three classes of members: the workers, the jerkers, and the shirkers.

———◆———

There are four classes of church members: the tired, the retired, the tiresome, and the tireless.

———◆———

It seems that some church members have been starched and ironed, but too few have been washed.

——— **CHURCH BULLETIN BOARDS** ———

Come in and have your faith lifted.

———◆———

Come in and let us prepare you for your finals.

———◆———

A miser is a rich pauper.

———◆———

Ask about our pray-as-you-go plan.

———————◆———————

We hold sit-in demonstrations every Sunday.

———————◆———————

No matter how much you nurse a grudge, it won't get better.

———————◆———————

Start living to beat hell.

———————◆———————

If some people lived up to their ideals, they would be stooping.

———————◆———————

Everything you always wanted to know about heaven and hell but were afraid to ask.

———————◆———————

Pray up in advance.

———————◆———————

Patience is the ability to stand something as long as it happens to the other fellow.

——— **CHURCH MEMBERS** ———

First Man: Are the members of your church united?
Second Man: Yes.
First Man: Praise the Lord for that.
Second Man: I don't know about that. They're united because they are all frozen together.

Man: Pastor, how many active members do you have?
Minister: They're all active. Half of them are working with me and half are working against me.

——— CHURCH SERVICE ———

Pastor: Isn't this a beautiful church? Here is a plaque for the men who died in the service.

Man: Which one? . . . morning or evening?

——— CHURCHGOER ———

Q: What do you call a non-churchgoer?
A: A Seventh-Day Absentist.

——— CIGARS ———

A defendant in a lawsuit involving a large sum of money was talking to his lawyer.

"If I lose the case, I'll be ruined," he said.

"It's in the judge's hands now," said the lawyer.

"Would it help if I sent the judge a box of cigars?"

"Oh, no," said the lawyer. "This judge is a stickler for ethical behavior. A stunt like that would prejudice him against you. He might even hold you in contempt of court. In fact, you shouldn't even smile at the judge."

Within the course of time, the judge rendered a decision in favor of the defendant.

As the defendant left the courthouse with his lawyer, he said, "Thanks for the tip about the cigars. It worked."

"I'm sure we would have lost the case if you had sent them."

"But I did send them."

"You did?"

"Yes. That is how we won the case."

"I don't understand," said the lawyer.

"It's easy. I sent the cigars to the judge, but enclosed my opponent's business card."

——— CIVIL SERVANT ———

Q: What is the difference between a chess player and a civil servant?
A: A chess player moves every now and then.

——— CLEAVER ———

Did you hear about the inventor who came up with a knife that would slice two loaves of bread at the same time? He sold it to a large bakery. He then developed a knife that could slice three loaves of bread at the same time. He sold that idea, too.

Finally, the ultimate. He made a huge knife that could cut four loaves of bread at the same time! And so was born the world's first four-loaf cleaver.

——— CLERGY ———

Two men named Richard Hanson lived near each other in the same community. One was a minister and the other was a businessman. The minister passed away at about the same time as the businessman went on a trip to Florida.

When the businessman arrived in Florida he sent a telegram to his wife informing her of his safe arrival. Unfortunately, the message was delivered in error to the wife of the recently deceased minister.

The telegram read, "ARRIVED SAFELY; HEAT HERE TERRIFIC."

(The following is a story that can be told about a clergyman or friend.)
One day I had a dream about my friend _____.
I dreamed that he died and went to heaven. But in the dream the way to heaven was to climb a ladder. And as anyone climbed the ladder he was supposed to take a piece of chalk and make a mark on each rung for each sin he had committed.

As I looked in my dream, I saw _____ coming down the ladder. I asked him what he was doing. He said he was coming down for more chalk.

Clergyman: someone who still preaches against modern dress even though there's not enough left to talk about.

An airliner flew into a violent thunderstorm and was soon swaying and bumping around the sky. One very nervous lady happened to be sitting next to a clergyman and turned to him for comfort.

"Can't you do something?" she demanded forcefully.

"I'm sorry, ma'am," said the reverend gently. "I'm in sales, not management."

——— **CLOVERLEAF** ———

California's state flower.

——— **COACH** ———

During the review of the football plays before a big game, one of the star running backs spent most of the time reading a comic book. The coach noticed but didn't say anything about it.

It was a very exciting and important game, but the coach made the running back sit on the bench until the last quarter. When the last quarter started the coach said to the running back, "Warm up!"

After a series of warm-up moves, the running back said, "I'm ready, coach."

The coach reached into his coat pocket and pulled out a comic book. "Here," he said. "Sit over there at the end of the bench and read it."

——— **COLD** ———

"I have a cold or something in my head."
"I bet it's a cold."

——— **COLD CASH** ———

A woman's husband asked her what she wanted for her birthday the next week. She thought for a moment, then said, "This year I want cold, hard cash for a change."

The following day her husband filled her request. He put $20 in nickels, dimes, and quarters into a quart jar, then filled it with water. On her birthday he handed his wife a solidly frozen bottle of change from the freezer.

——— **COLD CUTS** ———

"You're only as old as you think."
"In that case you must be about three months old."

———◆———

Of course I'm listening to you; don't you see me yawning?

I think you're the greatest, but then again, what do I know?

"Some boys think I'm pretty and some think I'm ugly. What do you think?"
"A bit of both."

The only reason we invited him here tonight is to remind you that every 60 seconds mental illness strikes!

You know, if brains were dynamite, he wouldn't have enough to blow his nose!

His breath was so bad that his dentist had to work on his teeth through his ear.

She's a rag, a bone, and a hank of hair—and he's a brag, a groan, and a tank of air.

—— COLLEGE ——

Father: My son just received his B.A.
Neighbor: I suppose now he'll be looking for a Ph.D.
Father: No, now he's looking for a J.O.B.

Letter from son at school:

Dear Dad,
    Gue$$ what I need mo$t. That'$ right. $end it $oon.
                    Be$t Wi$he$
                    Jay

Reply:

Dear Jay,

NOthing ever happens here. We kNOw you like school. Write aNOther letter soon. Mom was asking about you at NOon.

NOw I have to say good-bye.

Dad

———————◆———————

Professor to students: If you get this information in your brain, you will have it in a nutshell.

———————◆———————

Professor: Give me three collective nouns.
Student: Flypaper, wastebasket, and vacuum cleaner.

——— **COLLEGE CHEER** ———

Money from home.

———————◆———————

Two editors of local newspapers did not get along and used their newspapers to do battle.

"The editor of the *Daily Express* is mean enough to steal the swill from a blind hog," wrote the editor of the *Daily Post*.

The next day the following appeared in the *Daily Express*:

"The editor of the *Daily Post* knows that we never stole his swill."

——— **COMEDIAN** ———

A person who has a good memory for old jokes.

——— **COMMERCIAL** ———

A minister asked a little girl what she thought of her first church service.

"The music was nice," she said, "but the commercial was too long."

—— COMMITTEE ——

A committee is a group of the unprepared, appointed by the unwilling, to do the unnecessary.

—— COMMUTERS ——

Two elderly women on a commuter train got into an argument about the window: One insisted that it had to be open or she would suffocate; the other demanded that it be closed so she would not catch a cold. The conductor was asked to settle the noisy dispute.

A commuter nearby called to the conductor, "Open the window first, and let one of them catch cold and die. Then close it and let the other one suffocate."

—— CONCENTRATE ——

Member: Pastor, how did you get that cut on your face?

Pastor: I was thinking about my sermon this morning and wasn't concentrating on what I was doing, and I cut myself while shaving.

Member: That's too bad! Next time you had better concentrate on your shaving and cut your sermon!

—— CONCLUSION ——

The troops were being taught to jump from a plane.

"What if my parachute doesn't open?" asked one rookie.

"That," said the instructor, "is known as jumping to a conclusion."

—— CONSCIENCE ——

Mark Twain used to tell the story of how he once stole a watermelon from a cart when the owner was not looking. He carried the melon to a secret spot, sat down, and was just about to bite into the melon when he realized that he should not do that. It just wasn't right.

So, he got up, took the watermelon back, replaced it on the cart, and took a ripe one.

—— CONTEMPT ——

A famous trial lawyer was asked to apologize to the court for some remarks he had made. With dignity, he bowed to the judge and said, "Your

Honor is right, and I am wrong, as Your Honor generally is."

The judge never figured out whether he should be satisfied with this remark or cite the lawyer for contempt of court.

——— COOK ———

Bride: The two best things I cook are meatloaf and apple dumplings.
Groom: Well, which is this?

——— COUGH ———

People who cough incessantly never seem to go to a doctor—they go to banquets, concerts, and church.

——— COUNTESS ———

A newspaper columnist was found guilty and fined for calling a countess a cow. When the trial ended and the man paid his fine, he asked the judge if, since it was now clear he could not call a countess a cow, he could call a cow a countess.

The judge said that that was all right to do. Whereupon the newspaperman turned toward the countess in the courtroom, bowed elaborately, and said, "How do you do, Countess."

——— COW ———

A man's car stalled on a country road. When he got out to fix it, a cow came along and stopped beside him. "Your trouble is probably in the carburetor," said the cow.

Startled, the man jumped back and ran down the road until he met the farmer. He told the farmer his story.

"Was it a large red cow with a brown spot over the right eye?" asked the farmer.

"Yes, yes," the man replied.

"Oh! I wouldn't listen to Bessie," said the farmer. "She doesn't know anything about cars."

——— CRAZY, MAN, CRAZY ———

Today more and more hippies are looking to religion for the answer to their problems. Last Sunday, a hippie went to church and was so overwhelmed by the sermon he grabbed the preacher's hand when he left the church and said, "Dad, I read you; that sermon was the most; it was gone; you were right on." The preacher said, "I'm afraid I don't understand." The hippie said, "Yes, you do, dad. In fact, I liked it so gone, I put 20 samolas in the collection plate." The preacher said, "Oh, crazy, man, crazy!"

——— CREEP ———

He's the kind of guy who can really creep into your heart and mind. In fact, you'll never meet a bigger creep!

——— CRITICIZE ———

When the family returned from Sunday morning service, father criticized the sermon, daughter thought the choir's singing was off-key, and mother found fault with the organist's playing. The subject had to be dropped when the small boy of the family said, "But it was a good show for a nickel, don't you think, Dad?

——— CUFF LINKS ———

For my birthday my wife gave me three sets of cuff links. The only trouble is that I do not have shirts with French cuffs. So I had to have my wrists pierced.

——— CUPID ———

Cupid's dart hurt more coming out than going in.

——— CURRENCY ———

A substance which isn't current enough.

——— CUTIE PIE ———

One afternoon the boss' wife met him at the office. As they were going down the elevator, it stopped, and a luscious blonde secretary got on, poked the boss in the ribs, and said, "Hello, cutie pie."

The wife, without blinking, leaned over and said, "I'm Mrs. Pie."

——— CZECHOSLOVAKIAN MIDGET ———

A Czechoslovakian midget was running through the side streets, trying to escape the secret police. At last he came to a small cafe and rapped on the door.

"I know it's late," he said to the astonished proprietor. "But do you suppose you could cache a small Czech?"

––––––– **DANIEL WEBSTER** –––––––

Daniel Webster was once bested by one of the farmers of his native state. He had been hunting at some distance from his inn, and rather than make the long trip back, he approached a farmhouse some considerable time after dark and pounded on the door. An upstairs window was raised and the farmer, with head thrust out, called, "What do you want?"

"I want to spend the night here," said Webster.

"All right. Stay there," said the farmer. Down went the window.

––––––– **DATSUN** –––––––

Unable to find a replacement cog for his car engine, a Datsun owner was told that he would have to go to Japan to get one.

He didn't want to make the trip for so little, so he decided to buy six-dozen cogs, bring them back to America, and sell them to help pay for the flight.

On the flight back, there was engine trouble and to save fuel the pilot gave orders to jettison all baggage. This meant that the cogs had to go also.

On the ground below, an elderly couple looked up at the sky. They saw all the baggage falling from the plane.

"Look, Sarah," said the old man. "It's raining Datsun cogs."

––––––– **DEACON** –––––––

A Baptist deacon had advertised a cow for sale.

"How much are you asking for it?" inquired a prospective purchaser.

"A hundred and fifty dollars," said the advertiser.

"And how much milk does she give?"

"Four gallons a day," he replied.

"But how do I know that she will actually give that amount?" asked the purchaser.

"Oh, you can trust me," reassured the advertiser. "I'm a Baptist deacon."

"I'll buy it," replied the other. "I'll take the cow home and bring you back the money later. You can trust me; I'm a Presbyterian elder."

When the deacon arrived home he asked his wife, "What is a Presbyterian elder?"

"Oh," she explained, "a Presbyterian elder is about the same as a Baptist deacon."

"Oh, dear," groaned the deacon, "I have just lost my cow!"

◆

Pastor: Say, deacon, a mule died out in front of the church.

Deacon: Well, it's the job of you ministers to look after the dead. Why tell me?

Pastor: You're right; it is my job. But we always notify the next of kin.

DEADBEAT

A doctor spotted a deadbeat patient while he was out to dinner. He called the patient aside and reminded him that he owed $250 for the work done more than two years earlier. He insisted that the man pay up. To the doctor's astonishment, the patient pulled a checkbook from his pocket and wrote a check to the doctor for the full amount.

Skeptical about the man's good faith, the doctor went directly to the bank the next morning and presented the check for payment. The teller handed back the check with the explanation that the patient's account was $25 short of the amount of the check. The doctor smiled, stepped back to the customer desk for a few minutes, came back to the teller, deposited $35 to the account of his former patient, and then again presented the $250 check. He walked out with a net gain of $215.

DEAL

A farmer and his wife went to a fair. The farmer was fascinated by the airplane rides, but he balked at the $10 tickets.

"Let's make a deal," said the pilot. "If you and your wife can ride without making a single sound, I won't charge you anything. Otherwise you pay the $10."

"Good deal!" said the farmer.

So they went for a ride. When they got back the pilot said, "If I hadn't been there, I never would have believed it. You never made a sound!"

"It wasn't easy, either," said the farmer. "I almost yelled when my wife fell out."

——— DEGREES ———

A girl at Bennington named Louise
Weighed down with Ph.D.'s and D.D.'s
Collapsed from the strain.
Said her doctor, "It's plain
You are killing yourself—by degrees."

——— DEMOCRATS ———

The rumor was started that the Democrats were against religion and for atheism. In fact, they might even destroy the Bible.

An old lady, wondering how the Scriptures could be preserved in such an event, called on a Democrat friend in her town and asked him to hide her Bible.

After scoffing at the idea that Democrats would suppress and destroy all the Bibles, the Democrat asked the old lady why she wanted him to hide her Bible.

"Because," she said, "they'll never think of looking for a Bible in the house of a Democrat."

——— DENOMINATOR ———

Son: Dad, will you help me find the least common denominator in this problem?

Dad: Good heavens, son, don't tell me that hasn't been found. They were looking for it when I was a kid.

——— DENTIST ———

Dentist: Good grief! You've got the biggest cavity I've ever seen—the biggest cavity I've ever seen.

Patient: You don't have to repeat it, doc!

Dentist: I didn't—that was the echo.

——— DEVILED HAM ———

Q: Where was deviled ham mentioned in the Bible?
A: When the evil spirits entered the swine.

——— DIAMOND RING ———

Mr. Smith bought a beautiful diamond ring for his wife and at lunch showed it to his friend Mr. Jones. Jones offered to buy it for more than Smith had paid. Smith later regretted the sale and bought it back from Jones at a still higher price, but Jones again bought it back from Smith at a much higher price. Finally Jones sold the ring to a person unknown to Smith.

When Smith heard of this final transaction he protested. "How could you do such a stupid thing!" he said. "That was crazy. We were both making such a good living from that ring!"

——— DIET ———

You know it is time for a diet when:
You dive into a swimming pool so your friends can go surfing.
You have to apply your makeup with a paint roller.
Weight Watchers demands your resignation.
You step on a penny weight scale that gives you your fortune and it says, "One at a time, please!"
Your face is so full that you look like you're wearing horn-rimmed contact lenses.
The bus driver asks you to sit on the other side because he wants to make a turn without flipping over.
You're at school in the classroom and turn around and erase the entire blackboard.
They throw puffed rice at your wedding.
You get a hiccup while in your bathing suit . . . and it looks like someone adjusting a venetian blind.
You fall down and try to get up, rocking yourself to sleep in the process.
A shipbuilder wants to use you as a model.
You step on a penny weight scale that gives you your fortune and it says, "You are very fond of food. You lack willpower and you overdo everything. Either that or a baby elephant has just collapsed on this scale."

——— DIETER'S PSALM ———

My weight is my shepherd;
I shall not want low calorie foods.
It maketh me to munch on potato chips and bean dip;
It leadeth me into 31 Flavors;
It restoreth my soul food;
It leadeth me in the paths of cream puffs in bakeries.
Yea, though I waddle through the valley of weight watchers,
I will fear no skimmed milk;
For my appetite is with me;
My Hostess Twinkies and Ding Dongs they comfort me;
They anointeth my body with calories;
My scale tippeth over!
Surely chubbiness and contentment shall follow me
All the days of my life.
And I shall dwell in the house of Marie Callender Pies . . . forever!

——— DIFFERENCE ———

Teacher: What's the difference between a porpoise and a dolphin?
Student: That's what I say. What's the difference?

——— DISAGREE ———

Wife: I'm afraid the mountain air would disagree with me.
Husband: My dear, it wouldn't care.

——— DISCUSSION ———

Angry wife to husband: No! Every time we discuss something sensibly, I lose!

——— DISHES ———

Wife: Would you help me with the dishes?
Husband: That isn't a man's job.
Wife: The Bible suggests that it is.
Husband: Where does it say that?
Wife: In 2 Kings 21:13 it says, " I will wipe Jerusalem as a man wipeth a dish, wiping it, and turning it upside down."

—— DIVORCE ——

"Have you ever thought about divorcing your wife?"
"Divorce? . . . No. Murder? . . . Yes!"

—— DOCTOR ——

Dr. Hanson: So the operation on the man was just in the nick of time?
Dr. Poure: Yes, in another 24 hours he would have recovered.

A lady with a pain in her side went to see a doctor. He told her she had appendicitis and must have an operation. She decided to get another doctor's opinion. The second doctor told her she had heart trouble. "I'm going back to the first doctor," she replied. "I'd rather have appendicitis."

A doctor was called in to see a very busy patient. "Well, sir, what's the matter?" he asked cheerfully.
"That's for you to find out," the patient snapped.
"I see," said the doctor. "Well, if you'll excuse me a minute, I'll phone a friend of mine—a veterinarian. He's the only man I know who can make a diagnosis without asking questions."

Nurse: Doctor, there's a man in the waiting room who claims he's invisible.
Doctor: Tell him I can't see him.

My doctor is an eye, ear, nose, throat, and wallet specialist.

Did you hear about the man who complained that every time he put on his hat he heard music? The doctor fixed him up. He removed the hat band.

My husband, a marriage counselor, often refuses to accompany me to parties and get-togethers. He says that so many people spoil his evening by asking him for advice. One day I saw my doctor and I asked him if this happened to him also. He told me that it happened to him all the time. I then asked him how he got rid of those people.

"I have a wonderful remedy," the doctor grinned. "When someone begins to tell me his ailments, I stop him with one word: 'Undress.' "

———◆———

My wife was very sick so we called Dr. Griffin. He gave her some medicine and she got worse. I then called Dr. Kurth and he gave her some more medicine and she still got worse. I thought she was going to die, so I called Dr. Cross and he was too busy, and finally my wife got well.

———◆———

My doctor is a very generous man. He gave me four months to live. When I told him that I didn't think I would be able to pay his bill before I died, he gave me another six months.

———◆———

Patient: Doc, am I getting better?
Doctor: I don't know—let me feel your purse.

———◆———

One day a well-to-do society lady visited a mental hospital. As she was walking around, a distinguished-looking man offered his services as a guide on her tour.

In the course of several hours of careful inspection, the society lady became impressed by the knowledge and intelligence of her guide. She was pleased by his gentle manners and obvious good breeding. In taking her leave she thanked him and expressed her belief that the hospital was in good hands.

"Oh, but I am not a hospital official," the man said. "I am a patient." He then told her how he had been unjustly committed by greedy members of his family who only had designs on his personal fortune. His detailed and reasonable account of the conspiracy touched the society woman's heart. She thought that it was a terrible wrong for the man to have been committed. She promised to get help and go to a judge to correct whatever injustice had been done. The kindly man thanked her for her warm kindness.

As she turned to go down the steps, she received a vigorous kick in the bottom. This caused her to stumble and nearly fall down the entire flight of stairs.

Gasping and in shock, she turned toward the man and demanded, "Why did you do that? I might have been seriously hurt."

The patient smiled gently. "I didn't want to hurt you. I did that so you would not forget to tell the judge about my case."

Patient: Every night when I get into bed I think that someone is under my bed. I then get up and look. There is never anyone there. When I crawl under the bed and lie down, I get the idea that there is someone on top of the bed. I then get up and look and I never find anyone on top of the bed. This goes on all night, up and down, up and down; it's driving me out of my mind. Do you think you can help?

Psychiatrist: I think I can. All you have to do is visit me twice a week for the next two years and I think I can cure you. The visits will cost $75 an hour.

Patient: That is an awful lot of money for a working man like me. I'll have to talk it over with my wife and let you know.

The next week the patient phoned the psychiatrist.

Patient: I won't be back, doc. My wife solved the problem. She cut the legs off the bed.

Patient: Doctor, I've got trouble with my throat.

Doctor: Go in the other room and disrobe. I'll be there in a minute.

Patient: But, doctor, it's just my throat!

Doctor: Get in the other room and disrobe and I'll examine you.

So the man went in and disrobed. As he was sitting there in his shorts, he looked around. Next to him was another guy sitting there in his shorts also, with a big package in his hands.

Patient: Can you imagine that doctor! I've got trouble with my throat and he tells me to disrobe!

Other man: What are you complaining about? I only came in here to deliver a package.

———— DONKEY ————

One day some soldiers from a nearby Army camp saw a boy leading a donkey. They thought they would have some fun with him.

"Say, boy," called out one of the soldiers. "You sure are keeping a tight rein on your brother, aren't you?"

"I sure am," said the boy. "If I didn't he would probably join the Army."

———— DREAM HOUSE ————

We've just moved into our dream house. It costs twice as much as we ever dreamed it would.

———— DRIVE-IN CONFESSIONAL ————

Have you heard of the new drive-in confessional? It is called "Toot and Tell!"

———— DRIVING ————

A man who was driving an auto with his wife in the backseat stalled his car on a railroad track. A train was coming down the track. His wife screamed, "Go on! Go on!"

The husband responded, "You've been driving all day from the backseat. I've got my end across the track. See what you can do with your end."

———————◆———————

If I were honest, there are a number of red lights that I have driven through. But on the other hand, I've stopped at a lot of green lights that I've never gotten credit for.

———— DRUGGIST ————

So this druggist is filling a prescription, hands his customer a little bottle with 12 pills in it, and says, "That'll be $4.50." Suddenly the phone rings and as the druggist turns to answer it, the customer puts 50 cents on the counter, walks out. The druggist turns back, spots the 50 cents and yells: "Sir! Sir! That's $4.50 not 50 cents. Sir!" The guy is gone. The druggist picks up the half a buck, looks at it, shrugs, flips it into the till, and mumbles: "Oh, well, 40 cents profit is better than nothing."

——— **DULL** ———

It is always dullest just before the yawn.

——— **DUMB** ———

I didn't say he was dumb . . . I said he was 20 years old before he could wave good-bye.

———◆———

Hokum: What do you mean by telling everyone I am deaf and dumb?
Yokum: That's not true. I never said you were deaf.

——— **DUNLAP'S DISEASE** ———

"He is suffering from Dunlap's disease."
"What is Dunlap's disease?"
"His stomach done-laps over his belt!"

——— **DUST** ———

On the way home from church a little boy asked his mother, "Is it true, Mommy, that we are made of dust?"
"Yes, darling."
"And do we go back to dust again when we die?"
"Yes, dear."
"Well, Mommy, when I said my prayers last night and looked under the bed, I found someone who is either coming or going."

E

——— **EASEL** ———

An artist decided to buy a new easel. He wasn't too sure what type to get. At the art shop they offered him two, a big one and a small one. He pondered for a while and finally decided on the lesser of two easels.

———— ECCENTRICS ————

Wife: Everyone is talking about the Carlsons' quarrel. Some people are taking his side and others are taking her side.

Husband: And I suppose a few eccentrics are minding their own business.

———— EDITOR ————

A person employed on a newspaper, whose business is to separate the wheat from the chaff—and see that the chaff is printed.

———— EGYPT ————

Gary: A man just sold me the Nile River.

Larry: Egypt you.

———— ELECTRIC BLANKET ————

Husband: How do you want the electric blanket tonight, dear . . . rare, medium, or well done?

———— ELEPHANT ————

Christy: What's the difference between an elephant and a matterbaby?

Mark: What's a matterbaby?

Christy: Nothing. I didn't know you cared.

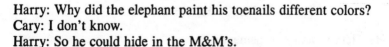

Harry: Why did the elephant paint his toenails different colors?

Cary: I don't know.

Harry: So he could hide in the M&M's.

———————◆———————

One day a large elephant saw a turtle near a pond. The elephant lumbered over and squashed the turtle under its large foot.

A jackal who saw the murder ran over to the elephant and said, "Why did you do that?"

The elephant replied, "This is the same turtle that bit off the tip of my trunk 17 years ago, when I went to get a drink out of the river."

The jackal's eyes widened. "The same one? You must have an incredible memory!"

Raising its head proudly, the elephant said, "Turtle recall."

——— **ELEPHANT EAR SANDWICH** ———

Customer: Your sign says, "$50 to anyone who orders something we can't furnish." I would like to have an elephant ear sandwich.

Waiter: Ohhh... we're going to have to pay you the $50.

Customer: No elephant ears, huh?

Waiter: Oh, we've got lots of them... but we're all out of those big buns!

——— **EMBARRASS** ———

Two girls boarded a crowded bus and one of them whispered to the other, "Watch me embarrass a man into giving me his seat."

Pushing her way through the crowd, she turned all her charms upon a gentleman who looked like he might embarrass easily. "My dear Mr. Wilson," she gushed, "fancy meeting you on the bus. Am I glad to see you. Why, you're almost a stranger. My, but I'm tired."

The sedate gentleman looked up at the girl. He had never seen her before but he rose and said pleasantly, "Sit down, Mary, my girl. It isn't often I see you on washday. No wonder you're tired. Being pregnant isn't easy. By the way, don't deliver the wash until Thursday. My wife is going to the District Attorney's office to see whether she can get your husband out of jail."

——— **ENGAGEMENT RING** ———

He: Here is your engagement ring.

She: But this diamond has a flaw in it.

He: You shouldn't notice that—we are in love and love is blind.

She: Not stone blind.

——— **EPISTLE** ———

Sunday school teacher: What are Epistles?

Student: I guess they are the wives of the Apostles.

——— ETHICS ———

Son: Dad, what is ethics?
Dad: Well, son, you know that your uncle and I are in business together. Suppose a customer comes in and buys something worth $10 but by mistake gives me a $20 bill and leaves without waiting for his change. If I split the extra $10 with your uncle, that's ethics.

——— EVERYDAY FACE ———

The popular preacher, Charles Spurgeon, was admonishing a class of divinity students on the importance of making the facial expressions harmonize with the speech in delivering sermons. "When you speak of heaven," he said, "let your face light up and be irradiated with a heavenly gleam. Let your eyes shine with reflected glory. And when you speak of hell . . . well, then your everyday face will do."

——— EXCUSES ———

Jones came into the office an hour late for the third time in one week and found the boss waiting for him. "What's the story this time, Jones?" he asked sarcastically. "Let's hear a good excuse for a change."

Jones sighed, "Everything went wrong this morning, boss. The wife decided to drive me to the station. She got ready in ten minutes, but then the drawbridge got stuck. Rather than let you down, I swam across the river (look, my suit's still damp), ran out to the airport, got a ride on Mr. Thompson's helicopter, landed on top of Radio City Music Hall, and was carried here piggyback by one of the Rockettes."

"You'll have to do better than that, Jones," said the boss, obviously disappointed. "No woman can be ready in ten minutes."

One day an employee arrived late with one eye closed, his left arm in a sling, and his clothes in tatters. "It's 9:30," pointed out the president, "and you were due at 8:30." The employee explained, "I fell out of a tenth-story window." The president snorted, "It took you a whole hour?"

In order to take care of all the excuses for not attending church, the following information was placed in a local newspaper.

1. Beds will be placed in the fellowship hall for those who say, "Sunday is my only day to rest."
2. Eye drops will be available for those with tired eyes from watching TV too late on Saturday night.
3. Steel helmets will be provided for those who say, "The roof would cave in if I ever went to church."
4. Blankets will be furnished for those who think that church is too cold and air-conditioning for those who say that it is too hot.
5. We will reserve the front pews for those who like the pastor's sermons and the back pews with earplugs for those who dislike his sermons.
6. Scorecards will be available for those who list the hypocrites present.
7. TV dinners will be available for those who can't go to church and cook the noon meal for the family.
8. We will have a selection of trees and shrubs for those who like to see God in nature.

––––––– EYE –––––––

Policeman: I'm looking for a man with one eye named Carnell.
Bystander: What's his other eye called?

––––––– EYE CHART –––––––

"Simply read the letters on that chart," ordered the draft board doctor.
"I don't see any chart," answered the draftee happily.
"You're absolutely right," snapped the doctor. "There isn't any chart. You're 1-A."

––––––– FAINTED –––––––

A man rose from his seat in a crowded bus so a lady standing nearby could sit down. She was so surprised she fainted.

When she revived and sat down, she said, "Thanks." Then he fainted.

——— FAMILY ———

The average American family consists of 4.1 persons. You have one guess as to who constitutes the .1 person.

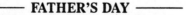

I have been told that insanity is hereditary. Parents get it from their children.

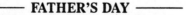

A young mother asked her husband to take the two-year-old for a walk. The husband was busy working on a project, but with a deep sigh (the kind that let his wife know he was not pleased), he grabbed the baby carriage and began walking around the block in the hot sun.

"Honey," shouted the young mother from the second-story window.

"Leave me alone!" he called back. "We're all right."

An hour later his wife once again pleaded, "Honey."

"Well, what do you want?" he replied in a gruff way. "Is there anything wrong in the house?"

"No, honey," replied his wife. "But you've been wheeling little Suzie's doll all afternoon. Isn't it time for the baby to have a turn?"

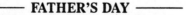

Father calling to his daughter as her date waits: Dreamboat! Your barnacle is here!

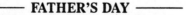

I think there is insanity in my family. They keep asking me for money.

——— FATHER'S DAY ———

First wife: How would you describe Father's Day?

Second wife: Just like Mother's Day . . . only you don't spend as much money.

FICTIONAL

Note from writer to editor: The characters in this novel are entirely too fictional and have no resemblance to any person living or dead.

Note from editor to writer: That's what is wrong with them.

FINGERS

My wife bawled me out for eating with my fingers. But I've always said that if food isn't clean enough to pick up with your fingers, it isn't fit to eat.

———◆———

Sister: Is it good manners to eat chicken with your fingers?

Brother: No, you should eat your fingers separately.

FIRST HUSBAND

The grief-stricken man threw himself across the grave and cried bitterly, "My life, how senseless it is! How worthless is everything about me because you are gone. If only you hadn't died, if only fate had not been so cruel as to take you from this world, how different everything would have been."

A clergyman happened by and to soothe the man he offered a prayer. Afterward he said, "I assume the person lying beneath this mound of earth was someone of importance to you."

"Importance? Indeed it was," moaned the man. "It's my wife's first husband!"

FIT FOR A PIG

Customer: This food isn't fit for a pig!

Waiter: I'm sorry, sir. I'll bring you some that is.

FLIRTING

Peggy: I caught my boyfriend flirting.

Sharon: Yes, that's the way I caught mine, too.

——— FLYSWATTER ———

Little Billy was left to fix lunch. When his mother returned with a friend, she noticed that Billy had already strained the tea.

"Did you find the tea strainer?" his mother asked.

"No mother, I couldn't, so I used the flyswatter," replied Billy.

His mother nearly fainted, so Billy hastily added, "Don't get excited, Mother. I used an old one."

——— FOOL ———

Rev. Henry Ward Beecher received a letter with one word written on it. It said, "Fool." The next Sunday he read the letter from the pulpit and said, "I have received many letters from people who have forgotten to sign their names, but this is the first time I've received a letter from someone who signed his name but forgot to write the letter."

——— FOREMAN ———

The news that Bill had lost his job got around quickly, and a friend asked, "Why did the foreman fire you?"

"You know that a foreman is . . ." Bill shrugged, "the one who stands around and watches the other men work."

"What's that got to do with it?" his friend wanted to know.

"Well, he just got jealous of me," Bill explained. "Everyone thought I was the foreman."

——— FORGETFUL ———

"George is so forgetful," the sales manager complained to his secretary. "It's a wonder he can sell anything. I asked him to pick me up some sandwiches on his way back from lunch, and I'm not sure he'll even remember to come back."

Just then the door flew open, and in bounced George. "You'll never guess what happened!" he shouted. "While I was at lunch, I met old man Brown, who hasn't bought anything from us for five years. Well, we got to talking and he gave me this half-million dollar order!"

"See," sighed the sales manager to his secretary, "I told you he'd forget the sandwiches."

G

——— GAMBLING ———

The trouble with hitting the jackpot on a slot machine is that it takes so long to put the money back in the machine.

◆

The story is told of a corporal who reported to a new regiment with a letter from his old captain, saying, "This man is a great soldier, and he'll be even better if you can cure him of his constant gambling."

The new C.O. looked at him sternly and said, "I hear you're an inveterate gambler. I don't approve. It's bad for discipline. What kind of things do you bet on?"

"Practically anything, sir," said the corporal. "If you'd like, I'll bet you my next month's pay that you've got a strawberry birthmark under your right arm."

The C.O. snapped, "Put down your money." He then stripped to the waist, proved conclusively he had no birthmark, and pocketed the bills on the table. He couldn't wait to phone the captain and exult, "That corporal of yours won't be in a hurry to make a bet after what I just did to him."

"Don't be too sure," said the captain mournfully. "He just wagered me 20 to 200 he'd get you to take your shirt off five minutes after he reported."

——— GARAGE SALE ———

A garage sale is a technique for distributing all the junk in your garage among all the other garages in the neighborhood.

——— GARDEN TOOLS ———

Wife to husband: Look, Ralph, the first garden tools are peeping their heads above the snow.

——— GAS ———

"Hello! Is this the City Gas Works?"

"No, this is the Mayor's office."

"Well, I didn't miss it very far, did I?"

——— GAS SAVER ———

I have been having some trouble with the new car I bought. I added a carburetor that saved 30 percent on gas, a timer that saved 50 percent on gas, and spark plugs that saved 30 percent on gas. I drove 10 miles and the gas tank overflowed.

——— GASOLINE ———

A boy and a girl were out driving one evening. They came to a quiet spot on a country lane, and the car stopped. "Out of gas," said the boy.

The girl opened her purse and pulled out a bottle.

"Wow!" said the boy. "A bottle... what is it?"

"Gasoline," said the girl.

——— GENERATION ———

Little girl: Mother, you know that vase you said had been handed down from generation to generation?

Mother: Yes.

Little girl: Well, this generation just dropped it.

——— GIFTS ———

First girl: Weren't you kind of nervous when your boyfriend gave you all those beautiful gifts?

Second girl: No. I just kept calm and collected.

——— GLACIER ———

"Dear me," said the old lady on a visit to the mountains, "look at all those rocks. Where did they all come from?"

"The glaciers brought them down," said the guide.

"But where are the glaciers?"

"The glaciers," said the guide with a weary voice, "have gone back for more rocks."

——— GLARE ———

Matt: Did you see that conductor? He glared at me as if I hadn't paid my fare.

Pat: And what did you do?

Matt: I glared right back as if I had.

——— GLASSES ———

The proprietor of a highly successful optical shop was instructing his son as to how to charge a customer.

"Son," he said, "after you have fitted the glasses, and he asks what the charge will be, you say, 'The charge is $10.' Then pause and wait to see if he flinches.

"If the customer doesn't flinch, you then say, 'For the frames. The lenses will be another $10.'

"Then you pause again, this time only slightly, and watch for the flinch. If the customer doesn't flinch this time, you say firmly, 'Each.'"

——— GNU ———

Mama Gnu was waiting for Papa Gnu as he came home for dinner one evening. "Our little boy was very bad today," she declared. "I want you to punish him."

"Oh no," said Papa Gnu. "I won't punish him. You'll have to learn to paddle your own gnu."

——— GOATS ———

Two goats in the desert found a tin can full of film. One of them nuzzled it until the lid came off. The film leader loosened around the spool, and the goat ate a few frames.

The second goat ate some, too. Soon they pulled all the film off the reel and consumed the whole of it.

When nothing was left but the can and the spool, the first goat said, "Wasn't that great?"

"Oh, I don't know," replied the second goat. "I thought the book was better."

——— GOLF ———

Golf is a lot of walking, broken up by disappointment and bad arithmetic.

———◆———

"You think so much of your old golf game you don't even remember when we were married."

"Of course I do, my dear; it was the day I sank that 30-foot putt."

————◆————

A pastor and one of his parishioners were playing golf at a local country club. It was a very close match. At the last hole, the pastor teed up, addressed the ball, and swung his driver with great force. The ball stubbornly rolled off the tee and settled slowly some 12 feet away instead of sailing down the fairway.

The clergyman frowned, glared after the ball, and bit his lip, but said nothing.

His opponent regarded him for a moment and sighed, "Pastor, that is the most profane silence I have ever heard!"

————◆————

"Reverend, I'm sorry I swore like that. That's what I like about you— when your golf ball goes into the rough, you don't swear."

"That may be—but where I spit, the grass dies!"

————◆————

I shoot golf in the low 70s. When it gets any colder, I quit.

————◆————

Wife: George, you promised you'd be home at 4:00. It's now 8:00.

George: Honey, please listen to me. Poor ol' Fred is dead. He just dropped over on the eighth green.

Wife: Oh, that's awful.

George: It surely was. For the rest of the game it was hit the ball, drag Fred, hit the ball, drag Fred.

————◆————

Two men were beginning a game of golf. The first man stepped to the tee, and his first drive gave him a hole-in-one. The second man stepped up to the tee and said, "Okay, now I'll take my practice swing, and then we'll start the game."

——— **GOOD SAMARITAN** ———

Sunday school teacher: In the story of the Good Samaritan, why did the Levite pass by on the other side?

Student: Because the poor man had already been robbed.

Sunday school teacher: Now class, you remember the story of the Good Samaritan. What would you do if you saw a man lying on the ground bleeding to death?
Little girl: I think I'd throw up.

GOOD NEWS / BAD NEWS

Doctor: I have some good news and some bad news.
Patient: What is the bad news?
Doctor: We had to cut off both of your legs.
Patient: What is the good news?
Doctor: There is a woman upstairs who would like to buy your shoes.

Agent to writer: I've got some good news and some bad news.
Writer: First tell me the good news.
Agent: Paramount just loved your story, absolutely ate it up.
Writer: That's fantastic—and the bad news?
Agent: Paramount is my dog.

The soldiers had been on the battlefield for weeks when the sergeant made an announcement.

"Men, I have some good news and some bad news for you. First the good news: Everyone will receive a change of socks. And now for the bad news. Walters, you will change with Hanson... Hanson you will change with Douglas... Douglas you will change with Kroeker... Kroeker you will change with Pedillia... Pedillia... "

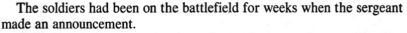

The loudspeaker of the big jet clicked on and the captain's voice announced in a clear, even tone: "Now there's no cause for alarm but we felt you passengers should know that for the last three hours we've been flying without the benefit of radio, compass, radar, or navigational beam due to the breakdown of certain key components. This means that we are, in the broad sense of the word, lost, and are not quite sure in which

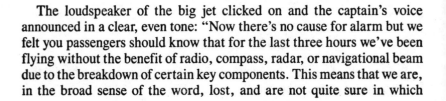

direction we are heading. I'm sure you'll be glad to know, however . . . on the brighter side of the picture . . . that we're making excellent time!"

——— GOTCHA ———

A man sitting at his window one evening casually called to his wife: "There goes that woman Ken Roberts is in love with."

His wife in the kitchen dropped the plate she was drying, ran into the living room, knocked over a vase, and looked out the window. "Where, where?" she said.

"Over there," said the husband. "The woman in the blue dress standing on the corner."

"Why, you big idiot," she replied, "that's his wife."

"Yes, of course," answered the husband with a satisfied grin.

——— GOUT ———

A local minister was troubled by one of his members who was constantly drinking alcohol. They happened to run into each other at a shopping mall. The drinker came up to the minister and asked, "Pastor, what causes gout?"

The minister thought that this would be a good opportunity to admonish the man about his drinking. "It comes from drinking too much alcohol."

"Oh, I see," said the man. "I just read in the paper that the pope and the president were both suffering from gout.

——— GRASS HOUSES ———

Did you hear about the tribe in Africa that stole the king's throne from a rival tribe? They hid the throne in the rafters of their grass hut. The men who stole the throne were having a party in the hut. They were feeling happy about their successful theft when all of a sudden the rafters broke and the throne fell down and killed all of the men.

Moral: Those who live in grass houses shouldn't stow thrones.

——— GROCERY MONEY ———

Husband: What have you been doing with all the grocery money I gave you?

Wife: Turn sideways and look in the mirror.

——— GUARDIAN ANGEL ———

Wife: Aren't you driving a little too fast, dear?
Husband: Don't you believe in a guardian angel? He'll take care of us.
Wife: Yes, I do. But I'm afraid we left him miles back!

——— GUEST TOWELS ———

The most embarrassing moment in the life of Jane Wyman happened when she was entertaining very special guests. After looking over all the appointments carefully, she put a note on the guest towels, "If you use these I will murder you." It was meant for her husband. In the excitement she forgot to remove the note. After the guests departed, the towels were discovered still in perfect order, as well as the note itself.

H

——— HAIRDO ———

We're constantly amazed at these young things with their fancy hairdos and skintight pants. And the girls are even worse.

——— HALT ———

A very new soldier was on sentry duty at the main gate of a military outpost. His orders were clear: No car was to enter unless it had a special sticker on the windshield. A big Army car came up with a general seated in the back. The sentry said, "Halt, who goes there?"

The chauffeur, a corporal, said, "General Wheeler."

"I'm sorry, I can't let you through. You've got to have a sticker on the windshield."

The general said, "Drive on."

The sentry said, "Hold it. You really can't come through. I have orders to shoot if you try driving in without a sticker."

The general repeated, "I'm telling you, son, drive on."

The sentry walked up to the rear window and said, "General, I'm new at this: Do I shoot you or the driver?"

——— HAMMER FROM SEARS ———

A man was sitting in a cafe when all of a sudden someone came in and beat him up. When he woke up he said to the owner, "Who was that?"

"That was Kung Fu from China," replied the owner.

Next week the man was eating in the same cafe when a different person entered and beat him up. When he woke up he said to the owner, "Who was that?"

The owner said, "That was Kuang Chow from Taiwan."

Several weeks later Kung Fu and Kuang Chow were eating in the cafe. The man who had been beaten by both of them entered and did his work. He said to the owner, "When they wake, tell them that was a hammer from Sears."

——— HANDWRITING ———

Teacher: Really, Tommy, your handwriting is terrible! You must learn to write better.

Tommy: Well, if I did, you'd be finding fault with my spelling.

——— HAPPY ENDING ———

"Did the movie have a happy ending?"

"Yes, everyone was glad it was over."

——— HELL ———

"There will be weeping, wailing, and gnashing of teeth among the wicked who pass on to the next world."

"What about those who haven't got any teeth?"

"Teeth will be provided."

———◆———

An American tourist was looking down the crater of a large volcano in Greece and said, "It looks like hell."

The Greek guide responded, "You Americans have been everywhere."

——— HELP! POLICE ———

Policeman: Name, please.

Motorist: Wilhelm Von Corquerinski Popolavawitz.

Policeman: Well, don't let me catch you speeding again.

———— HENPECKED ————

A new group of male applicants had just arrived in heaven.

Peter looked them over and gave this order: "All men who were henpecked on earth, please step to the left; all those who were bosses in their own homes, step to the right."

The line quickly formed on the left. Only one man stepped to the right.

Peter looked at the frail little man standing by himself and inquired, "What makes you think you belong on that side?"

Without hesitation, the meek little man explained, "Because this is where my wife told me to stand."

———— HERE COMES THE JUDGE ————

Judge: Haven't I seen you before?

Man: Yes, Your Honor. I taught your daughter how to play the piano.

Judge: Thirty years.

———— HIGH HEELS ————

The invention of a girl who had been kissed on the forehead too many times.

———— HIJACK ————

About a month ago I was flying to Miami and a nervous little guy sitting next to me took out a gun and said, "Tell the pilot to take me to Rio de Janeiro."

I said, "You mean Havana."

He said, "Don't mix me up. This is my first hijack."

———◆———

Teacher: Where's your homework this morning?

Student: You'll never believe this, but on the way to school I made a paper airplane out of it and someone hijacked it to Cuba!

———— HISTORICAL ————

"But, pastor," lamented the young husband in for counseling, "whenever Joan and I quarrel, she becomes historical."

"You mean, hysterical."

"No, historical. She is always digging up my past."

———— HIT-AND-RUN ————

When the traffic cop asked the prostrate man if he got the number of the hit-and-run driver, he said, "No, but I'd recognize my wife's laugh anywhere."

———— HITLER ————

Adolph Hitler was an avid believer in astrology and consulted with his special astrologer before making any decisions.

One day in consulting with him, Hitler asked, "On what day will I die?"

"You will die on a Jewish holiday," replied the astrologer.

"How can you be so sure of that?" asked Hitler.

"Any day you die will be a Jewish holiday," replied the astrologer.

———— HOG CALLER ————

A local pastor joined a community service club and the members thought they would have some fun with him. Under his name on the badge they printed "Hog Caller" as his occupation.

Everyone made a big fanfare as the badge was presented. The pastor responded by saying, "I usually am called 'Shepherd of the Sheep' . . . but you know your people better than I do."

———— HOLY MATRIMONY ————

A minister forgot the name of a couple he was going to marry so he said from the pulpit, "Will those wishing to be united in holy matrimony please come forward after the service?"

After the service 13 old maids came forward.

———— HOMESICK ————

"I'm homesick! I'm homesick!"

"But you're at home!"

"I know—and I'm sick of it!"

———— HONORARY DEGREE ————

An honorary degree is like the curl in the tail of a pig:

- It follows the main part of the animal.
- It is highly ornamental.
- In no way does it improve the quality of the ham.

——— HORSE ———

If everyone owned a horse, this country would be more stabilized.

——— HOURGLASS FIGURE ———

"Olive has the same hourglass figure she had when we were married, except now it could hold more sand."

——— HOUSEWIFE DEPRESSION ———

Three causes of housewife depression: ABC... NBC... CBS.

——— HOW MANY WHEELS? ———

Husband: That man is really stupid.
Wife: Why do you say that?
Husband: He thinks that a football coach has four wheels.
Wife: Isn't that silly. How many wheels does it have?

——— HOW'S THAT? ———

"Our paper is two days late this week," wrote an Idaho newspaper editor, "owing to an accident. When we started to run the press Monday night, one of the guy ropes gave way, allowing the forward glider fluke to fall and break as it struck the flunker flopper. This, of course, as anyone who knows anything about a press will readily understand, left the gangplank with only the flip-flap to support it, which also dropped and broke off the wooper-cock. This loosened the fluking between the ramrod and the flibber-snatcher, which caused trouble with the mogus.

"The report that the delay was caused by our overindulgence in stimulants is a tissue of falsehoods. The redness in the appearance of our right eyes was caused by our going into the hatchway of the press in our anxiety to start it, and pulling the coppling pin after the slap-bang was broken, which caused the dingus to rise up and welt us in the optic. We expect a brand new glider fluke on this afternoon's train."

——— HUCK ———

Finn and Huck were friends. Finn up and died. No one was worried, however. They said, "Huck'll bury Finn."

——— HUMAN ERRORS ———

The airline company was disturbed over a high percentage of accidents, and decided to eliminate human errors by building a completely mechanical plane.

"Ladies and gentlemen," came a voice over a loudspeaker on the maiden voyage, "it may interest you to know that you are now traveling in the world's first completely automatic plane. Now just sit back and relax because nothing can possibly go wrong . . . go wrong . . . go wrong . . . go wrong."

——— HUMORIST ———

A person who originates old jokes.

I

——— IRS ———

A businessman who was near death asked that his remains be cremated and the ashes be mailed to the Internal Revenue Service with the following note attached: "Now You Have It All."

———◆———

Q: What do you need when you have an IRS auditor buried to his neck in concrete?
A: More concrete.

——— I COME QUICKLY ———

A new preacher had just begun his sermon. He was a little nervous and about ten minutes into the talk his mind went blank. He remembered to do what they had taught him in seminary when a situation like this arose—repeat your last point. Often this would help you remember what should come next. So he thought he would give it a try.

"Behold, I come quickly," he said. Still his mind was blank. He thought he would try it again. "Behold I come quickly." Still nothing.

He tried it one more time with such force he fell forward, knocking the pulpit to one side, tripping over a flower pot, and falling into the lap of a little old lady in the front row.

The young preacher apologized and tried to explain what had happened. "That's all right, young man," said the little old lady. "It was my fault. I should have gotten out of the way. You told me three times you were coming!"

——— I REMEMBER ———

Father: When I was your age, I was up at five every morning. I fed the chickens, cleared the snow from around the house, and then did my six-mile paper route. And I thought nothing of it.

Son: I don't blame you, Dad. I don't think much of it, either.

——— IDEAL WIFE ———

What every man expects his wife to be:

- Always beautiful and cheerful. Could have married movie stars but wanted only you.
- Hair that never needs curlers or beauty shops.
- Beauty that won't run in a rainstorm.
- Never sick, just allergic to jewelry and fur coats.
- Insists that moving the furniture by herself is good for her figure.
- Expert in cooking, cleaning house, fixing the car or TV, painting the house, and keeping quiet.
- Favorite hobbies: mowing the lawn and shoveling snow.
- Hates charge plates.
- Her favorite expression: "What can I do for you, dear?"

- Thinks you have Einstein's brain but look like Mr. America.
- Wishes you would go out with the boys so she could get some sewing done.
- Loves you because you're so-o-o sexy.

But actually:
- She speaks 140 words a minute with gusts up to 180.
- She once was a model for a totem pole.
- She's a light eater—as soon as it gets light she starts eating.
- Where there's smoke, there she is—cooking.
- If you get lost, open your wallet—she'll find you.

——— IDIOT ———

"When I was a child I used to bite my fingernails, and the doctor told me if I didn't quit I'd grow up to be an idiot."

"And you couldn't stop, huh?"

———◆———

Do you know how to keep an idiot in suspense? I'll tell you tomorrow.

——— I'M FINE ———

I'm fine, I'm fine.
There's nothing whatever the matter with me,
I'm just as healthy as I can be.
I have arthritis in both of my knees
And when I talk, I talk with a wheeze.
My pulse is weak and my blood is thin
But I'm awfully well for the shape I'm in.
My teeth eventually will have to come out
And I can't hear a word unless you shout.
I'm overweight and I can't get thin
But I'm awfully well for the shape I'm in.
Arch supports I have for my feet
Or I wouldn't be able to walk down the street.
Sleep is denied me every night
And every morning I'm really a sight.

My memory is bad and my head's a-spin
And I practically live on aspirin.
But I'm awfully well for the shape I'm in.
The moral is, as this tale unfolds,
That for you and me who are growing old,
It's better to say, "I'm fine," with a grin
Than to let people know the shape we're in!

——— INADMISSIBLE ———

Judge: Did you see the shot that was fired?
Witness: I only heard it.
Judge: That is pure hearsay and inadmissible as evidence.
As the witness left the stand and as his back was turned to the judge, he laughed out loud. At once the judge called him back and was about to hold him in contempt of court.
Witness: Did you see me laugh?
Judge: No, but I heard you.
Witness: Isn't that the same kind of inadmissible evidence, Judge?

——— INCOME TAX ———

Don't be surprised if your next income tax form is simplified to contain only four lines:
1. What was your income last year?
2. What were your expenses?
3. How much do you have left?
4. Send it in.

———◆———

Did you hear about the man from the income tax bureau who phoned a certain Baptist minister to say, "We're checking the tax return of a member of your church, Deacon X., and noticed that he lists a donation to your building fund of $300. Is that correct?"
The minister answered without hesitation, "I haven't got my records available, but I'll promise you one thing: If he hasn't, he will!"

——— INDIAN SQUAW ———

There were three Indian squaws, one sitting on an elk hide, one on a deer hide, and one on a hippopotamus hide. The squaws on the elk and deer hides had one papoose each, while the squaw on the hippopotamus hide had two papooses.

Moral: The squaw on the hippopotamus equals the sum of the squaws on the other two hides.

——— INFALLIBILITY ———

The pope would have never introduced papal infallibility if he had ever been married.

——— INNOCENT ———

Policeman: Here is your parking ticket.
Woman: And just what do you do when you catch a real criminal?
Policeman: I don't know . . . all I ever catch are the innocent ones.

——— INSANE ASYLUM ———

A home for old joke-book writers.

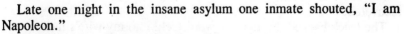

A policeman saw an old man pulling a box on a leash down a busy street. "Poor man," he thought. "I'd better humor him."

"That's a nice dog you've got there," he said to the old man.

"It isn't a dog, it's a box," said the man.

"Oh, I'm sorry," said the policeman, "I thought you were a bit simple-minded," and he walked on.

The old man turned and looked at the box. "We sure fooled him that time, Rover," he said.

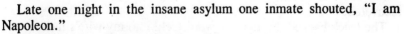

Late one night in the insane asylum one inmate shouted, "I am Napoleon."

Another said, "How do you know?"

The first inmate said, "God told me."

Just then, a voice from the next room shouted, "I did not."

—— **INSOMNIA** ——

As they were leaving church one Sunday, a man confided to his friend that he was suffering from insomnia. The friend asserted that he had no trouble getting to sleep.

"Really?" the first man inquired. "Do you count sheep?"

"No," was the retort. "I talk to the shepherd."

———◆———

"Do you know of any cures for insomnia?"

"Try talking to yourself."

—— **INSTRUCTIONS** ——

Pilot: Pilot to tower... pilot to tower... I am 300 miles from land and... 600 feet high and running out of gas... please instruct... over."

Tower: Tower to pilot... tower to pilot... repeat after me... Our Father, which art in heaven...

—— **INSURANCE** ——

The following quotations were taken from a Toronto newspaper. They are samples of comments that individuals wrote down on their claim forms following their auto accidents:

I misjudged a lady crossing the street.

Coming home, I drove into the wrong house and collided with a tree I don't have.

I collided with a stationary streetcar coming the opposite direction.

The other car collided with mine without giving warning of its intentions.

I heard a horn blow and was struck in the back—a lady was evidently trying to pass me.

I thought my window was down, but found it was up when I put my hand through it.

My car was stolen, and I sent up a human cry but it has not been recovered.

The truck backed through my windshield into my wife's face.

A pedestrian hit me and went under my car.

The guy was all over the road. I had to swerve a number of times before I hit him.

If the other driver had stopped a few yards behind himself, the accident would not have happened.

In my attempt to kill a fly, I drove into a telephone pole.

I had been shopping for plants all day, and was on my way home. As I reached an intersection, a hedge sprang up, obscuring my vision. I did not see the other car.

I had been driving my car for 40 years when I fell asleep at the wheel and had an accident.

I was on my way to the doctor's with rear-end trouble when my universal joint gave way, causing me to have an accident.

My car was legally parked as it backed into the other vehicle.

An invisible car came out of nowhere, struck my vehicle, and vanished.

I told the police that I was not injured, but on removing my hat, I found that I had a skull fracture.

I was sure the old fellow would never make it to the other side of the roadway when I struck him.

The pedestrian had no idea which way to go, so I ran over him.

The indirect cause of this accident was a little guy in a small car with a big mouth.

I was thrown from my car as it left the road. I was later found in a ditch by some stray cows.

The telephone pole was approaching fast. I was attempting to swerve out of its path when it struck my front end.

I was unable to stop in time, and my car crashed into the other vehicle. The driver and passengers then left immediately for a vacation with injuries.

I pulled away from the side of the road, glanced at my mother-in-law, and headed over the embankment.

——— INTERVIEW ———

"Now this is the verbal part of your employment test. What does Aurora Borealis mean?"

"It means I don't get the job!"

———◆———

"Were you hired by the radio station?"

"N-n-no, they s-s-said I w-w-wasn't t-t-tall enough!"

——— INTRODUCTION ———

Introducing a speaker: There isn't anything that I wouldn't do for Mr. _____, and there isn't anything he wouldn't do for me. That's why we have gone through life not doing anything for each other.

Speaker: After an introduction like that, I can hardly wait to hear what I am going to say, to myself.

———◆———

In his last appearance, he drew a line three blocks long. Then they took his chalk away.

———◆———

You have heard it said before that this speaker needs no introduction. Well, I have heard him and he needs all the introduction he can get.

———◆———

You haven't heard nothing until you've heard our speaker of the evening. Then you've heard nothing.

———◆———

Our speaker for the evening gives the most refreshing talks. Everywhere he goes the audiences always feel good when they wake up.

———◆———

A Londoner wound up a business trip to the Orient with a visit to Taipei. At a luncheon he was asked to say a few words. Since he spoke not a word of Chinese, his address was to be translated by an interpreter sentence by sentence.

"Well," he began, "I just want you to know that I'm tickled to death to be here."

A look of agony appeared on the interpreter's face. "This poor man," he said in halting Chinese, "scratches himself until he dies, only to be with you."

—— INVALID ——

Christy: I was an invalid once.
Lisa: You were? When was that?
Christy: When I was a baby I couldn't walk until I was a year old.

—— ISAIAH ——

Q: Do you know what the name of Isaiah's horse was?
A: Is Me. He said, "Woe, is me."

—— ISMS ——

Communism: If you have two cows, you give both cows to the government, and then the government sells you some of the milk.
Socialism: If you have two cows, you give both cows to the government, and then the government gives you some of the milk.
Naziism: If you have two cows, the government shoots you and takes both cows.
Facism: If you have two cows, you milk both of them and give the government half of the milk.
New Dealism: If you have two cows, you kill one, milk the other and pour the milk down the drain.
Capitalism. If you have two cows, you sell one cow and buy a bull.

—— IT'S THE PLUMBER ——

Once upon a time there was a parrot who could say only three little words: "Who is it?" One day when the parrot was alone in the house, there was a loud knock on the door. "Who is it?" screeched the parrot.
"It's the plumber," the visitor responded.
"Who is it?" repeated the parrot.
"It's the plumber, I tell you," was the reply. "You called me to tell me your cellar was flooded."
Again the parrot called, "Who is it?"
By this time, the plumber became so angry that he fainted. A neighbor rushed over to see the cause of the commotion and found the visitor had died because of a heart attack. He looked at the man and said, "Who is it?"
The parrot answered, "It's the plumber!"

J

——— JEWELS ———

A woman making arrangements with an artist to sit for her portrait said to him, "Although I have only a few items of jewelry; nevertheless, I want this painting to show me wearing diamond rings and earrings, an emerald brooch, and a multistrand necklace of pearls that look like they are priceless."

"I can do this all right," said the artist. "But do you mind telling me why you want this, when apparently you do not particularly care for jewelry?"

"You see, if I die first," said the woman, "and my husband marries again, I want that second wife to go out of her mind trying to find out where he hid the jewels."

——— JOAN OF ARC ———

A little boy, just back from Sunday school, asked his father if Noah had a wife.

"All the time, questions, questions, questions," replied the father. "Of course he did, Joan of Arc."

——— JOB ———

Q: Why was Job always cold in bed?
A: Because he had such miserable comforters.

"Did you know that Job spoke when he was a very small baby?"
"Where does it say that?"
"It says, 'Job cursed the day he was born.'"

——— JOKES ———

Dan: How do you like my jokes?

Stan: I can't see anything funny in them.
Dan: Oh well, you'll probably catch on after a while and laugh.
Stan: No, I laughed at them 20 years ago.

Gary: So you didn't like my jokes.
Harry: No, they were terrible.
Gary: Oh, I don't know about that—I threw a bunch of them in the furnace and the fire roared.

─── **JUDGE** ───

Judge: Thirty years in prison!
Prisoner: But, Judge, I won't live that long!
Judge: Don't worry, do what you can.

Judge: I've decided to give you a suspended sentence.
Prisoner: Thank you, Your Honor.
Judge: For what? You're going to be hanged.

─── **JUDGMENT** ───

Husband: You must admit, that men have better judgment than women.
Wife: Oh, yes. You married me, and I married you.

─── **JURY** ───

Mrs. Franklin had been called for jury duty. She declined to serve because, she said, she did not believe in capital punishment. The judge tried to persuade her to stay. "Madam," he said, "this is not a murder case. It is merely a case in which a wife is suing her husband because she gave him $4,000 to buy her a new fur coat and he lost it all at the racetrack instead."

"I'll serve," agreed Mrs. Franklin. "I could be wrong about capital punishment."

K

——— KAYAK ———

Did you hear about the Eskimo who put some oil heaters in his kayak and was surprised when they exploded and set fire to it? Which only goes to prove that you can't have your kayak and heat it, too.

——— KIBITZER ———

All evening long, four card players had been pestered by a kibitzer. When he went out of the room for a moment, they hit on a plan to silence him. "Let's make up a game no one ever heard of," one of them said. "Then he'll have to shut up."

The kibitzer returned. The dealer tore two cards in half and gave them to the man on his left. He tore the corners off three cards and spread them out in front of the man opposite him. Then he tore five cards in quarters, gave 15 pieces to the man on his right and kept five himself. "I have a mingle," he said. "I'll bet a dollar."

"I have a snazzle," the next man announced. "I'll raise you a dollar."

The third man folded without betting.

The fourth, after due deliberation, said, "I've got a farfle. I'll raise you two dollars."

The kibitzer shook his head vehemently. "You're crazy," he said. "You're never going to beat a mingle and a snazzle with a lousy farfle!"

——— KING ———

The lion went up to the rhinoceros and asked, "Who is the king of the jungle?"

"You are, O lion," came the answer.

The lion went up to the hippopotamus and asked, "Who is the king of the jungle?"

The hippo said, "You are, O lion."

The lion went up to the elephant and asked, "Who is the king of the jungle?"

For an answer the elephant seized the lion with his trunk, threw him high in the air, caught him on the way down, and slammed him hard against a tree.

The lion arose, half-dazed, shook himself, and said weakly, "Just because you don't know the right answer, you don't have to get sore."

——— KING OF SIAM ———

Rich: I once sang for the king of Siam. At least that's what he told me he was.

Dave: Yes, he said, "If you're a singer, then I'm the king of Siam."

——— KING OF THE WORLD ———

Husband: I know you are having a lot of trouble with the baby, dear, but keep in mind, "the hand that rocks the cradle is the hand that rules the world."

Wife: How about taking over the world for a few hours while I go shopping?

——— KISS ———

Girl: I'm sorry but I don't kiss on the first date.

Boy: How about on the last one?

Husband: I'd like to know whatever became of the old-fashioned girls who fainted when a man kissed them.

Wife: What I'd like to know is what happened to the old-fashioned men who made them faint.

Boy: I want to be honest. You're not the first girl I've kissed.

Girl: I want to be honest. You've got a lot to learn.

Father: When I was your age, I never kissed a girl. Will you be able to tell your children that?

Son: Not with a straight face.

A man entered a bank with a gun in his hand. He bellowed, "I'm going to rob every man in this bank, and I'm going to kiss every woman."

One of the men who had accompanied his wife to the bank said, "You may rob all of us men, but you're not going to kiss all of the ladies!"

His wife punched him in the ribs and said, "Now leave him alone, George. He's robbing the bank."

——— KISS A MULE ———

A little prospector wearing clean new shoes walked into a saloon. A big Texan said to his friend standing at the bar, "Watch me make this dude dance." He walked over to the prospector and said, "You're a foreigner, aren't you? From the East?"

"You might say that," the little prospector answered. "I'm from Boston and I'm here prospecting for gold."

"Now tell me something. Can you dance?"

"No, sir. I never did learn to dance."

"Well, I'm going to teach you. You'll be surprised how quickly you can learn."

With that, the Texan took out his gun and started shooting at the prospector's feet. Hopping, skipping, jumping, by the time the little prospector made it to the door he was shaking like a leaf.

About an hour later the Texan left the saloon. As soon as he stepped outside the door, he heard a click. He looked around and there, four feet from his head, was the biggest shotgun he had ever seen.

And the little prospector said, "Mr. Texan, have you ever kissed a mule?"

"No," said the quick-thinking Texan, "but I've always wanted to."

——— KNOCK-KNOCK ———

Knock, knock.
Who's there?
Wendy.
Wendy who?
Wendy red red robin, comes bob bob bobbin' along...

Knock, knock.
Who's there?
Tarzan.
Tarzan who?
Tarzan stripes forever.

——— **KNOWLEDGE** ———

He who knows but little shares it often.

L

——— **LADY-KILLER** ———

Guy: I'm a lady-killer.
Gal: Yeah, they take one look at you and drop dead.

——— **LAMPPOST** ———

First Russian: In America the people are so honest, you can hang your watch on a lamppost and come back in three weeks and it's still there.
Second Russian: You mean to say that in America you can hang your watch on a lamppost and come back in three weeks and your watch is still there?
First Russian: No, the lamppost is still there.

——— **LANCING MICHIGAN** ———

Q: What is the greatest surgical operation on record?
A: Lancing Michigan.

——— **LANDLORD** ———

"Twenty years from now," said a poor writer who was having trouble with his landlord, "people will come by and look at this house and say, 'Phillips, the famous writer, had a room here.' "
The landlord was unimpressed. "Phillips, I'm telling you that if you don't pay your rent, they'll be saying that the day after tomorrow!"

—— LARGE ——

"When I got on the bus three men got up to give me their seats."
"Did you take them?"

—— LAST WORDS ——

"Have you any last words," the warden asked the condemned man, "before we hang you?"

"Yes," panted the prisoner, "just get it over with quickly, please!"

The warden patted the man on the back, gave the signal, and the condemned man was dropped through the platform. But he didn't die. He kept bouncing up and down. So they drew him up and dropped him again. But still he didn't die; he just bounced up and down. Spectators began to faint as they heard the prisoner gasp, "C'mon and get through with this!"

So they lifted him up again and dropped him again, and once more he bobbed up and down at the end of the rope. The executioner was in a cold sweat and the guards had all they could do to keep the warden from passing out. When they drew him up for the eleventh time, the prisoner, eyeballs popping and tongue lolling out the side of his mouth, demanded, "C'mon and get through with this! What am I—a murderer or a yo-yo?"

—— LATE ——

Every day Mr. Smith's secretary was 20 minutes late. Then one day she slid snugly into place only five minutes tardy.

"Well," said Mr. Smith, "this is the earliest you've ever been late."

---◆---

Husband: I have tickets for the theater.
Wife: Wonderful, darling. I'll start dressing right away.
Husband: That's a good idea. The tickets are for tomorrow night.

—— LAUGH ——

"Did you see that young lady smile at me?"
"That's nothing. The first time I saw you, I laughed right out loud."

---◆---

From the moment I picked up your joke book until I laid it down I was convulsed with laughter. Some day I intend to read it.

—— LAWYER ——

Witness: Well, I think—
Lawyer: Don't think! In this courtroom you are to tell what you know, not what you think!
Witness: Well, I'm not a lawyer. I can't talk without thinking!

"And what do you do, sir?"
"I'm a criminal lawyer."
"Aren't they all!"

Did you hear that my lawyer was in an accident? The ambulance backed up without warning.

Do you know the difference between a dead chicken in the road and a dead lawyer in the road? There are skid marks in front of the chicken.

Do you know why they bury lawyers 16 feet deep in the ground? Because lawyers are real good down deep.

Did you hear about the man who was walking through a graveyard and noticed a gravestone that said, "Here lies a lawyer and a good man."
"Imagine that," said the man to himself, "two men buried in the same grave."

Did you hear the good news and the bad news? The good news is that a busload of lawyers just ran off the cliff. The bad news is that there were three empty seats on the bus.

"What do you have when you have 20,000 lawyers at the bottom of the ocean?"

"You have a good start."

——— LECTURE ———

At a lecture series a very poor speaker was on the platform. As he was speaking, people in the audience began to get up and leave. After about ten minutes there was only one man left. Finally the man stopped speaking and asked the man why he remained to the end. "I'm the next speaker," was the reply.

———◆———

A lecturer announced to his audience that the world would probably end in seven billion years.

"How long did you say?" came a terrified voice from the rear.

"Seven billion years."

"Thank goodness!" said the voice. "I thought for a moment you had said seven million."

———◆———

Interrupted by the sound of the bell announcing the end of the class, the professor was annoyed to see the students noisily preparing to leave even though he was in the middle of his lecture. "Just a moment, class," he said, "I have a few more pearls to cast."

——— LEFTOVERS ———

A preacher forgot his notes for the sermon he was going to deliver. In the midst of the sermon he got a few things twisted when he said that the Lord took 4000 barley loaves and 6000 fishes and fed 24 people, and had plenty left over.

Someone in the congregation called out, "Anybody could do that."

"Could you?" asked the minister.

"Certainly I could."

After the service, when the minister complained about the heckler's conduct, he was told of his error by a deacon.

"Well, next week I will not forget my notes. I'll fix that character."

The next week the minister stepped forward confidently and began his sermon. In the course of it, he brought up again the miracle of the loaves and fishes. He told how the five barley loaves and the two fishes had fed the multitude of probably 24,000 people. He then pointed to the heckler from the previous Sunday and asked, "Could you do that?"

"I sure could," said the heckler.

"And just how would you do that?" asked the minister.

"With the loaves and fishes leftover from last Sunday."

——— LIAR ———

The game warden was walking through the mountains when he encountered a hunter with a gun. "This is good territory for hunting, don't you think?" suggested the warden.

"You bet it is," said the hunter enthusiastically. "I killed one of the finest bucks yesterday—it weighed at least 250 pounds."

"Deer are out of season now," said the warden. "Do you know that you are talking to a game warden?"

"No, I was not aware of that," said the hunter. "And I'll bet you didn't know that you've been talking to the biggest liar in the state."

———◆———

A minister wound up the services one morning by saying, "Next Sunday I am going to preach on the subject of liars. And in this connection, as a preparation for my discourse, I should like you all to read the seventeenth chapter of Mark."

On the following Sunday, the preacher rose to begin and said, "Now, then, all of you who have done as I requested and read the seventeenth chapter of Mark, please raise your hands."

Nearly every hand in the congregation went up. Then said the preacher, "You are the people I want to talk to. There is no seventeenth chapter of Mark!"

——— LICENSE ———

Two fellows out hunting were stopped by a game warden. One of them took off running and the game warden went after him and caught him. The fellow then showed the warden his hunting license.

"Why did you run when you had a license?"

"Because the other fellow didn't have one."

——— LIE ———

A minister spoke to a deacon and said, "I'm told you went to the ball game instead of church this morning." "That's a lie," said the deacon, "and here's the fish to prove it."

——— LIE DETECTOR ———

First man: Have you ever seen one of those machines that can tell when a person is telling a lie?

Second man: Seen one? I married one!

——— LITTLE LIONS ———

A small man said to a large man, "If I were as big as you, I would go into the jungle, find me a big lion, and pull him limb from limb."

The big man replied, "There are some little lions in the jungle, too. Let's see what you can do."

——— LOAN ———

Stan: How about lending me $50?

Dan: Sorry, I can only let you have $25.

Stan: But why not the entire $50, Dan?

Dan: No, $25 only. That way it's even—each one of us loses $25.

———◆———

"Hello, this is George."

"Hello, George. What's on your mind?"

"I'm broke down in Los Angeles and I need $200 right away."

"There must be something wrong with the line. I can't hear you."

"I say, I want to borrow $200."

"I can't hear a word you're saying."

Operator (coming on the line): "Hello! This is the operator. I can hear your party very plainly."

"Then you give him the $200."

———◆———

A man came into the bank to get a loan. He went up to the teller and said, "Who arranges for loans?"

"I'm sorry, sir," the teller told him, "but the loan arranger is out to lunch."

"All right," said the man. "May I speak to Tonto?"

——— LONG EVENING ———

After a long evening of conversation the host said, "I hate to put you out, but I have to get up at six o'clock in the morning to catch a plane."

"Good heavens," said the guest. "I thought you were at my house!"

——— LORD'S PRAYER ———

Children's versions of the Lord's Prayer:
Our Father, Who are in heaven, hello! What be Thy name?
Give us this day our daily breath.
Our Father, Who art in heaven, Hollywood be Thy name.
Our Father, Who art in heaven, Harold be Thy name.
Give us this day our jelly bread.
Lead us not into creation.
Deliver us from weevils.
Deliver us from eagles.

———◆———

Two lawyers were bosom friends. Much to the amazement of one, the other became a Sunday school teacher. "I bet you don't even know the Lord's Prayer," he fumed.

"Everybody knows that," the other replied. "It's 'Now I lay me down to sleep—'"

"You win," said the other admiringly. "I didn't know you knew so much about the Bible."

——— LOST AND FOUND ———

Bill: I just found this nice new penknife on the sidewalk.
Dad: Are you sure it was lost?
Bill: I'm very sure. I saw the man looking for it.

——— LOT'S WIFE ———

The Sunday school teacher was describing how Lot's wife looked back and suddenly turned into a pillar of salt.

"My mother looked back once while she was driving," contributed little Johnny, "and she turned into a telephone pole."

——— LOVE ———

A little foolishness and a lot of curiosity.

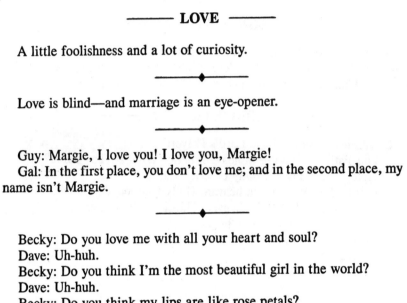

Love is blind—and marriage is an eye-opener.

Guy: Margie, I love you! I love you, Margie!
Gal: In the first place, you don't love me; and in the second place, my name isn't Margie.

Becky: Do you love me with all your heart and soul?
Dave: Uh-huh.
Becky: Do you think I'm the most beautiful girl in the world?
Dave: Uh-huh.
Becky: Do you think my lips are like rose petals?
Dave: Uh-huh.
Becky: Oh, you say the most beautiful things.

Better to have loved a short man than never to have loved a tall.

Love may not make the world spin around, but it certainly makes a lot of people dizzy.

——— LUCK ———

I believe in luck. How else can you explain the success of those you dislike?

—Jean Cocteau

Depend on the rabbit's foot if you will, but remember it didn't work for the rabbit.

—*R.E. Shay*

——— **LUNATICS** ———

Son: How do they catch lunatics, Dad?
Dad: With lipstick, beautiful dresses, and pretty smiles.

——— **MAD** ———

Ralph: The police shot my dog.
Gary: Was he mad?
Ralph: Well, he wasn't too pleased about it.

——— **MAHARAJA** ———

The maharaja of an Indian province decreed a ban on hunting wildlife, and soon the country was overrun with man-eating animals. When the people could stand it no longer, they gave the maharaja the heave-ho. This may be the first time in history when the reign was called on account of game.

——— **MAID** ———

Wife: I've been asked for a reference for our last maid. I've said she's lazy, unpunctual, and impertinent. How can I add anything in her favor?
Husband: You might say that she's got a good appetite and sleeps well.

——— **MANSLAUGHTER** ———

A man charged with murder bribed a friend on the jury to hold out for a verdict of manslaughter. The jury was out for a long period of time, but at last brought in a verdict of manslaughter.
Upon visiting the prisoner the following week, the friend was thanked.

120

"You must have had a tough time getting them to vote for manslaughter."
"Tough is right," replied the friend. "The other 11 wanted to acquit you."

——— MARBLEHEAD ———

"In Massachusetts they named a town after you."
"What is it?"
"Marblehead."

——— MARILYN MONROE ———

Wife: And Francois, the great expert on beautiful women, told me that I can match my legs with Marilyn Monroe.
Husband: How can you match your legs with Monroe? They don't even match each other!

——— MAROONED ———

"I had a terrible dream. I dreamed I was marooned on an island with 12 beautiful women."
"What's wrong with that?"
"Did you ever try and cook and wash for 12 women?"

——— MARRIAGE ———

Keep your eyes wide open before marriage—half-shut afterward.

Marriage is like the army...everyone complains, but you'd be surprised at how many reenlist.

Son: How much does it cost to get married, Dad?
Dad: I don't know. I'm still paying on it.

"Can you take dictation?"
"No, I've never been married."

She calls her husband "Henry." He's the eighth.

———————◆———————

Jay: I have half a mind to get married.
Bufe: That's all you need.

———————◆———————

"And at her request you gave up drinking?"
"Yes."
"And you stopped smoking for the same reason?"
"I did."
"And it was for her that you gave up dancing, card playing, and billiards?"
"Absolutely."
"Then, why didn't you marry her?"
"Well, after all this reforming I realized I could do better."

———————◆———————

First girl: My pastor said we could have 16 husbands.
Second girl: Are you sure about that?
First girl: Why, yes. At the last wedding at the church I heard him say, "Four better, four worse, four richer, and four poorer!"

———————◆———————

Marriage is like a railroad sign—you see a girl and stop. Then you look. And after you're married you listen.

———————◆———————

Husband: Why do you weep and snuffle over a TV program and the imaginary woes of people you have never met?
Wife: For the same reason you scream and yell when a man you don't know makes a touchdown.

———————◆———————

Wife: I read about a man who speaks eight languages who married a woman who speaks two.
Husband: That seems to be about the right handicap.

———————◆———————

The most dangerous year in married life is the first. Then follows the second, third, fourth, fifth . . .

———————◆———————

Marriage is like horseradish—men praise it with tears in their eyes.

———————◆———————

"Now that looks like a happily married couple."
"Don't be too sure, my dear. They're probably saying the same thing about us."

———————◆———————

Marriage is like a violin—after the music stops, the strings are still attached.

———————◆———————

Wife: At least you could talk to me while I sew.
Husband: Why don't you sew to me while I read?

———————◆———————

Wife: If you had it to do over again, would you marry me, dear?
Husband: Of course, if I had to do it over again.

———————◆———————

A couple's happy married life almost went on the rocks because of the presence in the household of old Aunt Emma. For seven long years she lived with them, always crotchety, always demanding. Finally the old girl died.

On the way back from the cemetery, the husband confessed to his wife, "Darling, if I didn't love you so much, I don't think I would have put up with having your Aunt Emma in the house all those years."

His wife looked at him, aghast. "My Aunt Emma!" she cried. "I thought she was your Aunt Emma!"

———————◆———————

One night a wife found her husband standing over their baby's crib. Silently she watched him. As he stood looking down at the sleeping infant, she saw on his face a mixture of emotions: disbelief, doubt, delight, amazement, enchantment, skepticism.

Touched by this unusual display and the deep emotions it aroused, with eyes glistening she slipped her arm around her husband.

"A penny for your thoughts," she said.

"It's amazing!" he replied. "I just can't see how anybody can make a crib like that for only $46.50."

Tom: If a wedding means showers for the bride, what does it mean for the groom?

Jerry: Curtains.

A knock came at the door. "Who is it?" asked the wife.

A gruff voice replied, "It's Jack the Ripper."

She turned to her husband and said, "It's for you, dear."

My wife puts so much grease on her face at night you'd think she was going to swim the English Channel.

A wife sought the advice of a fortune-teller, who said, "Prepare yourself for widowhood. Your husband is about to die a violent death."

The wife sighed deeply and asked, "Will I be acquitted?"

A woman offered a brand-new Porsche for sale for a price of $10. A man answered the ad, but he was slightly disbelieving.

"What's the gimmick?" he inquired.

"No gimmick," the woman answered. "My husband died, and in his will he asked that the car be sold and the money given to his secretary."

"I understand the government is going to handle marriages."

"Yes."

"I wonder what department they'll be in?"

"I think it will be the War Department."

124

Wife: I can't sleep, dear. I keep thinking there's a mouse under the bed.
Husband: Well, start thinking there's a cat under the bed and go to sleep.

Wife: I should have listened to my mother's advice and never married you.
Husband: Good grief! How I've misjudged that woman.

Attendant: Doctor, there is a man outside who wants to know if we've lost any of our men from the insane asylum.
Doctor: Why's that?
Attendant: He says that someone has run off with his wife.

My wife told the neighbors that 30 years ago she had a close encounter with a subhuman alien creature from outer space, but never reported it to the authorities. Instead, she married it.

——— **MARRIAGE COUNSELOR** ———

Marriage counselor: Do you enjoy talking to each other?
Counselee: Oh, we enjoy talking to each other all right. The problem is listening to each other.

Marriage counselor: Do you encourage your husband in his work?
Counselee: I do my best. I keep telling him he ought to ask for a raise.

——— **MARTIAN** ———

A Martian wandered from his spaceship in the desert into Las Vegas and arrived when one of the slot machines was spewing forth a bunch of nickels. When the exploding gadget had subsided, the Martian went over to it and said, "With a cold like that, you ought to take some aspirin and get into bed."

—————— MATCH ——————

Writer: Can't you suggest something to put a finishing touch on my story?
Editor: Yes. A match.

—————— MATHEMATICS ——————

A Missouri farmer passed away and left 17 mules to his three sons. The instructions left in the will said that the oldest boy was to get one-half, the second eldest one-third, and the youngest one-ninth. The three sons, recognizing the difficulty of dividing 17 mules into these fractions, began to argue.

The uncle heard about the argument, hitched up his mule, and drove out to settle the matter. He added his mule to the 17, making 18. The eldest son therefore got one-half or nine; the second got one-third or six; and the youngest got one-ninth or two. Adding up 9, 6, and 2 equals 17. The uncle, having settled the argument, hitched up his mule and drove home.

—————— MECHANIC ——————

Motorist: What will it cost to fix my car?
Mechanic: What's wrong with it?
Motorist: I don't know.
Mechanic: $79.95!

—————— MEDICALLY EXEMPT ——————

A draftee went in for his physical wearing a truss and with papers that were stamped "M.E." for Medically Exempt.

Afterward a friend borrowed the truss to wear for his physical.

At the end of the examination the doctor stamped M.E. on his papers. "Does that mean I'm Medically Exempt?" he asked the doctor.

"No," replied the doctor. "M.E. stands for Middle East. Anyone who can wear a truss upside down can ride a camel."

—————— MEDICARE ——————

A sample of what might happen if we had socialized medicine is currently making the rounds. It goes something like this:

A man feeling the need of medical care went to the medical building for that purpose, and upon entering the front door found himself faced with a battery of doors, each marked with the names of ailments such as appendicitis, heart, cancer, etc.

He felt sure his trouble could be diagnosed as appendicitis, so he entered the door so marked. Upon entering, he found himself faced with two more doors, one marked male and the other female. He entered the door marked male and found himself in another corridor where there were two doors, one marked Protestant and the other Catholic.

Since he was a Protestant, he entered the proper door and found himself facing two more doors, one marked taxpayer and the other marked nontaxpayer. He still owned equity in his home, so he went through the door marked taxpayer, and found himself confronted with two more doors marked single and married.

He had a wife at home, so he entered the proper door and once more there were two more doors, one marked Republican and the other Democrat.

SINCE HE WAS A REPUBLICAN HE ENTERED THE DOOR AND FELL NINE FLOORS TO THE ALLEY.

——— MELLOW ———

A church soloist was delighted when one of the members spoke to him after church and said, "You have a very mellow voice."

The soloist went home and looked up the definition of the word "mellow" in his dictionary. He read, "Mellow: overripe and almost rotten."

——— MELODY IN "F" ———

(The Prodigal Son)

> Feeling footloose and frisky, a feather-brained fellow
> Forced his fond father to fork over the farthings,
> And flew far to foreign fields
> And fabulously frittered his fortune with faithless friends.
> Fleeced by his fellows in folly, and facing famine,
> He found himself a feed-flinger in a filthy farmyard.
> Fairly famishing, he fain would've filled his frame
> With foraged food from fodder fragments.

"Fooey, my father's flunkies fare far finer,"
The frazzled fugitive forlornly fumbled, frankly facing facts.
Frustrated by failure, and filled with foreboding,
He fled forthwith to his family.
Falling at his father's feet, he forlornly fumbled, "Father, I've flunked,
And fruitlessly forfeited family fellowship favor."
The far-sighted father, forestalling further flinching,
Frantically flagged the flunkies.
"Fetch a fatling from the flock and fix a feast."
The fugitive's fault-finding brother frowned
On fickle forgiveness of former folderol.
But the faithful father figured,
"Filial fidelity is fine, but the fugitive is found!
What forbids fervent festivity?
Let flags be unfurled! Let fanfares flare!"
Father's forgiveness formed the foundation
For the former fugitive's future fortitude!

—— **MEMBERSHIP DRIVE** ——

We had a membership drive in our church. Last week we drove off 35.

—— **MEMBRANE** ——

The part of your brain you remember with.

—— **MEMOIRS** ——

There's nothing a man can do to improve himself so much as writing his memoirs.

—— **MEMORY** ——

A tourist was introduced to an Indian in New Mexico who was said to have a perfect memory. Skeptical, the tourist asked, "What did you have for breakfast on September 10, 1943?"
The Indian answered, "Eggs."
The man scoffed, "Everyone eats eggs for breakfast. He's a phony."

Thirteen years later the traveler's train stopped again in the small New Mexico town, and he saw the same Indian sitting on the train platform. The tourist went up to him and said jovially, "How!"
The Indian answered, "Scrambled."

Teacher: What was George Washington most famous for?
Student: His memory.
Teacher: That's an odd answer. What makes you think Washington's memory was so remarkable?
Student: Well, they sure put up a lot of monuments to it.

——— MEMORY VERSE ———

A little boy was writing the memory verse for the day on the blackboard: "Do one to others as others do one to you."

Sunday school teacher: Do you remember your memory verse?
Student: I sure do. I even remember the zip code ... John 3:16.

——— MEN ———

Wife: All men are fools.
Husband: Of course, dear. We are made like that so you girls won't have to be old maids.

——— MENTAL BLOCK ———

A street on which several psychiatrists live.

——— MENTAL PATIENTS ———

When a busload of people entered a large restaurant, the leader of the group approached the manager.
"Sir, I'm Mr. Phillips of the Kingsview Mental Hospital. These nice folks are mental patients in our halfway house program. They've all been

cured, but they do have one small problem: They will want to pay you in bottle caps. So if you'll be so kind as to humor them in this way, I'll take care of the bill when they are through."

The manager, wanting to be a good citizen, went along and collected the bottle caps. The leader returned and with gratitude said, "Thank you so very much. I'll pay the bill now. Do you have change for a hubcap?"

——— MESS ———

College boy to his mother: "I decided that I want to be a political science major and that I want to clean up the mess in the world!"

"That's very nice," purred his mother. "You can go upstairs and start with your room."

———◆———

First husband: Does your wife keep a messy home?
Second husband: Let's put it this way—when the toast pops out of the toaster, it takes an hour to find it.

——— METAL AGE ———

We live in the Metal Age:
- silver in the hair.
- gold in the teeth.
- lead in the pants.
- iron in the veins.

——— METRIC COOKIE ———

A gram cracker.

——— MID-LIFE CRISIS ———

You'll have to excuse me but I'm going through a very difficult time in a man's life. I'm too tired to work and too broke to quit.

———— MIDDLE AGE ————

Middle age is when all one's energy goes to waist.

————◆————

You're middle-aged when your stomach goes out for a career of its own.

————◆————

A middle-aged man's waistline is his line of least resistance.

————◆————

Middle age is that period when you are just as young as ever, but it takes a lot more effort.

————◆————

Middle age is when you still have the old spark, but it takes more puffing.

————◆————

Maybe they call it middle age because that's where it shows first.

————◆————

Middle age is the time when your idea of getting ahead is staying even.

————◆————

Middle age is when you know all the answers and nobody asks you the questions.

————◆————

The hardest decision in life is when to start middle age.

————◆————

Middle age is when the narrow waist and the broad mind begin to change places.

———— MIDDLE OF ROAD ————

A fellow who tries to straddle an issue is like one in the middle of the highway, subject to being hit by both lines of traffic.

MIDGET

During the days of the Salem, Massachusetts, witch hunts, a midget was imprisoned for fortune-telling. She later escaped from jail, and the headline in the local newspaper read: SMALL MEDIUM AT LARGE.

MILITARY

During a practical exercise at a military police base, the instructor was giving the class instruction in unarmed self-defense. After presenting a number of different situations in which they might find themselves, he asked a student, "What steps would you take if someone were coming at you with a big, sharp knife?"
The student replied, "Big ones!"

MILKMAN

Milkman: Are you sure you want 54 quarts of milk?
Lady: Yes. My doctor told me to take a bath in milk.
Milkman: Do you want it pasteurized?
Lady: No, just up to my chin.

MILKTOAST

Overpowering wife to milktoast husband: "You be quiet. When I want your opinion, I'll give it to you."

MILLION

"How many make a dozen?"
"Twelve."
"And how many make a million?"
"Very few."

MILLIONAIRE

A billionaire after taxes.

132

—— MIND ——

"Something came into my mind just now and went away again."
"Maybe it was lonely."

———◆———

"I believe I could write like Shakespeare if I had a mind to try it."
"Yes, nothing is wanting but the mind!"

—— MIND YOUR OWN BUSINESS ——

To keep your teeth in good shape, mind your own business.

—— MINE ENEMIES ——

The little young lady of the house, by way of punishment for some minor misdemeanor, was compelled to eat her dinner alone at a little table in a corner of the dining room. The rest of the family paid no attention to her presence until they heard her audible praying over her repast with the words, "I thank thee, Lord, for preparing a table before me in the presence of mine enemies."

—— MINISTER ——

Mother: Quick, Henry, call the doctor. Johnny just swallowed a coin.
Father: I think we ought to send for the minister. He can get money out of anybody.

———◆———

A minister preached a very short sermon. He explained, "My dog got into my office and chewed up some of my notes."
At the close of the service a visitor asked, "If your dog ever has pups, please let my pastor have one of them."

———◆———

Wife: Who was that at the door, dear?
Husband: It was that new minister. He has been by four times this week.
Wife: What is his name?
Husband: I think it's Pester Smith.

———◆———

Delivering a speech at a banquet on the night of his arrival in a large city, a visiting minister told several anecdotes he expected to repeat at meetings the next day. Because he wanted to use the jokes again, he requested that the reporters omit them from any accounts they might turn in to their newspapers. A cub reporter, in commenting on the speech, ended his piece with the following: "The minister told a number of stories that cannot be published."

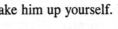

Q: What is the difference between a doctor and a minister?
A: One practices and the other preaches.

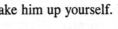

While the minister was speaking, a man fell asleep. The minister raised his voice and pounded the pulpit but the man would not wake up. Finally, the minister called to a deacon, "Go wake that man up."
The deacon replied, "Wake him up yourself. You put him to sleep!"

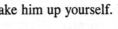

A minister was asked to inform a man with a heart condition that he had just inherited a million dollars. Everyone was afraid the shock would cause a heart attack and the man would die.
The minister went to the man's house and said, "Joe what would you do if you inherited a million dollars?" Joe responded, "Well, pastor, I think I would give half of it to the church."
And the minister fell over dead.

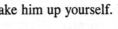

Minister at funeral service: Friends, in this coffin is the body of our beloved departed one. It is only the shell—the nut has gone!

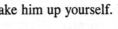

The minister of a large church asked the secretary to put his topic on the bulletin board so that everyone could see what his next Sunday's sermon would be. He said, "My topic is 'Are Ministers Cracking Up?'"

The secretary put up the following announcement: "Our Minister's Cracking Up."

Priest: Rabbi, when are you going to break down and eat ham?
Rabbi: At your wedding, Father.

Pastor: Mrs. Janelli, what did you think of the sermon?
Mrs. Janelli: Very good, pastor. It was so very instructive. You know, we really didn't know what sin was till you came here.

The new minister stood at the church door greeting the members as they left the Sunday morning service. Most of the people were very generous in telling the new minister how they liked his message, except for one man who said, "That was a very dull and boring sermon, pastor."

In a few minutes the same man appeared again in the line and said, "I didn't think you did any preparation for your message, pastor."

Once, again, the man appeared, this time muttering, "You really blew it. You didn't have a thing to say, pastor."

Finally the minister could stand it no longer. He went over to one of the deacons and inquired about the man.

"Oh, don't let that guy bother you," said the deacon. "He is a little slow. All he does is go around repeating whatever he hears other people saying."

A minister from the city was filling the pulpit in a small farm community. After his sermon he was invited over to the house of one of the members for lunch. In the course of the conversation, he mentioned with pride that his son had won first prize in the 100-yard dash.

"I know just how you must feel," declared the member understandingly. "I remember how pleased I was last year when our pig got the blue ribbon at the fair."

After the funeral a minister posted this notice on the church bulletin board: "Brother Poure departed for heaven at 3:30 A.M."

The next day he found the following written below his announcement: "Heaven, 8:00 P.M.—Mr. Poure has not arrived yet. Great Anxiety."

———◆———

Thirteen ministers were on a flight to New York. When they came into a large storm, they told the stewardess to tell the pilot that everything would be okay because 13 ministers were on board.

Later the stewardess returned from the cockpit.

"What did the pilot say?" one preacher asked.

"He said he was glad to have 13 ministers aboard but he would rather have four good engines."

——— MINK ———

I promised my wife a mink for her birthday—if she'd keep his cage clean.

——— MINOR OPERATION ———

One performed on somebody else.

——— MIRACULOUS ———

A traveling preacher was debating with a Texas oilman who doubted the miracle of divine chastisement. "Let me tell you of a remarkable occurrence," the preacher said. "In this morning's paper, there's an article about a politician who was struck by lightning while he was lying. Miraculous incident, wasn't it?"

"I don't know now," the Texan replied. "It would be more of a miracle if lightning struck a politician when he wasn't lying."

——— MIRROR ———

"I practice smiling in front of a mirror."

"I bet it works...I can't keep from laughing myself."

———◆———

"Is this one of your silly abstract paintings?"

"No, that's a mirror!"

———◆———

Mrs. Jones was standing in her kitchen with a friend. She looked out the window and pointed at the neighbor's wash hanging on the clothesline and said to her friend, "Just look at Mrs. Martin's wash. It sure looks dirty. Look at all those gray streaks on her laundry."

Her friend replied, "Those streaks aren't on your neighbor's wash—they're on your window!

──────── **MISBEHAVING** ────────

Misbehaving children are youngsters whose parents embarked on the sea of matrimony without a paddle.

──────── **MISCHIEF** ────────

The chief's daughter.

──────── **MISER** ────────

"Could you tell me how you became such a rich man?"
"Turn out the lights and I will tell you the story."
"You need not tell the story. I think I already know."

──────── **MISFIT** ────────

In a small town everyone made fun of a local misfit. They would hold out a dime and a nickel to him and ask him which he wanted. He would always choose a nickel. One day someone asked him why he always chose the nickel. The misfit replied, "If I ever took a dime, they'd quit giving me nickels."

──────── **MISJUDGE** ────────

A lady judge who's not married.

──────── **MISTAKE** ────────

What a doctor buries.

──────── ◆ ────────

A well-adjusted person is one who makes the same mistake twice without getting nervous.

———◆———

Man: Pastor, do you think it is right for one man to profit from another man's mistake?
Pastor: Why, most certainly not!
Man: Then would you mind returning the $25 I gave you last year for marrying me?

———◆———

Every married man should forget his mistakes. There is no use in two people remembering the same thing.

———◆———

Boss: How can one person make so many mistakes in a single day?
Employee: I get up early.

——— MODEL HUSBAND ———

Always some other woman's.

——— MODERN EDUCATION ———

Learning the three R's—rah, rah, rah!

——— MODESTY ———

The art of encouraging others to find out for themselves how important you are.

——— MONDAY ———

Prisoner: You mean they're going to hang me?
Guard: Yes, on Monday morning.
Prisoner: Can't you hang me on Saturday?
Guard: Why don't you want to hang on Monday?
Prisoner: Well, it seems like a terrible way to start the week.

—— MONEY ——

When someone says, "It's only money," it's usually your money he's talking about.

———◆———

Money used to talk—then it whispered. Now it just sneaks off.

———◆———

Most money is tainted. Taint yours and taint mine.

———◆———

The easiest way to teach children the value of money is to borrow some from them.

———◆———

Money has wings and most of us see only the tail feathers.

———◆———

There's something bigger than money—bills.

———◆———

Money brings only misery. But with money you can afford it.

———◆———

Photographer (to young man): It will make a much better picture if you put your hand on your father's shoulder.
Father: It would be much more natural if he had his hand in my pocket.

———◆———

Money isn't everything and don't let anybody tell you it is. There are other things such as stocks, bonds, letters of credit, traveler's checks, drafts...

———◆———

Wife to husband: Of course I spend more than you make, dear. I have great confidence in you.

———◆———

Money talks. It says good-bye.

Joe: Money doesn't bring happiness.
Moe: Can you prove it?
Joe: Sure, you take a guy with 40 million dollars. He ain't any happier than a man with 37 million dollars.

Credit manager: Are you going to pay us something on that account?
Customer: I can't just now.
Credit manager: If you don't, I'll tell all your other creditors that you paid us in full.

Blessed are the young, for they shall inherit the national debt.

A member of the Inca tribe was captured by the Spanish. The captain told his interpreter to say to the Inca Indian, "Tell him if he doesn't tell us where they have hidden all of their gold, we will burn both of his feet in the fire."

Through the interpreter the Inca Indian responded, "I'd rather die than tell you where the gold is." With that they burned his feet in the fire.

The captain then told the interpreter to say, "Tell him if he doesn't tell us where the gold is hidden, we will hang him from that noose on the tree over there."

The Inca Indian again responded, "I'd rather die than tell you where the gold is." With that, they took him over to the tree and hanged him until he could hardly breathe.

The Spanish captain then ordered the Indian to be brought to him again. This time he said to the interpreter, "Tell him if he doesn't tell us where the gold is, we will skin him alive."

The Inca Indian could stand it no longer and said, "The gold is hidden in a little cave just behind the large waterfall. The waterfall is one mile over the hill to the right."

The interpreter related the following to the captain, "He said that he would rather die than tell you where the gold is."

It takes twice as much money to live beyond your means as it used to.

If the president asks me to tighten my belt again, I'm liable to end up with gangrene of the stomach.

Today a dollar saved is a quarter earned.

Two men both grabbed for the check after eating lunch together. The man to get the check said, "Either you're losing your grip, or I don't know my own strength."

Martin: Haven't you forgotten that you owe me $500?
George: I should say not. Didn't you see me trying to duck into that alley to avoid you?

Sign in store: "Cash only, please. We know that your check is good, but we don't trust the banks."

Young man: I say, old man, could you lend me one dollar?
Old man: I'm a little deaf in that ear; go around to the other one.
Young man: Could you lend me five dollars?
Old man: Lend you what?
Young man: Five dollars.
Old man: Oh, you had better go back to the one-dollar ear.

Clarence: I'm looking for someone to lend me $50.
Richard: Well, you've got a nice day for it.

Show me a man who hides his wallet in the freezer, and I'll show you a guy who has cold cash to spend.

———◆———

Renter: I'll send you my check for the first of the month.
Manager: Could you give me a rough idea of what month?

———◆———

A theater manager found a wallet with no name and $700 in it. He announced to the audience, "Will the person who lost the $700 please form a double line at the box office?"

———◆———

The economy is terrible. At the beginning of the year, the politicians promised things would improve by the last quarter. Well, I'm down to my last quarter and they haven't improved.

———◆———

Reporter: Mr. Paul Getty, you are a very wealthy man. Would you say that your holdings would be worth a billion dollars?
Mr. Getty: I suppose so, but remember: A billion doesn't go as far as it used to.

———◆———

Visitor: Where is the capital of the USA?
Native: Spread all over the world.

———◆———

I hope they don't raise the standard of living any higher. I can't afford it now.

———◆———

The worst thing about history is that every time it repeats itself the price goes up.

———◆———

Things are so bad financially that one supermarket is putting in a recovery room.

———◆———

Doctor: Well, your examination is over and you are as sound as a dollar.
Banker: As bad as that! (And he fainted dead away!)

Willard: There are thousands of ways of making money, but only one honest way.
Donald: What's that?
Willard: Ah-ha—I knew you wouldn't know!

Joe: I bought this item at the 15-cent store.
Moe: You mean, the five-and-ten store.
Joe: Well, five and ten makes 15.

Money doesn't go as far as it used to, but at least it goes faster.

Money does make a difference. If you have two jobs and you're rich, it is called diversified interests. If you have two jobs and you're poor, you call it moonlighting.

Money may talk but it seems to be very hard of hearing when you call it.

The reason money is called "cold cash" is because we don't keep it long enough to get it warm.

Myles: Suppose you loan Ralph $10 and he agrees to repay you at the rate of a dollar a week. How much money would you have after seven weeks?
Jay: Nothing.
Myles: Nothing? You don't know very much about math.
Jay: You don't know much about Ralph.

Joe: Hello, Roger, what's new?
Roger: How about that $20 you owe me?
Joe: Nothing new, eh?

———◆———

"I want to have my face on some money."
"I would be glad if I had my hands on some."

——— **MONKEY** ———

"All the kids at school say I look like a monkey."
"Hush up and comb your face!"

——— **MONOLOGUE** ———

Son: What is a monologue, Dad?
Dad: That's a conversation between a husband and a wife.
Son: But our teacher said that was a dialogue.
Dad: Your teacher isn't married.

——— **MOODS** ———

My husband has three moods . . . hungry, thirsty, and both.

——— **MOONSHINE** ———

The prosecution and defense had both presented their final arguments in a case involving a Kentucky moonshiner.

The judge turned to the jury and asked, "Before giving you your instructions, do any of you have any questions?"

"Yes, Your Honor," replied one of the jurors. "Did the defendant boil the malt one or two hours, does he cool it quickly, and at what point does he add the yeast?"

——— **MORNING** ———

I hate mornings . . . they're so early.

MORTGAGE

A small house is better than a large mortgage.

MOSQUITO

The mosquito has no preference,
He bites folks fat or thin.
But the welt that he raises, itches like blazes,
And that's where "the rub" comes in.

MOTHER

Mother to fussy son: Twenty years from now you'll be telling some girl what a great cook your mother was . . . now eat your dinner.

MOTHER'S DAY

Mother's Day brings back memories of maternal advice and admonition. Picture the scene with these famous offspring.

Alexander the Great's mother: How many times do I have to tell you—you can't have everything you want in this world!

Franz Schubert's mother: Take my advice, son. Never start anything you can't finish.

Achilles' mother: Stop imagining things. There's nothing wrong with your heel.

Madame de Pompadour's mother: For heaven's sake, child, do something about your hair!

Sigmund Freud's mother: Stop pestering me! I've told you a hundred times the stork brought you!

MOTHER-IN-LAW

A woman who is never outspoken.

———◆———

My mother-in-law sent me two sweaters for Christmas. When she came for a visit, I put on one of the sweaters. The first thing she said was, "What's the matter? Didn't you like the other one?"

———◆———

I didn't mind it when my wife and my mother-in-law both said, "I do" at the wedding . . . but when I had to carry the two of them over the threshold, that was too much.

Did you hear about the man who was driving down the street, when all of a sudden he came across a long line of people. They were all walking single file in the middle of the road. He drove past 100, 200, 300, until he lost count. All of them were walking single file down the yellow line in the center of the street.

Finally, up ahead he saw the line slowing down to a standstill. At the head of the line he saw a hearse, and then another hearse, and then a big black limousine. The limousine had a flat tire and the driver was changing the tire. The man's curiosity was so great that he pulled his car over to the side of the road, got out, walked over to the limousine, and knocked on the window.

The window rolled down, and he saw a man in a black suit and next to him on the seat was a dog. Finally the man spoke to the fellow in the black suit. "Pardon me, sir," he said. "But I have never seen a funeral like this before. Could you tell me what is going on?"

The man in the suit replied, "Well, in the first hearse is my wife. The dog sitting next to me killed her."

"Oh, I'm terribly sorry," said the man. "But what about the second hearse?"

The man in the suit said, "In the second hearse is my mother-in-law, and the dog next to me killed her also."

"I'm so sorry," said the man. He then started to walk back to his car. About halfway there, he turned around and went back to the limousine. He said, "Excuse me, sir, but would it be possible to borrow your dog for awhile?"

(Short pause) The man in the black suit replied, "Get in line."

"My mother-in-law passed away last week."
"What was the complaint?"
"There was no complaint. Everybody was satisfied."

——— MOTIVATION ———

A young man had a job with a company that required him to work very late at night. In going home after work, he found that it was fastest to walk through a cemetery near his home. One night when he was very tired, he accidently fell into a freshly dug grave.

At first he was not too concerned, but when he realized that he could not get out because the hole was too deep, he became somewhat hysterical. Finally, in complete exhaustion, he sat down in the corner of the grave and fell asleep.

Shortly thereafter another man decided to walk through the cemetery and happened to fall into the same grave. He too went through great effort to get out but could not. He then moved around the grave until he stepped on the first man who was asleep. The first man woke up and shouted, "You can't get out of here."

But he did.

MOTORCYCLE

Two men were traveling on a motorcycle on a windy winter day. When it became too breezy for one, he stopped and put his overcoat on backward to keep the wind from ballooning it away from him. A few miles further on, the motorcycle hit a tree, killing the driver and stunning the fellow with the reversed coat. Later, when the coroner visited the scene, he said to a rookie policeman standing nearby, "What happened?"

"Well," the officer replied, "one of them was dead when I got here, and by the time I got the head of the other one straightened around, he was dead, too."

MOUNTAIN CLIMBING

Max looked up at the steep, icy mountainside. "I can't do it," he said.

His companions begged him to climb the mountain with them. But he refused to move. "I'm against mountain climbing," he said.

Now they call him "Anti-climb Max."

MOUSE

Teacher: Robert Burns wrote "To a Field Mouse."
Student: I'll bet he didn't get an answer.

——— MOUSETRAP ———

Young wife: Don't forget to bring home another mousetrap.
Husband: What's the matter with the one I brought yesterday?
Young wife: It's full!

——— MOUTH ———

It's better to keep your mouth shut and appear stupid than to open it and remove all doubt.

———◆———

To avoid trouble, breathe through your nose, and keep your mouth shut.

——— MOVIE ———

Wife: I thought the movie and the acting stank!
Husband: I can't say I liked it that well.

———◆———

Actor: Do come and see my picture and you'll leave the theater a happier man.
Friend: Yes, I always do feel much better after a good sleep.

———◆———

I went to one of those new movies last week. It was so bloody that it was rated "O-positive."

———◆———

They show movies on the planes these days. Coming from Chicago last week, the pilot wouldn't get on. He'd already seen the picture.

———◆———

A mother and daughter were watching a 1930s film on TV. As it ended with the usual romantic clinch and fadeout of that era, the teenager said, "Gosh, Mom, your movies ended where ours begin."

——— MUD PIE ———

A distraught mother went to a psychiatrist and said that her son was always making mud pies, and when he had finished them he ate them.

148

"That's not too unusual," said the psychiatrist. "Lots of boys make mud pies and try to eat them."

"I'm not so sure of that," said the mother, "and neither is my son's wife."

––––––– **MUGGING** –––––––

Then there's the city where crime has gotten so bad that citizens figure muggings into their budgets.

––––––– **MUGWUMP** –––––––

One who sits on a political fence with his mug on one side and his wump on the other.

––––––– **MULE** –––––––

Cutting off a mule's ear won't make him a horse.

––––––– **MURDERER** –––––––

One who is presumed innocent until he is proved insane.

––––––– **MUSIC** –––––––

Nowadays, whatever is not worth saying is sung.

–––––◆–––––

"Are you fond of music?"
"Yes, but keep right on playing."

–––––◆–––––

Notice in the church bulletin: "Mrs. Smith will sink two numbers. She will be accompanied by the choir."

––––––– **MUSTACHE** –––––––

Teacher: Can any bright pupil tell me why a man's hair turns gray before his mustache?
Student: 'Cause his hair has a 20-year head start on his mustache.

–––––◆–––––

Suzie: George's mustache made me laugh.
Jeanie: Yeah. It tickled me, too.

———— MUZZLED ————

A bear never knows until he is muzzled how many people are not afraid of him.

———— MY COUNTRY ————

Sometimes you wonder what kids are really learning. Yesterday a teacher pointed at the flag, turned to my six-year-old, and asked him what it was.
He answered, "It is the flag of my country."
The teacher couldn't leave well enough alone. She said, "Now tell me the name of your country."
And he said, " 'Tis of Thee!"

———— MY WIFE ————

Joe: My wife has been using a flesh-reducing roller for nearly two months.
Moe: Can you see any results?
Joe: Yes, the roller is much thinner.

———◆———

"I wouldn't say my wife is a poor housekeeper, but she doesn't turn on the stove. She just lights the grease."

———◆———

Customer: I've come back to buy that television I was looking at yesterday.
Salesman: That's good. May I ask what the one dominating thing was that made you want this set?
Customer: My wife.

———◆———

I don't know what to get my wife anymore. First she wanted a mink; I got her a mink. Then she wanted a silver fox; I got her a silver fox. It was ridiculous . . . the house was full of animals.

———◆———

My wife just had plastic surgery . . . I took away all her credit cards.

———◆———

My wife talks so much I get hoarse just listening to her.

———◆———

My wife is the sweetest, most tolerant, most beautiful woman in the world. This is a paid political announcement.

———◆———

I walked into a store and said, "This is my wife's birthday. I'd like to buy her a beautiful fountain pen."
The clerk winked at me and said, "A little surprise, eh?"
I said, "Yes, she's expecting a Cadillac."

———◆———

"My wife always has the last word."
"You're lucky. Mine never gets to it."

———◆———

One day my wife drove up the side of a building and there was another woman driver coming down.

———◆———

"Every once in awhile my wife puts on one of those mud packs."
"Does it improve her looks?"
"Only for a few days—then the mud falls off!"

———◆———

"Why are you adding up those figures?"
"My wife said she is going to lose four pounds a month. I figure that in 32 months I'll be rid of her!"

———◆———

My wife thinks she's Teddy Roosevelt. She runs from store to store, yelling, "*Charge!*"

———◆———

"My wife has been cooking a chicken for two days."
"For two days?"

"Yeah! The cookbook said to cook it one-half-hour to the pound—and my wife weighs 110 pounds!"

Bob: My wife treats me like an idol.
Ray: Why do you say that?
Bob: She feeds me burnt offerings at meals.

"My wife says if I don't chuck golf, she'll leave me!"
"That's too bad."
"Yes, I'll miss her."

When we first married my wife was not a very good cook. She would make new desserts and have me try them before dinner.

One day I came home and she told me that she had just made a pumpkin pie. She told me to try some. I said, "How about after dinner?" She said, "No, I want you to try it now."

I don't want to say it was bad, but I had to drink four glassfuls!

I miss my wife's cooking . . . as often as I can.

My wife's meals are something to behold . . . not to eat, just behold.

My wife had a terrible accident in the kitchen the other night . . . and I ate it!

Joe: My wife is very touchy. The least little thing will set her off.
Moe: You're lucky. Mine is a self-starter.

My wife spends a fortune on cold creams and oils—puts them all over her body. I went to grab her; she slid out of bed.

My wife and I just celebrated our Tin Anniversary . . . 12 years eating out of cans.

My wife will never find where I hid my extra money. I hid it in my socks that need mending!

"Why are you so sad, Bill?"
"My wife said she wouldn't talk to me for 30 days."
"Why should that make you sad?"
"Today is her last day!"

———◆———

"My wife is always asking for money," complained a man to his friend. "Last week she wanted $200. The day before yesterday she asked me for $125. This morning she wanted $150."
"That's crazy," said the friend. "What does she do with it all?"
"I don't know," said the man, "I never give her any."

———◆———

My wife puts cold cream on at night, an inch thick. Then she puts those curlers in her hair, puts a fishing net over the whole thing, and says, "Kiss me."
I say, "Take me to your leader."

———◆———

I came home last night and there was the car in the dining room. I said to my wife, "How did you get the car in the dining room?"
She said, "It was easy. I made a left turn when I came out of the kitchen."

My wife likes those little foreign cars. I bought her two . . . one for each foot.

My wife changes her hair so many times she has sort of a convertible top.

———◆———

"I try to do everything to make my wife happy. She complained about the housework so I bought her an electric iron, an electric dishwasher, and an electric dryer. Then she complained there were so many gadgets around the house she had no room to sit down. What could I do?"

"Buy her an electric chair!"

─────── MYSTIC ───────

Attendant: Do you wish to consult with Wing Tong Fong, the great Chinese mystic?

Lady: Yes, tell him his mother is here from the Bronx.

N

─────── NAG ───────

A woman with no horse sense.

──────◆──────

Man: Do you serve breakfast here?

Waitress: Sure; what'll it be?

Man: Let me have watery scrambled eggs... and some burnt toast... and some weak coffee, lukewarm.

Waitress: Whatever you say, sir.

Man: Now, are you doing anything while that order is going through?

Waitress: Why—no, sir.

Man: Then sit here and nag me awhile... I'm homesick!

─────── NAIL POLISH ───────

Q: What would you use to shine a nail?

A: Nail polish.

─────── NAIL-BITING ───────

"I finally made my son stop biting his nails."

"How did you manage to do that?"
"I made him wear shoes."

———— NAILS ————

"Do you file your nails?"
"No, I just cut them off and throw them away."

———— NAME ————

First cowboy: My name's Tex.
Second cowboy: You from Texas?
First cowboy: Nope, I'm from Louisiana, but who wants to be called Louise?

———————◆———————

If you are looking for a name for a new pet, try one of these:

A white mouse	Mousey Tung
A collie	Flower
A collie	Melon
A boxer	Shorts
A rabbit	Transit
A donkey	Shane
A pigeon	Toad
A frog	Horn
A horse	Greeley
A rooster	Shire Sos
A gopher	Broke
A crow	Magnon
A sparrow	Agnew
A kitten	Kaboodle
A cat	Mandu
A rat	Frank Lloyd
A rat	Fink

———————◆———————

Lady of the house: I want you to stand at the front door and call the guests' names as they arrive.
Butler: Very well, madam. I've been wanting to do that for years.

——— NARROW ———

A narrow mind and a wide mouth usually go together.

——— NASTY LETTER ———

After receiving a nasty letter, a pastor sent it back to one of his members with this note: "The enclosed letter arrived on my desk a few days ago. I am sending it to you because I think you should know that some idiot is sending out letters over your signature. Cordially . . ."

——— NATURAL SELECTION ———

To take the largest piece.

——— NAVY ———

Two sailors were adrift on a raft in the ocean. They had just about given up hope of rescue. One began to pray, "O Lord, I've led a worthless life. I've been unkind to my wife and I've neglected my children, but if you'll save me, I promise . . ."

The other shouted, "Hold it. I think I see land."

◆

A young naval student was being put through the paces by an old sea captain:

"What would you do if a sudden storm sprang up on the starboard?"

"Throw out an anchor, sir."

"What would you do if another storm sprang up aft?"

"Throw out another anchor, sir."

"And if another terrific storm sprang up forward, what would you do?"

"Throw out another anchor."

"Hold on," said the captain. "Where are you getting all those anchors from?"

"From the same place you're getting your storms, sir."

——— NEARSIGHTED ———

Jack: I'm so nearsighted I nearly worked myself to death.

Elmer: What's being nearsighted got to do with working yourself to death?

Jack: I couldn't tell whether the boss was watching me or not, so I had to work all the time.

——— NECESSITY ———

Almost any luxury you see in the home of a neighbor.

——— NECKING ———

The dean of women at a large coeducational college posted an announcement that started with the sentence: "The president of the college and I have decided to stop necking on the campus."

——— NEIGHBOR ———

The man in the repair shop said, "Here it is, Mr. Wilson. Your lawn-mower is now in perfect condition. Just one precaution, however. Don't ever lend it to a neighbor."

"That's just the trouble," said Mr. Wilson. "I am the neighbor."

◆

Mother: I don't think the man upstairs likes Mike to play on his drums.
Father: Why do you say that?
Mother: Because this afternoon he gave Mike a knife and asked him if he knew what was inside the drum.

——— NERVOUS ———

He's so nervous, he keeps coffee awake.

◆

I got nervous after the copilot asked me how to get to the cockpit.

◆

Sheriff: "Excuse me for being nervous," he apologized as he slipped the noose over the condemned man's head. "This is my first hanging."
Man: "Mine too!"

——— NEUROTIC ———

Now there's a list of the ten most neurotic people. It's called "The Best-Stressed List."

◆

My fourth husband is more neurotic than my third husband. I should have never left my third husband.

——— **NEW ORLEANS** ———

A number of children from the neighborhood were invited to Mrs. Johnson's for a Thanksgiving dinner. She decided to do something different while serving the meal.

"Where are you originally from?" she asked one child.

"California," said the boy.

"Well then, I will give you the left wing."

She turned to another boy.

"Where are you from?"

"New York," he answered.

"You get the right wing."

She turned to the third boy. "Where are you from?"

"I'm from New Orleans and I ain't hungry."

——— **NEWS** ———

Wife to husband: Shall we watch the six o'clock news and get indigestion, or wait for the eleven o'clock news and have insomnia?

———◆———

A rich newspaper owner decided to give his newspaper to one of his three sons. He told them that he would give the paper to the one who could come up with the most sensational headline of only three words. The following is what they came up with:

First son: REAGAN TURNS COMMUNIST!

Second son: KHOMEINI BECOMES CHRISTIAN!

The winner was the third son who submitted only two words:

Third son: POPE ELOPES!

——— **NICKEL** ———

If a nickel knew what it is worth today, it would feel like two cents.

———◆———

About all you can get with a nickel these days is heads or tails.

——— **NIGHT** ———

Late-staying guest: Well, good night. I hope I have not kept you up too late.

Yawning host: Not at all. We would have been getting up soon, anyway.

──── NIGHT SCHOOL ────

Did you hear about the graduation ceremony at night school? Everybody wore a nightcap and nightgown.

──── NINE ────

Teacher: If two's company and three's a crowd, what are four and five?
Student: Nine.

──── NITRATE ────

Cheapest price for calling long-distance.

──── NITWIT ────

A nitwit is a person who tells you the first half of a joke, pauses to laugh for a few minutes, and then forgets the punch line.

──── NO HARM ────

A burglar entered the house of a Quaker and proceeded to rob it. The Quaker heard noises and took his shotgun downstairs and found the burglar. He aimed his gun and said gently: "Friend, I mean thee no harm, but thou standest where I am about to shoot."

──── NO-CAL SHAMPOO ────

Have you ever considered No-Cal shampoo? It's especially made for fatheads.

──── NOAH ────

Noah's remark as the animals were boarding the ark: Now I've herd everything.

Teacher: Do you know who built the ark?
Student: No.
Teacher: Correct.

Noah was standing at the gangplank checking off the pairs of animals when he saw three camels trying to get on board.

"Wait a minute!" said Noah. "Two each is the limit. One of you will have to stay behind."

"It won't be me," said the first camel. "I'm the camel whose back is broken by the last straw."

"I'm the one people swallow while straining at a gnat," said the second.

"I," said the third, "am the one that shall pass through the eye of a needle sooner than a rich man shall enter heaven."

"Come on in," said Noah, "the world is going to need all of you."

—————— NONSENSE ——————

A little nonsense now and then,
Is relished by the wisest men.

—————— NOODLE SOUP ——————

Customer: Yes, I know that fish is brain-food. But I don't care much for fish. Isn't there some other kind of brain-food?
Waiter: Well, there's noodle soup.

—————— NOSE ——————

Cleopatra's nose: Had it been shorter, the whole aspect of the world would have been altered.
—*Blaise Pascal*

————◆————

"So you had an operation on your nose?"
"Yes, it was getting so I could hardly talk through it."

—————— NOT RAISING HOGS ——————

I Would Like to Not Raise Hogs!
(Letter sent to the Secretary of Agriculture)
Dear Mr. Secretary:
My friend Bordereaux received a $1,000 check from the government for not raising hogs and so I am going into the not-raising-hogs business.

What I want to know is, what is the best kind of land not to raise hogs on and what is the best kind of hogs not to raise? I would prefer not to raise razorbacks, but if this is not the best kind not to raise, I will just as gladly not raise Durocs or Poland Chinas.

The hardest part of this business is going to be keeping an individual record on each of the hogs I do not raise.

My friend Bordereaux has been raising hogs for more than 20 years and the most he ever made was $400 in 1918, until this year when he received $1,000 for not raising hogs. Now, if I get $1,000 for not raising 50 hogs, I assume I will get $2,000 for not raising 100 hogs, etc.

I plan to start off on a small scale, holding myself down to not raising 4,000 hogs for which I will, of course, receive $80,000.

Now these hogs I will not raise will not eat 100,000 bushels of corn. I understand you pay farmers for not raising corn. Will you pay me for not raising 100,000 bushels of corn, which I will not feed to the hogs which I am not raising?

I want to get started as soon as possible, as this looks like a good time of year for not raising hogs.

> Yours very truly,
> Octover Brussard

––––––– NOTE –––––––

The following note was fastened to a defective parking meter by a rubber band:

"I put three nickels in this meter. License number 4761PQ."

"FRD719. Me, too!"

"So did I. JRY335."

"I'm not going to pay a nickel to find out if these guys are lying. WTM259."

––––––– NUDITY –––––––

Phyllis Diller says there's so much nudity in films that this year's Oscar for clothing design will probably go to a dermatologist.

——— NUMBERS ———

If the metric system ever takes over we may have to do the following:
A miss is as good as 1.6 kilometers.
Put your best 0.3 of a meter forward.
Spare the 5.03 meters and spoil the child.
Twenty-eight grams of prevention is worth 453 grams of cure.
Give a man 2.5 centimeters and he'll take 1.6 kilometers.
Peter Piper picked 8.8 liters of pickled peppers.

——— NUTS ———

There are more men than women in mental institutions—which goes to show who's driving whom nuts.

———◆———

A pastor got this note accompanying a box of goodies, addressed to him and his wife, from an elderly lady in the church.
Dear Pastor,
Knowing that you do not eat sweets, I am sending the candy to your wife—and nuts to you.

——— OARS ———

The fellow who's busy pulling on the oars hasn't got time to rock the boat.

——— OBEDIENCE ———

He that hath learned to obey will know how to command.

———◆———

There are two kinds of men who never amount to much: those who cannot do what they are told, and those who can do nothing else.

———◆———

One of the first things one notices in a backward country is that children are still obeying their parents.

––––––– **OBESITY** –––––––

Surplus gone to waist.

–––––◆–––––

One good thing you can say for his obesity is that a great deal of him is having a good time.

––––––– **OBSCENE** –––––––

What is this world coming to? I hear they just arrested a fellow who talks dirty to plants. Caught him making an obscene fern call!

––––––– **OBSCURITY** –––––––

Being the vice president of Italy.

––––––– **OBSTETRICIAN** –––––––

Sign in an obstetrician's office: "Pay-as-you-grow."

––––––– **OCTOPUS** –––––––

A cat with only eight lives left.

––––––– **ODD** –––––––

First boy: My dad is an Odd Fellow.
Second boy: Your mother is quite a peculiar character also.

––––––– **OFFERING** –––––––

An usher was passing the collection plate at a large church wedding. One of those attending looked up, very puzzled. Without waiting for the question, the usher nodded his head, "I know it's unusual, but the father of the bride requested it."

–––––◆–––––

Mother: Now remember to put some of your allowance in the offering at church.

Son: Why not buy an ice cream cone with it and let the cashier put it in the offering?

Minister before the morning offering: The Lord owns the cattle on a thousand hills. He only needs cowboys to round them up. Will the ushers please come forward for the offering?

A minister was just about ready to go into the church for the morning service when he discovered that he could not find the offering plates. He informed the chairman of the board of deacons.

"I can't find the offering plates. I have to start the service now. See if you can find something to collect the offering in."

The chairman of the board of deacons searched for something to collect the offering in. He could not find any plates, bags, or even boxes. He thought about someone's shoe, but dismissed that as not being too dignified.

When the time came for the offering, four ushers walked down the aisle wearing broad grins and carrying shiny receptacles. The chairman had resourcefully borrowed four hubcaps from a car in the parking lot.

A hat was passed around a church congregation for taking up an offering for the visiting minister.

Presently it was returned to him . . . conspicuously and embarrassingly empty. Slowly and deliberately, the parson inverted the hat and shook it meaningfully. Then raising his eyes to heaven, he exclaimed fervently, "I thank thee, dear Lord, that I got my hat back from this congregation."

OFFICE SIGN

In a very busy office there were three boxes for mail marked *Urgent*, *Frantic*, and *Most Frantic*.

OHIO

Teacher: Who discovered America?

164

Student: Ohio.

Teacher: Ohio? That's ridiculous. It was Columbus.

Student: Yes, sir. I know. But I didn't think it was necessary to mention the gentleman's first name, sir.

OIL

Wealth that slips through your fingers.

OLD

You're getting old if the gleam in your eye is the sun hitting your bifocals.

My husband is so old that he remembers Eve when she was just a rib.

Growing old doesn't seem so bad when you consider the alternative.

A trim-looking octogenarian was asked how he maintained his slim figure. "I get my exercise acting as a pallbearer for all my friends who exercise."

"My grandfather is 95 years old and every day he goes horseback riding—except during the month of July."

"Why not during July?"

"Because that is when the man who puts him on the horse goes on his vacation."

As you grow older you make a fool of yourself in a more dignified manner.

You can tell you are getting older when:

You sit in a rocking chair and can't get it going.

You burn the midnight oil after 8:00 P.M.
You look forward to a dull evening.
Your knees buckle and your belt won't.
Your little black book contains only names ending in M.D.
Your back goes out more than you do.
You decide to procrastinate and never get around to it.
Dialing long-distance wears you out.
You walk with your head held high, trying to get used to your bifocals.
You sink your teeth into a steak and they stay there.

——— OLD AGE ———

Patient: How can I live to be a hundred, doctor?
Doctor: Give up cookies, cake, and ice cream. Stop eating red meat, potatoes, and bread. And no soft drinks.
Patient: And if I do that, I will live to be a hundred?
Doctor: Maybe not, but it will certainly seem like it.

More people would live to a ripe old age if they weren't too busy providing for it.

Young man: Why did you live to be the age of 115?
Old man: Mainly because I was born in 1876.

"To what do you attribute your long life?" the reporter asked the centenarian.
"I don't rightly know yet," replied the old-timer. "I'm still dickering with two breakfast food companies."

The five "B's" of old age: bifocals . . . bunions . . . bridges . . . bulges . . . and baldness.

——— OLD CAR ———

Willy: Why did you bury your old car?
Billy: Well, the battery was dead, the pistons were shot, and then the engine died.

——— OLD DAYS ———

Nothing is more responsible for the good old days than a poor memory.

——— OLD FAITHFUL ———

He: Where are you going on your vacation?
Him: Yellowstone National Park.
He: Don't forget Old Faithful.
Him: She's going with me.

——— OLD MAID ———

A lady in waiting.

A lady in waiting and waiting and waiting.

A friend of an old maid asked her which she liked more in a man: brains, money, or appearance. The old maid responded, "Appearance—and the sooner the better."

——— OLD NATURE ———

A man was taken to court for stealing an item from a store. The man said to the judge, "Your Honor, I'm a Christian. I've become a new man. But I have an old nature also. It was not my new man who did wrong. It was my old man."

The judge responded, "Since it was the old man that broke the law, we'll sentence him to 60 days in jail. And since the new man was an accomplice in the theft, we'll give him 30 days also. I therefore sentence you both to 90 days in jail."

——— **OLD-TIMER** ———

One who remembers when people who wore blue jeans worked.

———◆———

You're an old-timer if you remember when the only babes politicians kissed were those in their mother's arms.

———◆———

You are an old-timer if you remember when a babysitter was called Mother.

——— **ONE FOOT** ———

Some speakers and most listeners would approve of the rule among certain tribes in Africa. Their regulation is that when a man rises to speak he must stand on one foot while delivering his speech. The minute the lifted foot touches the ground, the speech ends—or the speaker is forcibly silenced.

——— **ONE LESS** ———

Husband: Well, we have a tremendous party planned for tonight. I wonder how many truly great men will be here?
Wife: There will be one less than you think.

——— **ONE-HALF** ———

Trying hard to get on a bus, a woman snapped to the man in back of her, "If you were half a man, you'd help me onto this bus." He answered, "If you were half a lady, you wouldn't need any help."

——— **ONE-LINER** ———

A mini ha-ha.

——— **ONE-TRACK** ———

Most people operate on a one-track mind of two rails—*"me"* and *"I"*.

——— OOPS ———

Man: Just look at that young person with the short hair and blue jeans. Is it a boy or a girl?

Bystander: It's a girl; she's my daughter.

Man: Oh, please forgive me, sir. I had no idea you were her father.

Bystander: I'm not. I'm her mother.

———◆———

A tired guest at a formal function spoke to the man next to him: "Gee, this thing is a bore; I'm going to beat it!"

"I would, too," said the man, "but I've got to stay. I'm the host!"

———◆———

"Thank goodness that misery is over!"

"What misery?"

"Talking with the hostess. Have you been through it yet?"

"I don't have to. I'm the host."

———◆———

First man: Who is that awful-looking lady in the corner?

Second man: Why, that's my wife.

First man: Oh, I don't mean her (trying to get out of the situation), I mean the lady next to her.

Second man: That is my daughter.

——— OPERATION ———

Joe: I'm afraid I can't afford that operation now.

Moe: It looks like you'll have to talk about your old one for another year.

——— OPERETTA ———

Q: What is an operetta?

A: A girl who works for the telephone company.

——— OPINION ———

Writer: What do you think of my joke book? Give me your honest opinion.

Editor: It isn't worth anything.
Writer: I know, but give it to me anyway.

——— OPPORTUNIST ———

Any man who goes ahead and does what you always intended to do.

——— OPPORTUNITY ———

When your automobile engine develops a knock, chances are it's opportunity knocking for some mechanic.

———◆———

"May I ask you the secret of your success?"
"There is no easy street. You just jump at your opportunity."
"But how can I tell when my opportunity comes?"
"You can't. You've got to keep on jumping."

——— OPPOSITES ———

Your problem: When you get angry, it is because you are ill-tempered.
My situation: It just happens that my nerves are bothering me.

Your problem: When you don't like someone, it is because you are prejudiced.
My situation: I happen to be a good judge of human nature.

Your problem: When you compliment someone, it is because you use flattery.
My situation: I only encourage folks.

Your problem: When you take a long time to do a job, it is because you are unbearably slow and pokey.
My situation: When I take a long time, it is because I believe in quality workmanship.

Your problem: When you spend your paycheck in 24 hours, it is because you are a spendthrift.
My situation: When I do, it is because I am generous.

Your problem: When you stay in bed until 11 A.M., it is because you are a lazy, good-for-nothing.

My situation: When I stay in bed a little longer, it is because I am totally exhausted.

—— OPTIMIST ——

A person who thinks humorists will eventually run out of definitions of an optimist.

———◆———

He who thinks a housefly is looking for the way out.

———◆———

A man who goes into a restaurant without a dime and figures on paying for the meal with the pearl he hopes to find in the oyster.

———◆———

Twixt optimist and pessimist,
The difference is droll;
The optimist sees the doughnut,
The pessimist the hole.

———◆———

Q: What do they call a woman who runs the motor of her car while waiting for her husband?
A: An optimist.

———◆———

An optimist is someone who tells you to cheer up when things are going his way.

———◆———

An optimist is a fellow who grabs a fishing pole when he discovers that his basement is flooded.

—— ORANGES ——

Customer: Three of those oranges you sent me were rotten. I'll bring them back.

Merchant: That's all right, you needn't bring them back. Your word is just as good as the oranges.

——— ORATOR ———

One who misses many fine opportunities for keeping quiet.

——— ORATORY ———

The art of making deep noises from the chest that sound like important messages from the brain.

——— ORDEAL ———

What some ideal marriages turn out to be.

——— ORDER ———

Judge: Order in this court! I'll have order in this court!
Man: I'll have a hamburger with onions!

——— ORGANIST ———

The organist wanted to make an impression on the visiting clergyman with her musical accomplishment. She wrote a note to the old sexton who had been a little slack in his work of pumping enough air for the organ, and handed it to him just before the service started. But, making a natural mistake, the sexton passed the note on to the visiting clergyman, who opened it and read: "Keep blowing away until I give the signal to stop."

——— ORGANIZED ———

Don't confuse this confusion with disorganization . . . because we're not that organized yet.

——— ORTHOPEDIST ———

Orthopedists get all the breaks.

——— OURS ———

Wife: And another thing I want to tell you. I've noticed every time you talk, you say *my* house, *my* automobile, *my* chair, *my* shoes—everything's yours. You never say ours. I'm your partner. I'm your wife. It should be ours.

The husband paid no attention to his wife and just kept looking around the room for something.

Wife: What are you looking for?

Husband: Our pants.

——— OUT OF BUSINESS ———

Going out of business has become so profitable for one merchant that he's opening a chain of going-out-of-business stores.

——— OUTLYING ———

Gone to court.

——— OVERCOAT ———

A meek little man in a restaurant timidly touched the arm of a man putting on an overcoat. "Excuse me," he said, "but do you happen to be Mr. Smith of Newport?"

"No, I'm not!" the man answered impatiently.

"Oh-er-well," stammered the first man, "you see, I am, and that's his overcoat you're putting on."

——— OVERDRAWN ———

Husband: I just got a notice from the bank saying I'm overdrawn.

Wife: Try some other bank. They can't all be overdrawn.

——— OVEREATING ———

The destiny that shapes our ends.

——— OVERPOPULATION ———

Wife: This article on the overpopulation of the world says that somewhere in the world there is a woman having a baby every four seconds!

Husband: I think they ought to find that woman and stop her!

——— OVERTIME ———

Employer: How long did you work at your other job?

Job seeker: Fifty-five years.
Employer: How old are you?
Job seeker: Forty-five.
Employer: How could you work 55 years when you are only 45 years old?
Job seeker: Overtime.

--------- **OVERWEIGHT** ---------

He was so overweight that the only job he could get was pilot on the Goodyear blimp.

I don't want to say she is fat—but she is definitely overemphasized.

A fat man made a mad rush through the gate for an airplane. As he came back perspiring and frowning, the gateman said, "Just missed it, huh?" "No, I like to chase airplanes."

If he's not overweight, then he's certainly six inches too short.

--------- **PAIN IN THE NECK** ---------

"How is the pain in your neck?"
"He's out playing golf."

--------- **PAINT** ---------

Over bench: "Wet paint. Watch it or wear it."

——— PAINTING ———

Phil: Aren't you rather warm doing your painting all bundled up like that?
Bill: Well, it says right here on the paint can to be sure to put on three coats.

——— PAL ———

Dave: I'll never forget the time we were ice skating on the lake. Suddenly the ice broke and I plunged into the water. You threw off your coat and shoes, and jumped in after me. What a pal.

Walter: What do mean, pal? Why wouldn't I jump in after you? You had my jacket and skates on.

——— PANAMA CANAL ———

An inside strait.

——— PANHANDLER ———

A fellow walked up to a panhandler and politely remarked: "You're not too old and you look reasonably fit. Why don't you try to get a job?"

"I can't. I inherited this business from my father!"

——— PANTS ———

Pants are made for men and not for women. Women are made for men and not for pants. When a man pants for a woman and a woman pants for a man, that makes a pair of pants. Pants are like molasses, they are thinner in hot weather and thicker in cold weather. There has been much discussion as to whether pants is singular or plural; but it seems to us that when men wear pants it's plural, and when they don't, it's singular. If you want to make the pants last, make the coat first.

———◆———

Kenny: I just bought a new suit with two pairs of pants.
Lenny: Well, how do you like it?
Kenny: Fine, only it's too hot wearing two pairs.

——— PAPERWEIGHTS ———

A London street-market vendor posts this sign at his stall: "Lovely glass paperweights! The only way to keep housekeeping bills down!"

——— PARACHUTE JUMP ———

Just before a drafted farmboy made his first parachute jump, his sergeant reminded him, "Count ten and pull the first rip cord. If it snarls, pull the second rip cord for the auxiliary chute. After you land, our truck will pick you up."

The paratrooper took a deep breath and jumped. He counted to ten, and pulled the first cord. Nothing happened. He pulled the second cord. Again, nothing happened. As he careened crazily earthward, he said to himself, "Now I'll bet that truck won't be there either!"

——— PARADISE ———

Two ivory cubes with dots all over them.

——— PARALYZE ———

Two untruths.

——— PARDON ———

"I beg your pardon for coming so late."
"My dear, no pardons are needed. You can never come too late."

——— PARENTS ———

Wrinkles are hereditary. Parents get them from their children.

———◆———

I've wanted to run away from home more often since I've had kids than when I was a boy.

———◆———

The quickest way for a parent to get a child's attention is to sit down and look comfortable.

———◆———

My parents are in the iron and steel business. Mom irons and Dad steals.

——— PARKING ———

I solved the parking problem—I bought a parked car.

——— PARKING SPACE ———

Unoccupied space on the other side of the street.

——— PARROT ———

A dignified old clergyman owned a parrot of whom he was exceedingly fond, but the bird had picked up an appalling vocabulary of cuss words from a previous owner and, after a series of embarrassing episodes, the clergyman decided he would have to kill his pet.

A lady in his parish suggested a last-ditch remedy. "I have a female parrot," she said, "who is an absolute saint. She sits quietly on her perch and says nothing but, 'Let's pray.' Why don't you bring your parrot over and see if my own bird's good influence doesn't reform him?"

The clergyman said it was worth a trial, and the next night he arrived with his pet tucked under his arm. The bird took one look at the lady parrot and chirped, "Hi, toots. How about a little kiss?"

"My prayers have been answered," said the lady parrot gleefully.

——— PARSON ———

The parson of a tiny congregation in Arkansas disappeared one night with the entire church treasury, and the local constable set out to capture him. This he did, dragging the culprit back by the collar a week later. "Here's the varmint, folks," announced the constable grimly. "I'm sorry to say he's already squandered our money, but I drug him back so we can make him preach it out."

Operator: Do you wish to make a station-to-station call, sir?
Minister: No, parson-to-parson.

——— PARTING ———

Two partners had come to the parting of the ways over social and business differences.

"You stole my accounts," shouted one. "You crook."
"And you stole my wife," shouted the other. "You horse thief."

——— PASSION ———

Passion makes idiots of the cleverest men, and makes the biggest idiots clever.

——— PASSPORT PHOTO ———

A way to see yourself as others see you.

——— PAST TENSE ———

When you used to be nervous.

——— PASTOR ———

Friend: Pastor, how do you let off steam when you miss a shot and your golf ball goes into a sand trap?
Pastor: I just repeat the names of some of the members of my congregation . . . with feeling!

———◆———

Friend: Say, pastor, how is it that you're so thin and gaunt while your horse is so fat and sleek?
Pastor: Because I feed the horse and the congregation feeds me.

———◆———

Did you hear about the young pastor who fouled up the established routine? He didn't stand at the door and shake hands with the worshipers after the service. He went out to the curb and shook hands with the red-faced parents waiting for their children to come out of Sunday school.

———◆———

The pastor asked his congregation to participate in the morning offering and said, "Let us give generously—according to what you reported on your income tax."

———◆———

178

When the assistant pastor made the announcements he said, "The pastor will be gone tonight, and we will be having a service of singing and praise."

Notice in the church bulletin: There will be no healing service this Sunday due to the pastor's illness.

Remark to the pastor after the morning service: Every sermon you preach is better than the next one.

Greg: We call our pastor Reverend. What do you call yours?
Fred: We call ours Neverend.

Our pastor suffers from foot-and-mouth disease: He won't visit and he can't preach.

A pastor wired all his pews with electricity. One Sunday from his pulpit he said, "All who will give $100 toward the new building, stand up." He touched a button and 20 people sprang up.

"Fine, fine," the preacher beamed. "Now all who will give $500, stand up." He touched another button and 20 more jumped to their feet.

"Excellent," he shouted. "Now all who will give $1000, stand up." He threw the master switch and electrocuted 15 deacons.

A pastor, burdened by the importance of his work, went into the sanctuary to pray. Falling to his knees, he lamented, "O Lord, I am nothing! I am nothing!"

The minister of education passed by, and overhearing the prayer, was moved to join the pastor on his knees. Shortly he, too, was crying aloud, "O Lord, I too am nothing. I am nothing."

The janitor of the church, awed by the sight of the two men praying, joined them, crying, "O Lord, I also am nothing. I am nothing."

At this, the minister of education nudged the pastor and said, "Now look who thinks he's nothing!"

Frances: What do you think of our new pastor?

Sharon: On six days of the week he is invisible, and on the seventh day he is incomprehensible.

The minister's little daughter was sent to bed with a stomachache and missed her usual romp with her daddy. A few minutes later she appeared at the top of the stairs and called to her mother, "Mama, let me talk with Daddy."

"No, my dear, not tonight. Get back in bed."

"Please, Mama."

"I said no. That's enough now."

"Mother, I'm a very sick woman, and I must see my pastor at once."

PASTORAL VISIT

A minister habitually told his congregation that if they needed a pastoral visit to drop a note in the offering plate. One evening after services he discovered a note that said: "I am one of your loneliest members and heaviest contributors. May I have a visit tomorrow evening?" It was signed by his wife.

PATIENCE

It is easy finding reasons why other folks should be patient.

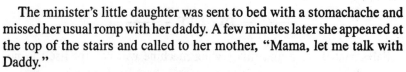

Patience is the art of concealing your impatience.

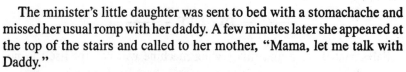

Patience is the ability to "count down" before "blasting off."

——— PAUL REVERE ———

A Texan was trying to impress on a Bostonian the valor of the heroes of the Alamo. "I'll bet you never had anything so brave around Boston," said the Texan.

"Did you hear of Paul Revere?" asked the Bostonian.

"Paul Revere?" said the Texan. "Isn't he the guy who ran for help?"

——— PAWNBROKER ———

One who lives off the flat of the land.

——— PAY OFF ———

Salesman: Believe me, this sewing machine will pay for itself in no time.

Customer: Good. When it does, send it to me.

——— PAYMENTS ———

Rod: I've got the worst kind of car trouble anybody could have.

Ron: What kind is it?

Rod: The engine won't start and the payments won't stop.

———◆———

The latest thing for a man who has everything is a calendar to remind him when the payments are due.

——— PEACEFUL COEXISTENCE ———

Visitors to a zoo were amazed to find a cage which was entitled "Peaceful Coexistence." It held a fox and four chickens. The zookeeper explained that it was easy to maintain the arrangement—all they had to do was to occasionally toss in a few more chickens.

——— PEANUT BUTTER ———

A bread spread.

——— **PEARLY GATES** ———

A minister and a congressman arrived at the pearly gates. Saint Peter greeted both of them and gave them their room assignments.

"Pastor, here are the keys to one of our nicest efficiency units. And for you, Mr. Congressman, the keys to our finest penthouse suite."

"What is the deal?" asked the minister. "This is unfair!"

"Listen," said Saint Peter, "ministers are a dime a dozen up here, but this is the first congressman we've ever seen."

——— **PEASHOOTER** ———

A baby blowgun.

——— **PEDESTRIAN** ———

A father who has kids who can drive.

——— **PEDIATRICIAN** ———

A man with little patients.

——— **PEEKABOO** ———

The act of spying on a ghost.

——— **PEEP** ———

He who peeps through the keyhole may lose his eye.

——— **PEN** ———

There's no wound deeper than a pen can give,
It makes men living dead, and dead men alive.

——— **PENICILLIN** ———

The best present for a man who's got everything is penicillin.

——— **PENNY A POINT** ———

A man arrived home early to find his wife in the arms of his best friend. The best friend commented how much he and the man's wife were in love with each other.

"Tell you what I'll do," said the best friend. "I'll play a game of cards for her. If I win, you divorce her, and if you win, I promise never to see her again. O.K.? How about playing gin rummy?"

"That's all right with me," agreed the husband. "And how about a penny a point to make the game a bit interesting?"

——— PENNY PINCHER ———

A Scotchman was arguing with a conductor as to whether the fare was 25 or 50 cents. Finally the disgusted conductor picked up the Scotchman's suitcase and tossed it off the train, just as they passed over a bridge. It landed with a splash.

"Man," screamed the Scotchman, "isn't it enough to try to overcharge me, but now you try to drown my little boy!"

——— PERFECT ———

Preacher: Does anyone know anyone who is perfect?
A little man in the back of the church raised his hand.
Preacher: Who do you know that is perfect?
Little man: My wife's first husband.

———◆———

Teacher: Johnny, how much is three times three?
Johnny: Nine.
Teacher: That's pretty good.
Johnny: Pretty good? Say, "it's perfect."

——— PERFECT PAIR ———

Husband: Nancy and Mike make a perfect pair, don't you think?
Wife: Yes. He's a pill and she's a headache.

——— PERFECT TIMING ———

Perfect timing is the ability to turn off the "hot" and "cold" shower faucets at the same time.

——— PERFECTION ———

The closest anyone comes to perfection is when he or she fills out a job application form.

———— **PERFUME** ————

Anyone who thinks chemical warfare is something new doesn't know much about women's perfume.

———— **PERIOD FURNITURE** ————

"Give an example of period furniture."
"Well, I should say an electric chair because it ends a sentence."

———— **PERPETUAL YOUTH** ————

The secret of perpetual youth is to lie about your age.

———— **PESSIMIST** ————

A pessimist is one who feels badly when he feels good for fear he'll feel worse when he feels better.

————◆————

No one ought to be so pessimistic he can't see some good in the other fellow's troubles.

————◆————

A pessimist is a person who grows his own crabgrass.

————◆————

A lot of pessimists get that way from financing optimists.

————◆————

A pessimist on world conditions had insomnia so bad the sheep were picketing him for shorter hours.

————◆————

A pessimist complains about the noise made when opportunity knocks.

————◆————

A pessimist is always building dungeons in the air.

————◆————

Always borrow from a pessimist . . . he never expects it back anyhow.

———◆———

A pessimist is one who, when faced with two evils, chooses them both.

———◆———

The pessimist thinks he is taking a chance—the optimist thinks he is grasping an opportunity.

———◆———

A pessimist is an optimist on his way home from Las Vegas.

——— PEST ———

A person who always butts in has an infuriating complex.

——— PET ROCK ———

Larry: My father won't let me have a pet rock.
Steve: Why not?
Larry: He's afraid it might have pebbles.

——— PHILOSOPHY ———

Unintelligible answers to insoluble problems.

——— PHOENICIANS ———

Sunday school teacher: What were the Phoenicians famous for?
Student: Blinds.

——— PHONE ———

Teacher: If you weigh 150 pounds and you sit in the bath, what happens?
Student: The phone rings.

——— PHONY ———

First husband: I bought my wife a string of pearls for her birthday.
Second husband: Why didn't you buy her something practical like a car?
First husband: Did you ever hear of a phony car?

——— PHOTOGRAPH ———

Mary: My husband had my photograph over his heart during the war. In fact, it stopped a bullet one time and saved his life.
Jerri: I'm not surprised, dear. It would stop anything.

——— PHOTOGRAPH ALBUMS ———

The strange views people take of things.

——— PHRENOLOGY ———

The science of picking the pocket through the scalp.

——— PIANO ———

Jack: My wife used to play the piano a lot, but since the children came she doesn't have time.
Mack: Children are a comfort, aren't they?

———◆———

Mark: My brother has been playing the piano for three years.
Clark: Aren't his fingers tired?

——— PICK ———

"Believe me, I pick my friends."
"Yes . . . to pieces."

——— PICKPOCKET ———

Someone who never learned to keep his hands to himself.

———◆———

Jack: Somebody picked my pocket.
Mack: What did he get?
Jack: Practice.

———————◆———————

Pete: Does your wife pick your suits?
Mike: No, just my pockets.

——— **PIE** ———

Delighted by the gift she had received, the lady spoke warmly to the boy: "At church tomorrow, I'll thank your mother for this lovely pie."
"If you don't mind," the boy suggested nervously, "would you thank her for two pies?"

——— **PIERCED EARS** ———

"Have you ever had your ears pierced?"
"No, but I have often had them bored."

——— **PIG IRON** ———

An iron for smoothing wrinkles off pigs.

——— **PIG TOES** ———

In a small town the farmers of the community had gotten together to discuss some important issues. About midway through the meeting a wife of one of the farmers stood up and spoke her piece.
One old farmer stood up and said, "What does she know about anything. I would like to ask her if she knows how many toes a pig has?"
Quick as a flash the woman replied, "Take off your boots, man, and count them!"

——— **PIGEON-TOWED** ———

There was once a beautiful fairy who yearned to be a ballet dancer. When she heard that the Royal Ballet was holding auditions in a nearby town, she harnessed 100 white pigeons to her chariot and flew to the theater. The director took one look at her spectacular entrance and told her to go away.

"But why?" she wailed.

"Because I've got enough pigeon-towed dancers in the company already."

——— PIGS ———

A city family decided to spend their vacation on a farm for the experience. The only thing they did not like was the noise that the pigs made.

The father wrote to the farmer the next year about coming again for another vacation. He asked if the pigs were still there. He received the following note from the farmer.

"Don't worry. We haven't had pigs on the farm since you were here."

"Do you know anything about pigs?"

"My father raised a big hog once."

"You're telling me."

——— PIGSTY ———

Traveler: What does this pigsty cost?

Innkeeper: For one pig, $5; for two pigs, $9.

——— PILLS ———

A patient limped into the doctor's office. The doctor handed the patient a large pill. Just then his nurse asked him some questions. The patient limped over to the sink and choked down the pill. Then the doctor returned with a bucket and said, "Now drop the pill in the bucket and we'll soak your foot."

——— PILOT ———

The loquacious old gentleman boarded a transport plane and started a conversation with the pilot.

"This plane takes all my courage," he said. "I was almost killed twice in an airplane."

"Once would have been enough," replied the bored pilot.

"I used to be a pilot in a stable."

"That's ridiculous."

"Really, I was a pilot in a stable. I used to pilot here, pilot there . . .

——— **PIN** ———

Lem: I just sat down on a pin.
Clem: Did it hurt?
Lem: No, it was a safety pin.

———◆———

Mark Twain said that when he was young he was impressed by the story of a young man who landed a job when the employer saw him pick up several pins from the sidewalk outside the firm's office.

So Twain went to the street alongside the office windows of a firm he wanted to work for and began almost ostentatiously to pick up pins he had earlier placed on the sidewalk. After a good number of pins had been picked up, a clerk came out and said, "The boss asked me to tell you to move along. Your idiotic behavior is distracting the people working in the office."

——— **PINCH** ———

A man and his little girl were on an overcrowded elevator. Suddenly a lady in front turned around, slapped him, and left in a huff. The little girl remarked, "I didn't like her either, Daddy. She stepped on my toe so I pinched her."

———◆———

As the crowded elevator descended, Mrs. Wilson became increasingly furious with her husband, who was delighted to be pressed against a gorgeous blonde.

As the elevator stopped at the main floor, the blonde suddenly whirled, slapped Mr. Wilson, and said, "That will teach you to pinch!"

Bewildered, Mr. Wilson was halfway to the parking lot with his wife when he choked, "I . . . I . . . didn't pinch that girl."

"Of course you didn't," said his wife, consolingly. "I did."

———◆———

"It's happened," cried the bishop in anguish as he sat playing bridge one evening with some charming people.

"What's happened?" asked the young woman next to him.

"A stroke: My left side is paralyzed."

"Are you sure?" asked the young lady.

"Yes, yes," groaned the bishop. "I've been pinching my left leg for the past few minutes and feel no sensation whatsoever."

"Relax," said the young lady. "That was my leg you were pinching."

——— PINE TREE ———

A tree that mopes.

——— PITCH ———

He who pitches too high won't get through his song.

——— PITCHFORK ———

In defending a client charged with assault, a lawyer told the jury his client was walking down the road with a pitchfork on his shoulder. A large dog that was very fierce attacked the man, and the man killed the dog with the pitchfork.

"Why did you kill my dog?" demanded the dog's owner.

"Because he tried to bite me."

"But why did you not go at him with the other end of the pitchfork?"

"Why didn't your dog come at me with his other end?"

——— PIZZA ———

Italian restaurant: "We offer you pizza and quiet."

—*Bennett Cerf*

———◆———

Cook: Do you want me to cut this pizza into six or eight pieces?

Man: You'd better make it six. I don't think I can eat eight pieces!

—— PLAGIARISM ——

When you take stuff from one writer, it's plagiarism; but when you take it from many writers, it's research.

—*Wilson Mizner*

—— PLANE ——

Customer: Where is your plane?
Pilot: Over there—the tri-motor plane.
Customer: What do you mean tri-motor plane?
Pilot: If one motor goes bad, we'll try the other.

—— PLANNING ——

The art of putting off until tomorrow what you have no intention of doing today.

—— PLANTS ——

In potted-plant section of a Fresno, California, nursery: "Please don't talk to the plants unless you're going to buy."

——◆——

Wife: Plants grow faster if you talk to them.
Husband: But I don't know how to speak Geranium.

—— PLEASE ——

Who would please all and please himself too,
Undertakes something he cannot do.

—— PLEASE STAND ——

A parishioner had dozed off to sleep during the morning service.
"Will all who want to go to heaven stand?" the preacher asked.
All stood, except the sleeping parishioner.
After they sat down, the pastor continued, "Well, will all who want to go to the other place stand?"

Someone suddenly dropped a songbook and the sleeping man jumped to his feet and stood sheepishly facing the preacher. He mumbled confusedly, "Well, preacher, I don't know what we're voting for, but it looks like you and I are the only ones for it."

PLEASURE

"Don't bother showing me to the door."
"It's no bother—it's a pleasure!"

◆

First employee: Are you going to the boss' funeral?
Second employee: Oh, no, I'm working today. My motto is business before pleasure.

PLEASURE TRIP

First mother: I just came back from a pleasure trip.
Second mother: Where did you go?
First mother: I drove my kids to camp.

PLEDGE

The deacon ran into the pastor's office and exclaimed excitedly, "Pastor, I have terrible news to report! Burglars must've broken in last night. They stole $90,000 worth of pledges!"

PLUM

Q: How do you tell a plum from an elephant?
A: A plum always forgets.

PLUMBER

Walter: Who put that statue under the sink?
Frances: That's no statue. That's the plumber.

◆

An absent-minded plumber is one who brings his tools with him.

Is it true that plumbers' fantasies are called pipe dreams?

PNEUMONIA

What you get after you've had old monia.

POET

A poet has a great imagination—he imagines people will read his poems.

POISE

The ability to be ill at ease inconspicuously.

Q: What is the definition of poise?
A: The ability to keep talking while the other guy takes the check.

POISON

A young mother paying a visit to a doctor friend and his wife made no attempt to restrain her five-year-old son, who was ransacking an adjoining room. But, finally, an extra loud clatter of bottles did prompt her to say, "I hope, doctor, you don't mind Johnny being in there."

"No," said the doctor calmly. "He'll be quiet when he gets to the poisons."

POLAR BEARS

Three polar bears were sitting on an iceberg. All were cold and quiet. Finally, the father bear said, "Now I've a tale to tell."

"I, too, have a tale to tell," said the mother bear.

The little polar bear looked up at his parents and said, "My tale is told!"

––––––– **POLICE** –––––––

A candidate for the police force was being verbally examined. "If you were by yourself in a police car and were pursued by a desperate gang of criminals in another car doing 40 miles an hour along a lonely road, what would you do?"

The candidate looked puzzled for a moment. Then he replied, "Fifty."

––––––––◆––––––––

At a commuter train station a policeman noticed a woman driver bowed over the steering wheel of her car in evident discomfort.

"Is there anything wrong?" said the policeman.

Half crying and half laughing the woman responded, "For ten years I have driven my husband to the station to catch his train. This morning I forgot him!"

––––––––◆––––––––

A jeweler watched as a huge truck pulled up in front of his store. The back came down and an elephant walked out. It broke one of the windows with its tusk and then using the trunk like a vacuum cleaner sucked up all the jewelry. The elephant then got back into the truck and it disappeared out of sight. When the jeweler finally regained his senses he called the police. The detectives came, and he told them his story.

"Could you describe the elephant?"

"An elephant is an elephant. You see one you've seen them all. What do you mean, 'describe him?' " asked the jeweler.

"Well," said the policeman, "there are two kinds of elephants, African and Indian. The Indian elephant has smaller ears and is not as large as the African elephant."

The jeweler said, "I can't help you out; he had a stocking pulled over his head."

––––––––◆––––––––

Officer: Miss, you were doing over 60 miles an hour!
Sweet young thing: Oh, isn't that neat. I only learned to drive yesterday.

––––––––◆––––––––

Things are so bad in our town that the police department now has an unlisted telephone number.

––––––––◆––––––––

Show me a policewoman with children and I will show you a pistol-packing mama.

POLICE HELICOPTER

The whirlybird that catches the worm.

POLITE

A polite man is one who listens with interest to things he knows all about when they are told to him by a person who knows nothing about them.

POLITICAL

I like political jokes—unless they get elected.

POLITICAL RALLY

After a political rally, a wife came home late and sank into a chair. "Everything is going great. We are going to sweep the country."

To which her husband responded, "Why not start with the living room?"

POLITICIAN

A politician was giving a speech in a rural district when a yokel tossed a cabbage onto the platform. The quick-thinking politician gave it a sidelong glance and said, "It appears that one of my opponents has lost his head."

◆

Politicians are the same all over. They promise to build a bridge even when there is no river.

—*Nikita Khrushchev*

◆

We need a law that will permit a voter to sue a candidate for breach of promise.

———————◆———————

Political orator: Yes, I have heard the voice of the people calling me to duty.

Heckler: Maybe it was an echo.

———————◆———————

"Well, election time will soon be here. I plan to run for office again. I guess the air will soon be full of my speeches."

"Yeah! . . . and vice versa!"

———————◆———————

"My father was a great Western politician in his day."

"Yeah? What did he run for?"

"The border."

———————◆———————

Political orator: All that I am or will be, I owe to my mother.

Heckler: Why don't you send her 30 cents and square the account?

———————◆———————

An important politician called to visit a friend at an insane asylum and while there tried to phone his office. But his connection was constantly delayed, and in exasperation he said to the operator, "Young lady, do you know who I am?"

"No," she replied. "But I know where you are."

———————◆———————

"Do you like conceited politicians as much as the other kind?"

"What other kind?"

———————◆———————

A policitian is someone whose greatest asset is his liability.

———————◆———————

The deaths of politicians should always appear in the public improvement section of the newspaper.

An honest politician is one who, when he is bought, will stay bought.

——— POLITICS ———

The most promising of all careers.

All political parties die at last of swallowing their own lies.

The difference between a Republican and a Democrat: One is IN and the other is OUT.

Some go into politics not to do good, but to do well.

There's one thing the Democrats and Republicans share in common—our money.

—Woody Allen

I wish the chemists who successfully removed the lead from gasoline would try the same with our congressmen.

A lobbyist browsing through an encyclopedia the other day came upon a stunning idea. In Ancient Greece, in order to prevent idiot statesmen from passing stupid laws upon the people, at one point in Greek history lawmakers were asked to introduce all new laws while standing on a platform with a rope around their neck. If the law passed, the rope was removed. If it failed, the platform was removed.

I stepped into the men's room once and found this sign posted over one of those hot air blowers for drying hands: "Push Button and Listen for a Short Message from the Vice President."

After giving what he considered a stirring, fact-filled campaign speech, the candidate looked out at his audience and confidently asked, "Now, are there any questions?"

"Yes," came a voice from the rear. "Who else is running?"

Minister: Before I vote and support you for sheriff, I'd like to know if you partake of intoxicating beverages.

Candidate for sheriff: Before I answer, tell me if this is an inquiry or an invitation.

Politics is the art of looking for trouble, finding it everywhere, diagnosing it wrongly, and applying unsuitable remedies.

——— POLYGAMY ———

A Mormon acquaintance once pushed Mark Twain into an argument on the issue of polygamy. After long and tedious expositions justifying the practice, the Mormon demanded that Twain cite any passage of Scripture expressly forbidding polygamy.

"Nothing easier," Twain replied. " 'No man can serve two masters.' "

——— POLYGON ———

A heathen who has many wives.

——— POOR BOX ———

The minister's brain is often the "poor box" of the church.

POOR PREACHER

Preacher: Please take it easy on the bill for repairing my car. Remember, I am a poor preacher.

Mechanic: I know; I heard you Sunday!

POP-EYED

A man sought medical aid because he had popped eyes and a ringing in the ears. A doctor looked him over and suggested removal of his tonsils. The operation resulted in no improvement, so the patient consulted another doctor who suggested removal of his teeth. The teeth were extracted but still the man's eyes popped and the ringing in his ears continued.

A third doctor told him bluntly, "You've got six months to live." In that event, the doomed man decided he'd treat himself right while he could. He bought a flashy car, a chauffeur, had the best tailor in town make him 30 suits, and decided even his shirts would be made-to-order.

"Okay," said the shirtmaker, "let's get your measurement. Hmm, 34 sleeve, 16 collar—"

"Fifteen," the man said.

"Sixteen collar," the shirtmaker repeated, measuring again.

"But I've always worn a 15 collar," said the man.

"Listen," the shirtmaker said, "I'm warning you. You keep on wearing a 15 collar and your eyes will pop and you'll have ringing in your ears."

POPOVER

The thing that happens when you put too much corn in the corn popper.

POSITIVE

Being mistaken at the top of one's voice.

POSSESSIONS

The wise man carried his possessions within him.

——— POST OFFICE ———

U.S. Snail.

——— POSTCARD ———

The following postcard was received:

Dear George,
We both miss you as much as if you were right here.

——— POSTDATED ———

A motorist driving by a Texas ranch hit and killed a calf that was crossing the road. The driver went to the owner of the calf and explained what had happened. He then asked what the animal was worth.

"Oh, about $200 today," said the rancher. "But in six years it would have been worth $900. So $900 is what I'm out."

The motorist sat down and wrote out a check and handed it to the farmer.

"Here," he said, "is the check for $900. It is postdated six years from now."

——— POSTPONED ———

When I was a boy, I'd rather be licked twice than postponed once.

——— POT HOLDER ———

A corset.

——— POT ROAST ———

I've heard so much about the bad effects of marijuana I'm afraid to eat pot roast.

——— POTLUCK ———

If you believe no two women think alike, you've never been to a potluck dinner.

——— POTATO ———

Did you hear about the man who crossed a potato with a sponge? It wasn't especially good eating, but it sure held a lot of gravy.

———◆———

Q: Why did the potatoes argue all the time?
A: They couldn't see eye-to-eye about anything.

——— POULTRY ———

Employee: Aren't you ashamed to give me such a poultry paycheck?
Boss: You mean paltry.
Employee: No, I mean poultry. It's chicken feed.

——— POVERTY ———

State of mind sometimes induced by a neighbor's new car.

———◆———

"Dad, what protects a man best from running wild . . . advice, restrictive laws, or stern counsel?"
"Poverty, son, poverty."

——— POWER ———

Power will intoxicate the best hearts, as wine the strongest heads. No man is wise enough, nor good enough, to be trusted with unlimited power.

———◆———

One day in the forest, three animals were discussing who among them was the most powerful.
"I am," said the hawk, "because I can fly and swoop down swiftly at my prey."
"That's nothing," said the mountain lion, "I am not only fleet, but I have powerful teeth and claws."
"I am the most powerful," said the skunk, "because with a flick of my tail, I can drive off the two of you."

Just then a huge grizzly bear lumbered out of the forest and settled the debate by eating them all... hawk, lion, and stinker.

——— PRACTICAL ———

City slicker: Is it right to say "a hen lays" or "a hen lies" eggs?
Farmer: Where I come from, the people just lift her up to see.

——— PRACTICAL JOKES ———

A man, fond of practical jokes, late one night sent his friend a telegram out of a clear sky, collect, which read: I am perfectly well.

A week later the joker received a heavy parcel...collect...on which he had to pay considerable charges. On opening it, he found a big block of concrete on which was pasted this message: This is the weight your telegram lifted from my mind.

Pranks for the memory.

——— PRACTICE ———

Daughter: Mom, may I have some money for a new dress?
Mother: Ask your father, dear. You are getting married in a month and the practice would do you good.

——— PRAISE THE LORD ———

Did you hear about the country parson who decided to buy himself a horse? The dealer assured him that the one he selected was a perfect choice. "This here horse," he said, "has lived all his life in a religious atmosphere. So remember that he'll never start if you order 'Giddyap.' You've got to say, 'Praise the Lord.' Likewise, a 'Whoa' will never make him stop. You've got to say, 'Amen.'"

Thus forewarned, the parson paid for the horse, mounted him, and with a cheery "Praise the Lord" sent him cantering off in the direction of the parson's parish. Suddenly, however, he noticed that the road ahead had been washed out, leaving a chasm 200 yards deep. In a panic, he forgot his instructions and cried "Whoa" in vain several times. The horse just cantered on. At the very last moment he remembered to cry "Amen" . . . and the horse stopped short at the very brink of the chasm. But alas! That's when the parson, out of force of habit, murmured fervently, "Praise the Lord!"

——— PRAY ———

An ocean liner was sinking and the captain yelled, "Does anybody know how to pray?"

A minister on board said, "I do."

"Good," said the captain. "You start praying. The rest of us will put on the life belts. We are one belt short."

One friend to another, "You drive the car and I'll pray."

"What's the matter; don't you trust my driving?"

"Don't you trust my praying?"

——— PRAYER ———

Little Dennis began falling out of a tree and cried, "Lord, save me, save me!" There was a pause and then he said, "Never mind, Lord, my pants just caught on a branch."

A little girl told her mother that her brother had set traps to catch poor, harmless birds. The mother asked if she had done anything about it.

"Oh, yes," the girl replied, "I prayed that the traps might not catch the birds."

"Anything else?"

"Yes, then I prayed that God would keep the birds from getting into the traps."

"Was that all?"

"Then I went and kicked the traps all to pieces."

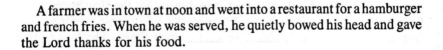

A farmer was in town at noon and went into a restaurant for a hamburger and french fries. When he was served, he quietly bowed his head and gave the Lord thanks for his food.

Some rough-looking fellows at the next table saw him and thought they would give him a hard time. One of them called out, "Hey, farmer, does everyone do that where you live?"

"No, son," answered the farmer, "the pigs and donkeys don't."

Daughter: Why is everyone getting down on their knees in church?
Mother: Shhh, they are going to say their prayers.
Daughter: With all their clothes on?

Noticing that just before the football game started both teams gathered together and prayed briefly, a fan, seated next to a minister, asked what he thought would happen if both teams prayed with equal faith and fervor.

"In that event," replied the minister, "I imagine the Lord would simply sit back and enjoy one fine game of football."

Little Susie concluded her prayer by saying: "Dear God, before I finish, please take care of Daddy, take care of Mommy, take care of my baby brother, Grandma, and Grandpa . . . and please, God, take care of yourself, or else we're all sunk!"

The teacher handed out the test papers and told the children they could start answering the questions.

She noticed little Billy sitting with his head bowed, his hands over his face. She approached him.

"Don't you feel well?" she inquired.

"Oh, I'm fine, teacher. Maybe it's unconstitutional, but I always pray before a test!"

Little William was saying his prayers one night. His mother tiptoed up and heard him say, "And please make Tommy stop throwing things at me. You may remember, I've mentioned this before. He's still doing it."

A Sunday school teacher asked a little girl if she said her prayers every night.

"No, not every night," declared the child. " 'Cause some nights I don't want anything!"

So this big-wheel Russian is riding along when he sees a peasant kneeling in the middle of a field, praying. He stops the car, stomps over, and says:

"Aha! You waste your time like this instead of plowing and planting for the Party!"

"But, Commissar, I'm praying for the Party!"

"Praying for the Party! Huh! And years ago, you probably prayed for the Czar!"

"I did, Commissar."

"Well . . . look what happened to him!"

"Right!"

The pastor was invited over for dinner and asked to lead in prayer for the meal. After the brief prayer, Junior said approvingly, "You don't pray so long when you're hungry, do you?"

———◆———

Radio prayer: Lord, comfort those who are afflicted by the radio today.

———◆———

Mother: That's no way to say your prayers.

Daughter: But Mom, I thought that God was tired of hearing the same old stuff every night . . . so I told Him the story of the Three Bears instead.

——— PRAYER MEETING ———

After attending a prayer meeting where everyone prayed very loud, a little boy remarked, "If they lived nearer to God they wouldn't have to pray so loud."

——— PREACH ———

First preacher: I think a pastor needs to study diligently for his Sunday morning message.

Second preacher: I disagree. Many times I have no idea what I am going to preach about but I go into the pulpit and preach and think nothing of it.

First preacher: And you are quite right in thinking nothing of it. Your deacons have told me they share your opinion.

———◆———

Pastor: How did the assistant pastor do Sunday morning?

Member: It was a poor sermon. Nothing in it at all.

(Upon seeing the assistant pastor, the following conversation took place.)

Pastor: How did it go Sunday morning?

Assistant: Excellent. I didn't have time to prepare anything myself, so I preached one of your sermons.

——— **PREACHER** ———

A preacher once asked an actor why he had such large audiences and he, the preacher, had only a small audience at church.

"I act as if I believe in what I say," said the actor, "while you preach as if you did not believe what you preached."

———◆———

Heckler: If I ever had a son who was a fool I'd make a preacher out of him.

Preacher: How come your father didn't send you to seminary?

———◆———

Visitor: Your preacher is sure long-winded.

Member: He may be long . . . but never winded.

———◆———

During a Christmas play: Not a preacher was stirring, not even a mouse.

———◆———

America still has more marriages than divorces, proving that preachers can still outtalk lawyers.

———◆———

"I am thankful that the Lord has opened my mouth to preach without my learning," said an illiterate preacher.

"A similar event took place in Balaam's time," replied a gentleman present.

———————◆———————

Notice in the local newspaper of a small town: "In the future the preacher for next Sunday will be found hanging on the bulletin board."

———————◆———————

A preacher spoke 20 minutes on Isaiah, 20 minutes on Ezekiel, 20 minutes on Jeremiah, and 20 minutes on Daniel. Then he said, "We now come to the 12 minor prophets. What place will I give Hosea?"

A man in the back of the church said, "I'm leaving. Give Hosea my place."

———————◆———————

Our preacher says things are getting better because he's getting much better buttons in the collection plate.

———————◆———————

Sammy: You know what it means when a preacher steps into the pulpit, removes his watch, and places it on the pulpit?

Danny: Yeah, nothing!

——————— PREACHING ———————

Did you hear about the minister who dreamed he was preaching a sermon and when he woke up, he was?

——————— PRECINCT ———————

Sunk before you could get there.

——————— PREGNANT ———————

An obviously pregnant woman and her husband were sitting in the obstetrician's waiting room. The wife looked at a lamp and commented on how lovely it was. Her husband gave her an anguished look and wailed, "Don't tell me you're starting to crave furniture!"

———————◆———————

The rather awkward freshman at a prom finally got up enough nerve to ask a sultry young beauty for a dance. "I never dance with a child," said the pretty little snob.

The freshman looked her over critically and said, "Please forgive me; I didn't realize you were pregnant."

——— PREJUDICE ———

I think prejudice is a great time-saver. It helps us form our opinions without bothering to get the facts.

——— PRESCRIPTION ———

Patient: You have been a great doctor. I want to leave you something in my will rather than insulting you by paying my bill.

Doctor: That's great! By the way, let me have the prescription I just gave you. I want to make a slight change in it.

———◆———

Young doctor: What is the secret of your success?

Old doctor: Always write your prescriptions illegibly and your bills very plainly.

——— PRESIDENT ———

When I was a boy, I was told anybody could become president. I'm now beginning to believe it!

———◆———

Pity poor old George Washington. He couldn't blame his troubles on the previous administration.

———◆———

A man walked up to the desk of a resort hotel and asked for a room.

"Have you a reservation?" asked the indifferent clerk.

"No. But I've been coming here every year for 12 years, and I've never had to have a reservation."

"Well, there is nothing available. We are filled up, and without a reservation you can't get a room."

"Suppose the president of the United States came in. You would have a room for him, wouldn't you?"

"Of course, for the president we would find a room—we would have a room."

"All right," said the man. "Now I'm telling you that the president isn't coming here tonight. So give me his room."

——— **PRINCE OF WALES** ———

Father: We have a new baby in our house.
Friend: I bet he reigns as king in your family now.
Father: No, Prince of Wails.

——— **PRISONER** ———

Counsel: Do you wish to challenge any of the jury?
Prisoner: Well, I think I could lick that little fellow on this end.

——— **PRIVILEGED** ———

Underprivileged: Not having remote control for your color television set.

——— **PROCRASTINATOR** ———

Is it true that a procrastinator is a man with a wait problem?

——— **PRODIGAL** ———

A Sunday school class was being quizzed on the prodigal son. The teacher asked one youngster, "Who was sorry when the prodigal son returned home?"

The boy gave it a lot of deep thought, then said, "The fatted calf."

——— **PROFESSION** ———

Surgeon: I think the medical profession is the first profession mentioned in the Bible. God made Eve by carving a rib out of Adam.

Engineer: No, engineering was first. Just think of the engineering job it was to create things out of chaos.

Politician: That's nothing. Who do you think created chaos?

─────── **PROFESSOR** ───────

A textbook wired for sound.

────────◆────────

One who talks in someone else's sleep.

────────◆────────

First student: What do they call old professor Jones?

Second student: They call him Sanka.

First student: Why do they call him that?

Second student: Because more than 98 percent of the active portion of the bean has been removed.

─────── **PROFIT** ───────

Q: What kind of money do fishermen make?

A: Net profits.

─────── **PROMISED LAND** ───────

Sunday school teacher: What do you think the "land flowing with milk and honey" will be like?

Student: Sticky!

─────── **PROMISES** ───────

First wife: Has your husband lived up to the promises he made to you before marriage?

Second wife: Just one.

First wife: Which one is that?

Second wife: He said he wasn't good enough for me.

——— PROPHETS ———

First Roman (at Christian massacre): We've got a capacity crowd, but still we're losing money. The upkeep on the lions must be pretty heavy.
Second Roman: Yes, sir, these lions sure do eat the prophets.

——— PROPOSAL ———

Boy: Why won't you marry me? Is there someone else?
Girl: There must be.

Wife: Do you remember the night you proposed to me?
Husband: Yes.
Wife: I was silent for a whole hour after.
Husband: That was the happiest hour of my life.

"Jim proposed to me last night."
"Doesn't he do it nicely?"

"What would you say if I asked you to be my wife?"
"Nothing. I can't talk and laugh at the same time."

"I've been asked to get married lots of times."
"Who asked you?"
"Mother and Father."

He: Will you marry me?
She: No.
And they lived happily ever after!

Him: There is one word that will make me the happiest man in the world. Will you marry me?

Her: No!
Him: That's the word!

———◆———

Boy: I would like to marry you.
Girl: Well, leave your name and address and if nothing better turns up, I will notify you.

———◆———

Daughter: Oh, Mother, please tell me if I should accept Joe's proposal.
Mother: Why don't you ask your father? He made a much smarter decision in marriage than I did.

———◆———

Girl one: I did not accept Jeff the first time he proposed.
Girl two: Of course not, my dear. You were not there.

——— **PROSPERITY** ———

Something you feel, fold, and forward to Washington.

———◆———

The sweet buy and buy.

——— **PROTECTION** ———

Son: Why is a man not allowed to have more than one wife?
Father: Because the law protects those who are incapable of protecting themselves.

——— **PROVERB** ———

Ozark proverb: Terrible is the fate to have a rooster who is silent and a hen who crows.

———◆———

Cheerfulness is the window cleaner of the mind.

———◆———

When life hands you a lemon, make lemonade.

A bright eye indicates curiosity and a black eye indicates too much curiosity.

Catty remarks often have more lives than a cat.

—— PSYCHIATRIST ——

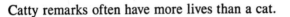

"I have been coming to your counseling sessions for two years and all you do is listen to what I have to say. You never say anything back."

"I didn't have to go to a psychiatrist for that. I could have stayed home with my husband. That's all he does, too."

A man walked into a doctor's office with a pelican on his head.

"You need help immediately," said the doctor.

"I certainly do," said the pelican. "Get this man out from under me."

A big-game hunter recently returned from Africa and went to a psychiatrist. He told the psychiatrist he didn't want to go through analysis, but would pay him $200 for answering two questions. The psychiatrist said this was highly irregular, but he agreed to do it.

"Is it possible," the hunter asked, "for a man to be in love with an elephant?"

The psychiatrist said, "Absolutely impossible. In all the annals of medicine, I've never heard of it. The whole idea is ridiculous. What's your second question?"

The man then asked meekly, "Do you know anyone who wants to buy a very large engagement ring?"

Two psychiatrists met in the street. One of them kept brushing his jacket.

"What's new?" asked one.

"Nothing, really, only I have these invisible insects crawling on me!"

"Well," said the other, jumping back, "don't brush them off on me!"

———————◆———————

Psychiatrist: Now, will you be able to pay this bill for the counseling I've given you?

Patient: Don't worry. Don't worry, doc. You'll get the money or my name isn't King Henry VIII.

———————◆———————

A psychiatrist was trying to comfort a new patient who was terribly upset. "You see, doc," the patient explained, "my problem is that I like shoes much better than I like boots."

"Why, that's no problem," answered the doctor. "Most people like shoes better than boots."

The patient was elated, "That's neat, doc. How do you like them, fried or scrambled?"

———————◆———————

A mother, visiting a department store took her son to the toy department. Spying a gigantic rocking horse he climbed up on it and rocked back and forth for almost an hour.

"Come on, son," the mother pleaded. "I have to get home to get your father's dinner."

The little lad refused to budge and all her efforts were unavailing. The department manager also tried to coax the little fellow without meeting with any success. Eventually, in desperation they called the store's psychiatrist. Gently he walked over and whispered a few words in the boy's ear and immediately the lad jumped off and ran to his mother's side.

"How did you do it?" the mother asked incredibly. "What did you say to him?"

The psychiatrist hesitated for a moment, then said, "All I said was, 'If you don't jump off that rocking horse at once, son, I'll knock the stuffing out of you!' "

———————◆———————

"Who is that strange-looking man who keeps staring at me?"
"Oh, that is Mr. Marconi, the famous expert on insanity."

Wife: My husband thinks he's a refrigerator.
Psychiatrist: I wouldn't worry as long as he is not violent.
Wife: Oh, the delusion doesn't bother me. But when he sleeps with his mouth open, the little light keeps me awake.

Wife: My husband frightens me the way he blows smoke rings through his nose.
Psychiatrist: That isn't unusual.
Wife: But my husband doesn't smoke.

Neurotics build air castles. Psychotics live in them. Psychiatrists collect the rent.

Anyone who goes to a psychiatrist ought to have his head examined!

The sad, quiet, big-eyed little lady sat in the psychiatrist's office. The good doctor questioned her gently as to why her family wanted her locked up.
"Now, tell me," he said, "just what your trouble is."
"It's just that...just that I'm so fond of pancakes, doctor."
"Is that all? Why, I'm very fond of pancakes myself."
"Oh, doctor, really? You must come over to our house. I've got trunks and trunks full of them!"

Psychiatrist: Congratulations, Mr. Young. You're finally cured of your delusion. But why are you so sad?
Patient: Wouldn't you be sad if one day you were president of the United States and the next day you were nobody?

Patient: I'm worried—I keep thinking I'm a pair of curtains.
Psychiatrist: Stop worrying and try to pull yourself together.

My psychiatrist told me he knows what makes me tick, but he can't explain what makes me chime on the hour.

Patient: I always feel that I'm covered in gold paint, doctor.
Psychiatrist: Oh, that's just your gilt complex.

Roger: I used to think I was a beagle. But the psychiatrist cured me.
Doger: How are you now?
Roger: Great. Just feel my nose.

My son is really growing up. Only last week he was able to go to the psychiatrist all by himself.

A man went to the psychiatrist because he had a fear of thunder. "Doc, I don't know what to do," said the man.
The doctor replied, "That's ridiculous. Thunder is a natural phenomenon. Nothing to be afraid of. Whenever you hear thunder, do like I do: Put your head under the pillow and it will go away."

Patient: Doctor, I think everyone tries to take advantage of me.
Psychiatrist: That's silly. It's a perfectly normal feeling.
Patient: Is it really? Thanks for your help, doctor. How much do I owe you?
Psychiatrist: How much do you have?

Patient (on phone): Doctor, I've decided to kill myself.
Psychiatrist: Don't do anything rash until you answer one question for me.
Patient: What's that?

Psychiatrist: Is your bill paid?

Patient: Nobody talks to me.
Psychiatrist: Next!

A man went to the psychiatrist and complained about feeling inferior because of his height. The psychiatrist reminded the short fellow about the great men in history, such as Napoleon and Lautrec, who were great men in spite of their height.

The little man felt completely cured after talking to the psychiatrist and everything would have worked out fine, but as he went out of the doctor's office a cat ate him.

Psychiatrist: Mr. Strange, I understand your problem is that you constantly contradict people. Right?
Patient: Wrong.
Psychiatrist: I must be mistaken then.
Patient: You are not.
Psychiatrist: Oh, I get it. You're contradicting everything I say.
Patient: That's ridiculous.
Psychiatrist: I see. Then you're perfectly sane.
Patient: Ha! I'm as crazy as a loon.
Psychiatrist: Ah, we're finally making some progress.

Sign outside of psychiatrist's office: "Two Couches—No Waiting."

Sign outside of psychiatrist's office: "Guaranteed Satisfaction or Your Mania Back."

The patient explained to the psychiatrist that he was haunted by visions of his departed relatives.

Patient: These ghosts are perched on the tops of fence posts around my garden every night. They just sit there and watch me and watch me and watch me. What can I do?

Psychiatrist: That's easy—just sharpen the tops of the posts.

Psychiatrist to patient: Did this feeling of being an insignificant person come on suddenly, or did it develop normally with marriage and parenthood?

A psychiatrist is a person who beats a psychopath to your door.

Patient: I'm dead.

Psychiatrist: That's impossible. You are talking to me right now.

Patient: I'm dead.

Psychiatrist: Now stand in front of that mirror and say, "Dead men don't bleed," for the next three hours.

At the end of that time the psychiatrist pricked the man's finger with a needle and it began to bleed.

Psychiatrist: There now, what does that prove?

Patient: Dead men do bleed.

Patient: Doctor, I get the feeling that people don't give a hoot about anything I say.

Psychiatrist: So?

Wife: You have got to help me, doctor. My husband keeps going around the house emptying ashtrays. He even does it in public places. I can't stand it!

Psychiatrist: That's not at all unusual; lots of people empty ashtrays.

Wife: Into their mouths?

Psychiatrist: I have treated you for six months and now you are cured. You will no longer have delusions of grandeur and imagine that you're Napoleon.

Patient: That's wonderful. I can hardly wait to go home and tell Josephine the good news.

——— PSYCHOLOGIST ———

A man who, when a good-looking girl enters the room, looks at everybody else.

A high school student wrote: "I would like to be a psychologist. I plan on taking as much psychology as possible in college and maybe someday emerge another Fraud."

——— PUN ———

A form of humor that causes everyone to groan and is meant to punish the hearers.

——— PUNISHMENT ———

Wife: Tomorrow is our twenty-fifth anniversary. I think I'll kill the big red rooster and bake him.

Husband: Now, now, honey; why punish the poor chicken for what happened 25 years ago?

Husband: Listen to this. This article states that in some of the old Roman prisons that have been unearthed, they found the petrified remains of the prisoners.

Wife: Gracious! Those must be what they call hardened criminals.

Dan: I'm named after my parents. My dad's name was Ferdinand and my mother's name was Liza.

Stan: What's your name, then?
Dan: Ferdiliza.

———◆———

"A man dropped off the eaves of this building and was killed."
"That's what he deserves for eavesdropping."

——— **PUPPY LOVE** ———

The beginning of a dog's life.

——— **PURSE** ———

A full purse makes the mouth run over.

——— **PUSH** ———

Mother: Did you push your little sister down the stairs?
Bobby: I only pushed her down one step. She fell the rest of the way.

———◆———

A Baptist minister rushed down to the train station every single day to watch the Sunset Limited go by. There was no chore he wouldn't interrupt to carry out his ritual. Members of his congregation deemed his eccentricity juvenile and frivolous, and asked him to give it up.

"No," he said firmly. "I preach your sermons, teach your Sunday school, bury your dead, marry you, run your charities, chairman every drive it pleases you to conduct. I won't give up seeing that Southern Pacific train every day. I love it! It's the only thing in this town I don't have to push!"

——— **QUACK** ———

A doctor who ducks the law.

———◆———

A quack was selling an elixir which he declared would make men live to a great age.

"Look at me," he shouted. "Hale and hearty. I'm over 300 years old."

"Is he really as old as that?" asked a listener of the youthful assistant.

"I can't say," replied the assistant. "I've only worked for him for 97 years."

QUADRUPLETS

Four crying out loud.

QUAKER

A Quaker became exasperated with his cow for kicking over a pail of milk.

He warned, "Thou knowest that, because of my religion, I can't punish thee. But if thee doeth that again, I will sell thee to a Baptist preacher and he will kick thee so thee won't be able to kick it over again!"

QUARREL

Never pick a quarrel even when it's ripe.

QUESTION

He must be very ignorant for he answers every question he is asked.

He who asks a question is a fool for five minutes; he who does not ask a question remains a fool forever.

To a quick question give a slow answer.

———— **QUIET** ————

A patient in a mental hospital placed his ear to the wall of his room, listening intently.

"Quiet," he whispered to an orderly and pointed to the wall.

The attendant pressed his ear against the wall, listened, and then said, "I don't hear anything."

"I know," replied the patient. "It's awful; it's been this way for days."

———— **QUININE** ————

A valuable medicine that comes from barking trees.

———— **QUITTING** ————

"My boss was sorry when I told him I was quitting next week."
"He was probably hoping it was this week."

———— **QUOTABLE QUOTES** ————

Why doesn't the fellow who says, "I'm no speechmaker," let it go at that, instead of giving a demonstration?

———————◆———————

Many can rise to the occasion, but few know when to sit down.

———————◆———————

When it comes to spreading gossip, the female of the species is much faster than the mail.

———————◆———————

Two feet on the ground are worth one in the mouth.

———————◆———————

Thrift is a wonderful virtue—especially in ancestors.

———————◆———————

While money isn't everything in life, it does keep you in touch with your children.

———————◆———————

The years that a woman subtracts from her age are not lost. They are added to the ages of other women.

Still, if nobody dropped out at the eighth grade, who would hire the college graduates?

To find out a girl's faults, praise her to her girlfriends.

Women's styles may change, but their designs remain the same.

———◆———

If a politician tries to buy votes with private money, he is a dirty crook; but if he tries to buy them with the people's own money, he's a great liberal.

———◆———

Many a child who watches television for hours will go down in history, not to mention arithmetic, English, and geography.

———◆———

People seldom think alike until it comes to buying wedding presents.

———◆———

A halo has only to fall 11 inches to become a noose.

———◆———

A man's horse sense deserts him when he is feeling his oats.

———◆———

Confucius say, ostrich who keep head in sand too long during hot part of day gets burned in end.

———◆———

He charged nothing for his preaching, and it was worth every penny of it.

———◆———

What this country needs is a good five-cent nickel.

———◆———

I do most of my work sitting down; that is where I shine.

———◆———

Running into debt doesn't bother me; it's running into my creditors that's upsetting.

———◆———

Many of our ambitions are nipped in the budget.

R

——— RABBIT'S FOOT ———

First husband: I carry a rabbit's foot in my pocket because it saves me lots of money.
Second husband: How is that?
First husband: Every time my wife sticks her hand in my pocket she thinks it's a mouse.

——— RACEHORSE ———

A racehorse can take several thousand people for a ride at the same time.

——— RADIO ———

Man has conquered the air but so has our neighbor's radio.

———◆———

Pete: Do you know who owned the smallest radio in the world?

Bill: No, who?

Pete: Paul Revere—he broadcast from one plug.

———— RAGMAN ————

Wife: There's an old-clothes man at the door.

Husband: Tell him I've got all the clothes I need.

———— RAILROAD ————

Jim: Say, can you tell me why there are fewer railroad accidents than automobile accidents?

Tim: Well, perhaps it's because the engineer isn't always hugging the fireman.

———— RAIN ————

"Is it raining outside?"

"Did you ever see it raining inside?"

———— RAINBOW TIE ————

"That's a beautiful rainbow tie you are wearing!"

"What do you mean by a 'rainbow tie'?"

"It has a big pot at the end!"

———— RAISE ————

Employee: I have been here 11 years doing three men's work for one man's pay. Now I want a raise.

Boss: Well, I can't give you a raise but if you'll tell me who the other two men are, I'll fire them.

Worker: Boss, I came to see if you could raise my salary.

Boss: Relax and don't worry. I've managed to raise it each payday so far, haven't I?

New employee to boss: Well, if I can't have a raise, how about the same pay more often?

———◆———

Employee: Sir, my wife...er...told me I must ask for an increase.
Employer: Well, I'll ask my wife if I can give you one.

———◆———

Employee (shaking a little): Could I have a raise?
Manager: You can't come in here like this and ask for a raise. You have only been with the company two weeks. You have to work yourself up first.
Employee: But I did...look...I'm trembling all over!

———◆———

"I am planning a salary increase for you, young man."
"When does it become effective?"
"Just as soon as you do!"

——— RAISIN BREAD ———

"Do you like raisin bread?"
"Don't know, I never tried raisin' any."

——— RAMPAGE ———

The page in the encyclopedia about male sheep.

——— RAMPART ———

Paintings displayed on a ramp.

——— RANSOM ———

Kidnapper: Lady, we are going to hold you until your husband ransoms you.
Woman: Oh, dear. I wish now that I had treated William a little better.

——— RATS ———

"I saw a big rat in my cookstove and when I went for my revolver, he ran out."

"Did you shoot him?"
"No. He was out of my range."

—— RATTAN ——

What a rat gets while vacationing in Florida.

—— RAVING BEAUTY ——

A girl who came out last in a beauty contest.

—— RAZOR ——

Jim: I got one of those new razors that has twin blades.
Tom: How do you like it?
Jim: Shaves good. But now instead of getting nicks, I get ditto marks.

—— RAZOR-BLADE THEME SONG ——

"Nobody Knows the Stubble I've Seen."

—— READING ——

Librarian: Please be quiet. The people next to you can't read.
Boy: What a shame! I've been reading since I was six.

—— REAL ESTATE AGENT ——

The first man to make a mountain out of a molehill was probably a real estate agent.

—— REAL PANE ——

A preacher was called upon to substitute for the regular minister, who had failed to reach the church because he was delayed in a snowstorm. The speaker began by explaining the meaning of a substitute. "If you break a window," he said, "and then place a piece of cardboard there, that is a substitute."

After the sermon, a woman who had listened intently shook hands with him, and wishing to compliment him, said, "You were no substitute. You were a real pane!"

——— **REALISM** ———

Artist: This is my latest painting. It is called Builders at Work. It is a piece of realism.
Customer: But, I don't see any of the men at work.
Artist: Of course not—that is the realism part of it.

——— **REALTORS** ———

Realtors . . . you have lots to be thankful for.

——— **REAPING** ———

The chaplain was passing through the prison garment factory. "Sewing?" he said to a prisoner who was at work. "No, chaplain," replied the prisoner gloomily, "reaping!"

——— **RECESSION** ———

Who is afraid of the recession? I've failed during boom times.

——— **RECKLESS DRIVER** ———

One who is seldom wreckless for long.

——— **RECOMMENDATION** ———

Diner: What would you recommend for tonight?
Waiter: Go someplace else . . . the cook is on strike.

——— **RECOUNT** ———

A recount is when the chairman can't believe his ayes.

——— **RECOVERY** ———

On August 7, 1990, the old gentleman suffered a stroke, but with the loving care of his family and his kind and efficient nurse, he never fully recovered.

——— **RED CROSS** ———

Despite warnings from his guide, an American skiing in Switzerland got separated from his group and fell—uninjured—into a deep crevasse. Several hours later, a rescue party found the yawning pit, and to reassure the stranded skier, shouted down to him, "We're from the Red Cross."

"Sorry," the imperturbable American echoed back, "I already gave at the office!"

——— **RED LIGHT** ———

The stalled car sat dead still at a traffic light as the lights went to red, to green, to yellow, to red, to green, to yellow, to red. Finally a cop came up and said, "Pardon me, sir, but don't we have any color you like?"

——— **REDEMPTION** ———

A man wanted to arrange for the disposal of a $5000 bond, so he called his bank.

"Sir," said the clerk, "is the bond for redemption or conversion?"

After a long pause the man said, "Well, am I talking to the First National Bank or the First Baptist Church?"

——— **REDSKINS** ———

People on the American bathing beaches.

——— **REDUCE** ———

The only sure way to reduce is to set the bathroom scale in front of the refrigerator.

——— **REDUCING DIET** ———

MONDAY
    Breakfast—Weak tea
    Lunch—1 bouillon cube in ½ cup diluted water
    Dinner—1 pigeon thigh & 2 oz. prune juice (gargle only)

TUESDAY
  Breakfast—Scraped crumbs from burned toast
  Lunch—1 doughnut hole (without sugar)
  Dinner—2 jellyfish skins & 1 glass dehydrated water

WEDNESDAY
  Breakfast—Boiled-out stains from table cover
  Lunch—½ doz. poppy seeds
  Dinner—Bees knees & mosquito knuckles sauteed with vinegar

THURSDAY
  Breakfast—Shredded eggshell skins
  Lunch—Bellybutton from a navel orange
  Dinner—3 eyes from Irish potatoes (diced)

FRIDAY
  Breakfast—2 lobster antennae
  Lunch—1 guppy fin
  Dinner—Jellyfish vertabrae a la book binders

SATURDAY
  Breakfast—4 chopped banana seeds
  Lunch—Broiled butterfly liver
  Dinner—Fillet of soft-shell crab slaw

SUNDAY
  Breakfast—Pickled hummingbird tongue
  Lunch—Prime ribs of tadpole and aroma of empty custard pie plate
  Dinner—Tossed paprika & clover leaf (1) salad

NOTE: All meals to be eaten under microscope to avoid extra portion.

——— **REFERENCE** ———

Letter of reference: This employee has worked for me for one week and I am satisfied.

——— **REFORM** ———

Nothing so needs reforming as other people's habits.

—Mark Twain

——— REGRET ———

Husband: If a man steals anything, he will live to regret it.
Wife: You used to steal kisses from me before we were married.
Husband: Well. . . .

——— REJECTION ———

There's a certain something about him that attracts women to other men.

——— RELATIVES ———

One of the great mysteries of life is how that idiot who married your daughter can be the father of the smartest grandchildren in the world.

——— RELATIVITY ———

When you are with a pretty girl for three hours, and it seems like only three minutes; and then you sit on a hot stove for a minute and think it's an hour.

——— RELAX ———

The time to relax is when you don't have time for it.

——— RELIEF ———

My small son approached me the other day and asked if there was anything he could do around the house to earn a little pocket money.
"I can't think of anything."
"Well, then, will you put me on relief?"

———◆———

Tom: Every time I pass a girl she sighs.
Jerry: With relief.

——— RELIGIOUS FREEDOM ———

To some people religious freedom means the choice of churches which they may stay away from.

——— REMARRIAGE ———

The triumph of hope over experience.

——— REMEMBER ———

A worker was called on the carpet by his supervisor for talking back to his foreman. "Is it true that you called him a liar?"
"Yes, I did."
"Did you call him stupid?"
"Yes."
"And did you call him an opinionated, bullheaded egomaniac?"
"No, but would you write that down so I can remember it?"

———◆———

An elephant never forgets, but what has he got to remember?

——— RENO ———

A large inland seaport in America with the tide running in and the untied running out.

———◆———

Where the honeymoon express is finally uncoupled.

——— RENT ———

Bill: How much are they asking for your apartment rent now?
Bob: About twice a day.

——— REPARTEE ———

An insult with a college education.

———◆———

Something great we think of 24 hours too late.

——— REPENTANCE ———

Most people repent their sins by thanking God they ain't so wicked as their neighbors.

—*Josh Billings*

———◆———

It is much easier to repent of sins that we have committed than to repent of those that we intend to commit.

—*Josh Billings*

——— REPLACEMENT ———

Employee: Say, boss, your assistant just died, and I was wondering if I could take his place?

Boss: It's all right with me if you can arrange it with the undertaker!

——— REPORT CARD ———

Son: Here's my report card, Dad, along with one of your old ones I found in the attic.

Father: Well, Son, you're right. This old report card of mine you found isn't any better than yours. I guess the only fair thing to do is give you what my father gave me.

A father was examining his son's report card. "One thing is definitely in your favor," he announced. "With this report card, you couldn't possibly be cheating."

——— REPORTER ———

A brand-new reporter was sent out by the editor to cover the story of a man who could sing opera without interruption while he was eating a seven-course meal.

The reporter came back and did not write-up the story.

The editor wanted to know the details.

"Oh, there was not much to it. The guy had two heads."

——— REPOSE ———

Whilst Adam slept, Eve from his side arose:
Strange his first sleep should be his last repose.

——— REPROACH ———

To remind a man of the good turns you have done him is very much like a reproach.

—Demosthenes

——— RESEMBLANCE ———

"Who is that homely boy who just walked into the room?"
"Why, that's my brother!"
"Oh, you must excuse me. I really hadn't noticed the resemblance."

——— RESOLUTION ———

Good resolutions are simply checks that men draw on a bank where they have no account.

—Oscar Wilde

——— RESORT ———

Place where people go for change and the landlord gets the rest.

◆

An Indian from a reservation in Arizona was visiting Washington, D.C. While wandering around the town, he was stopped by a native of the city who asked, "How do you like our town?"

"All right," said the Indian. "And how do you like our country?"

◆

——— RESPONSIBLE ———

Employer: We want a responsible man for this job.

Applicant: Well, I guess I'm your man. In all the other jobs I have worked at, whenever anything went wrong, they told me I was responsible.

——— REST ———

"My uncle was finally put to rest last week."
"I didn't know that he had passed away."
"He didn't, but my aunt did."

——— RESTAURANT ———

An institution for the distribution of indigestion.

Man in restaurant: I'll have the $5 dinner.
Waitress: Would you like that on white or dark bread?

Restaurant chains: Cook-alikes.

——— RESTITUTION ———

A home for chronically exhausted people.

——— RETORT ———

A very thin man met a very fat man in the hotel lobby.
"From the looks of you," said the fat man, "there might have been a famine."
"Yes," was the reply, "and from the looks of you, you might have caused it."

Two married girls were bothering a third girl who was still a spinster.
"Now, tell us truthfully," they badgered her, "have you ever really had a chance to marry?"
With a withering glance, she retorted, "Suppose you ask your husbands."

Mark Twain's hostess at the opera had chattered so much that no one in her box had been able to enjoy the singing. At the end of the performance she said, "Mr. Clemens, I want you to be my guest next Friday night, too. They are going to give 'Tosca' then."

"Charmed," said Twain, "I've never heard you in that."

A speaker was having a little trouble getting started in his speech. All of a sudden someone from the audience shouted: "Tell 'em all you know. It will only take a minute."

"I'll tell 'em all we both know," shot back the speaker. "It won't take any longer."

"Darling, I read your new book yesterday. I loved it. Who wrote it for you?"

"I'm glad you liked it. Who read it to you?"

"Oh, Sarah, I completely forgot about your little party last night."

"Weren't you there?"

---◆---

"Why darling, I was just wondering why you weren't invited to the party the Smiths had last week!"

"Isn't that a coincidence. I was just wondering why you were!"

---◆---

"You know, girls, a lot of men are going to be miserable when I marry."

"Really? How many men are you going to marry?"

---◆---

"The president has personally asked me to help beautify the United States on a special project."

"Really? And which country have you decided to move to?"

---◆---

Actor: As a matter of fact, I have received letters from ladies in almost every place in which I have appeared.

Rival: Landladies, I presume.

—— RETROACTIVE ——

This letter-to-the-editor appeared in a local newspaper: I have read recently that the word "obey" is now being omitted from the wedding ceremony. May I ask if you think the new wording for the wedding service is retroactive?

—— RETURN TO SENDER ——

A bookseller had a statement for a book curtly returned to him with this note written across it:

"Dear Sir: I never ordered this beastly book. If I did, you didn't send it. If you sent it, I never got it. If I got it, I paid for it. If I didn't, I won't!"

—— RETURNED CHECK ——

Husband: The bank returned the check you wrote.

Wife: Good. What shall we buy with it this time?

—— REVENGE ——

Did you hear about the man who burned the farmer's sugarcane field because he wanted sweet revenge?

——◆——

The 12-year-old boy stood patiently beside the clock counter while the druggist waited on all of the adult customers. Finally he got around to the youngster, who made his purchase and hurried out to the curb, where his father was impatiently waiting in his car.

"What took you so long in there, son?" he asked.

"The man waited on everybody in the store before me," the boy replied. "But I got even."

"How?"

"I wound all the alarm clocks while I was waiting," the youngster explained happily. "It's going to be a mighty noisy place at eight o'clock."

─────── REVENUE ───────

Internal Revenue man, eyeing taxpayer's expense claims: Shall we go over this item by item or would you prefer to chicken out right now?

─────── REVERSE REASON ───────

She married him because he was such a "dominating man"; she divorced him because he was such a "dominating male."

He married her because she was so "fragile and petite"; he divorced her because she was so "weak and helpless."

She married him because "he knows how to provide a good living"; she divorced him because "all he thinks about is business." He married her because "she reminds me of my mother"; he divorced her because "she's getting more like her mother every day."

She married him because he was "happy and romantic"; she divorced him because he was "shiftless and fun-loving."

He married her because she was "steady and sensible"; he divorced her because she was "boring and dull."

She married him because he was "the life of the party"; she divorced him because "he never wants to come home from a party."

─────── RHUBARB ───────

Bloodshot celery.

─────── RICE ───────

A product associated with the worst mistake of some men's lives.

─────── RICH ───────

Beverly: A scientist says that what we eat we become.
Melba: Oh, boy, let's order something rich.

───────◆───────

Better to live rich than to die rich.

———— RICH MAN ————

One who isn't afraid to ask the clerk to show him something cheaper.

———— RICH RELATIVES ————

The kin we love to touch.

————◆————

Q: What type of person lives the longest?
A: A rich relative.

———— RIDICULE ————

Ridicule is the first and last argument of fools.

———— RIDICULOUS ————

Wife: I got this girdle today for a ridiculous figure.
Husband: I know. But how much did it cost?

———— RIGHT ————

Boss: What do you mean by arguing with that customer? Don't you know our rule? The customer is always right.
Employee: I know it. But he insisted that he was wrong.

———— RIGHTEOUS INDIGNATION ————

Righteous indignation is your own wrath as opposed to the shocking bad temper of others.

———— RIGHTS ————

A man is endowed with certain inalienable rights, all of which he must fight for.

——— ROBBED ———

The teller had just been robbed for the third time by the same man, and the police officer was asking if he had noticed anything specific about the criminal.

"Yes," said the teller, "he seems to be better dressed each time."

——— ROCK BOTTOM ———

A rocking chair.

——— ROCK FESTIVAL ———

I went to a rock festival last summer and it was fascinating. There were 400 girls, 500 boys and 50 uncommitted.

——— ROCK 'N' ROLL ———

I guess you read about the rock 'n' roll show that turned into a riot. What bothers me is, how could they tell?

———◆———

Advertisement in newspaper: For sale cheap . . . my son's collection of rock 'n' roll records. If a boy's voice answers the phone, hang up and call later.

——— ROME ———

Teacher: When was Rome built?
Student: It was built during the night.
Teacher: The night? Where did you ever get such an idea?
Student: Well, everyone knows that Rome wasn't built in a day.

——— ROMEO AND JULIET ———

Man: I'm sorry I can't come to your party tonight. I have an engagement to see Romeo and Juliet.
Woman: That's all right. Bring them along, too.

——— ROOKIE ———

First rookie: I feel like punching that sarge in the nose again!

Second rookie: What do you mean, again?
First rookie: Well, I felt like it yesterday, too.

——— **ROOSTER** ———

Q: Why did the boy name his rooster Robinson?
A: Because it Crusoe.

——— **ROOT BEER** ———

Did you hear about the fellow who spilled some root beer on the stove?
Now he has foam on the range.

——— **ROPE** ———

"Did you ever hear the rope joke?"
"No."
"Skip it."

——— **ROSE** ———

Carl: What's that you have in your buttonhole?
Earl: Why, that's a chrysanthemum.
Carl: It looks like a rose to me.
Earl: Nope, you're wrong. It's a chrysanthemum.
Carl: Spell it.
Earl: K-r-i-s . . . by golly, that is a rose.

——— **ROUGH NEIGHBORHOOD** ———

I lived in such a rough neighborhood as a child that my mom would give
me a dollar each morning for the holdup man.

——— **ROUND** ———

Ruth: Where did Walter go?
Juliet: He's 'round in front.
Ruth: I know what he looks like, I just wanted to know where he went.

——— **RUBBER BAND** ———

Kathy: Did anyone around here lose a roll of bills with a rubber band?

Stan: Yes, I did.
Kathy: Well, I've found the rubber band.

——— RUBBER TREES ———

Stretch plants.

——— RUDOLPH ———

Mr. and Mrs. Smith were touring Russia. Their guide's name was Rudolph, and Mr. Smith and Rudolph argued all the time. As the couple was leaving Moscow, the husband said, "Look, it's snowing out."
The guide disagreed, "No, sir, it's raining out."
"I still think it's snowing," said Mr. Smith.
But his wife replied, "Rudolph the Red knows rain, dear."

——— RULE ———

First husband: Do you agree with the prediction that women will be ruling the world in the year 2000?
Second husband: Yes, they will still be at it.

——— RUMOR ———

A rumor goes in one ear and out many mouths.

———◆———

Rumor is one thing that gets thicker as you spread it.

———◆———

There is no such thing as an idle rumor.

———◆———

What dainty morsels rumors are. They are eaten with great relish!

——— RUN ———

Recent studies reveal that city-dwellers do not walk for their health—they run.

—— RUNNING WATER ——

Did you hear about the Indian chief named Running Water? He had two daughters, Hot and Cold, and a son named Luke.

—— RUSH HOUR ——

When the traffic stands still.

—— RUSSIANS ——

First Russian prisoner: What are you in for?
Second prisoner: I came to work late. How about you?
First prisoner: I came to work early, so they arrested me on suspicion.
Third prisoner: Well, I'm here because I arrived at work exactly on time.
Second prisoner: What kind of offense is that?
Third prisoner: They said I must own an American watch.

———◆———

If we're lucky the Russians will steal some of our secrets, and then they'll be two years behind us.

—— SPANKING ——

Stern punishment.

Son: Dad, you wouldn't spank me for something I didn't do, would you?
Father: Why, of course not.
Son: Good! I didn't do my homework.

———◆———

Father: Now, remember, I'm spanking you because I love you.
Son: I sure wish I was big enough to return your love.

—— SPEAKER ——

A manufacturer of bicycle tires was the speaker at a businessmen's luncheon. In response to a toast, he said, "I have no desire or intention to inflict upon you a long speech, for it is well known in our trade that the longer the spoke, the bigger the tire."

Some speakers are good. Some speakers are lousy. Some are good and lousy.

—— SPEAKING ——

Seated next to a blowhard at a UN dinner was an Oriental fellow dressed in the robes of one of the Far Eastern countries.

The blowhard, attempting to make conversation, leaned over and said: "You like soupee?" The Oriental fellow nodded his head. "You like steakee?" The Oriental nodded again.

As it turned out, the guest speaker at the dinner was our Oriental friend who got up and delivered a beautiful 50-minute address on the U.N. definition of encouragement to self-reliance by underdeveloped countries of the world. The speech was in flawless Oxford English.

He returned to his place at the head of the table, sat down, turned to his dinner partner, and said, "You like speechee?"

When he finally finished his speech, there was a great wakening.

Speaker: This is terrible! I am the speaker at this banquet and I forgot my false teeth!
Man: I happen to have an extra pair; try these.
Speaker: Too small!
Man: Well, try this pair.
Speaker: Too big!

Man: I have one pair left.
Speaker: These fit just fine. It sure is lucky to sit next to a dentist!
Man: I'm not a dentist. I am an undertaker.

Only one man applauded; he was slapping his head to keep awake.

History repeats itself—and so does this guy!

The fault with many speakers is that you can't hear what they're saying. The trouble with this one is that you can.

I was a young fellow when this speech started!

During a long lecture a speaker suffered many interruptions from a man in the balcony who kept yelling: "Louder! Louder!"
After about the fifth interruption, a gentleman in the first row stood up, looked back, and asked, "What's the matter, my friend, can't you hear?"
"No, I can't hear," came the answer from the balcony.
"Well, then, be thankful and shut up!"

"He's such a great speaker, I'd rather hear him speak than eat."
"Me, too. I sat at the head table with him. I've heard him eat."

"You heard my speech, Professor. Do you think it would improve my delivery if I followed the example of Demosthenes and practiced my diction and elocution with pebbles and marbles in my mouth?"
"I would recommend quick-dry cement."

The entire audience was hissing him except one man. He was applauding the hissing.

A lecture is something that can make you feel numb at one end and dumb at the other.

"Did his speech have a happy ending?"
"Sure, everybody was glad it was over."

At a banquet, several long-winded speakers covered almost every subject possible.

When yet another speaker rose, he said, "It seems to me everything has already been talked about. But if someone will tell me what to talk about, I will be grateful."

From the back of the room a voice shouted, "Talk about a minute!"

Did you hear about the wife of a speaker who took her husband's temperature with a barometer instead of a thermometer. It read Dry and Windy.

He's always offering "sound advice" . . . 99 percent sound and 1 percent advice.

He's suffering from I-strain.

He's an M.C. all right . . . a mental case.

He speaks straight from the shoulder. Too bad his remarks don't start from higher up.

Did you hear about the man who was speaking and someone in the audience went to sleep during his boring talk? He got so mad that he took the gavel and hit the sleeping man in the head. The sleeper woke up, took a long look at the speaker, and said, "Hit me again. I can still hear you."

Every time he opens his mouth, he puts his feats in.

He's an expert at handing out baloney disguised as food for thought.

He reminds you of a bee—a humbug.

He reminds you of a clarinet—a wind instrument.

Our speaker has not only all of the five senses but he has two more, horse and common.

He can wrap up a one-minute idea in a one-hour vocabulary.

An inexperienced speaker arose in confusion after dinner and murmured stumblingly, "M-m-my f-f-friends, when I came here tonight, only God and myself knew what I was about to say to you . . . and now only God knows."

"His last speech had the audience in the aisles."
"Applauding?"
"No, stretching and yawning."

If he said what he thought, he'd be speechless.

Speaker: Did you notice how my voice filled the town hall?
Man: Yes, in fact, I noticed several people leave to make room for it.

———————◆———————

They call him the "Mastoid of Ceremonies"—he's a pain in the ear.

———————◆———————

His wisecracks are always greeted with a tremendous burst of silence.

———————◆———————

Every year he takes a boast-to-boast tour.

———————◆———————

He holds people openmouthed with his conversations. They can't stop yawning.

———————◆———————

I have been told that the mind cannot absorb any more than the seat can endure.

———————◆———————

His ideas are sound—all sound.

———————◆———————

He was such a bad speaker the audience hissed the ushers.

———————◆———————

I have the microphone and there is the loud speaker!

———————◆———————

And now I'm going to say something in the public interest . . . Goodnight.

———————◆———————

I spoke to a group of hippies and they're a tough audience. They don't laugh or applaud . . . they're too busy scratching!

———————◆———————

Sign on speaker's table: "If you don't strike oil in 20 minutes, stop boring."

———◆———

Every time I stand up to speak my mind sits down!

———◆———

That was the sort of speech that gives failure a bad name.

———◆———

In biblical days, it was considered a miracle when a donkey spoke. Listening to him, you can't help but realize how times haven't changed.

———◆———

After a dinner program like this, a speaker is like parsley—not really needed.

———◆———

Chauncey Depew once played a trick on Mark Twain on an occasion when they were both to speak at a banquet. Twain spoke first for some 20 minutes and was received with great enthusiasm. When Depew's turn came immediately afterward, he said, "Mr. Toastmaster, Ladies and Gentlemen, before this dinner, Mark Twain and I made an agreement to trade speeches. He has just delivered mine and I'm grateful for the reception you have accorded it. I regret that I have lost his speech and cannot remember a thing he had to say."

He sat down with much applause.

——— SPECIALIST ———

A doctor whose patients are expected to confine their ailments to his office hours.

——— SPECTACLES ———

Wife: What are spectacles?
Husband: Spectacles are glasses that people look through.

Wife: If you looked through a window would you call it a spectacle?
Husband: It depends on what you saw.

—— SPEECH ——

Wife: How was your talk tonight?
Husband: Which one?
Wife: What do you mean, which one?
Husband: The one I was going to give, the one I did give, or the one I delivered so brilliantly to myself on the way home in the car?

"That was a great speech, sir . . . I liked the straightforward way you dodged those issues."

A wise man once said that the best way to save face is to keep the bottom part of it closed.

———◆———

Upon entering a room in a hotel, a woman recognized a well-known government official pacing up and down and asked what he was doing there. "I am going to deliver a speech," he said.
"Do you usually get very nervous before addressing a large audience?"
"Nervous?" he replied. "No, I never get nervous."
"In that case," demanded the lady, "what are you doing in the ladies' room?"

———◆———

World's Best After-Dinner Speech: "Waiter, give me both checks."

—— SPEEDING ——

"I know about a motorist, going 80, who tried to beat a speeding train to an intersection."
"Did the motorist get across?"
"He got a cross, all right . . . beautiful marble cross purchased by his beneficiaries."

———◆———

250

He: My wife just got a ticket for speeding.

Him: That's nothing! My wife is so bad the police gave her a season ticket.

——— SPELLING ———

Joe: Why did you fire your secretary?

Moe: She couldn't spell. She kept asking me how to spell every other word as she was taking dictation.

Joe: I suppose you couldn't stand the interruptions.

Moe: It wasn't that. I just didn't have time to look up all those words.

Employer: How's your spelling? Let me hear you spell Mississippi.

Secretary: The river or the state?

First boy: I couldn't learn to spell.

Second boy: Why not?

First boy: My teacher always changed the words.

——— SPHINX ———

Professor: Jones, can you tell me who built the Sphinx?

Student: I-I-I did know, sir, but I've forgotten!

Professor: Great guns, what a calamity! The only man living who knows, and he has forgotten!

——— SPINACH ———

Mother: Robbie, eat your spinach. It's good for growing children.

Robbie: Who wants to grow children?

——— SPINSTER ———

The most singular of women.

A woman who goes around and around looking for a man.

———◆———

A woman who is unhappily unmarried.

———◆———

First spinster: Why did you sell your double bed and buy twin beds?
Second spinster: Because every night I look under the bed to see if a man is there. With two beds, my chances are doubled.

——— **SPIRITUALIST** ———

A trance-guesser.

——— **SPLINTERS** ———

Chet: How did you get your hand full of splinters?
Jack: I was out hunting and caught a timber wolf barehanded.

——— **SPOKESMAN** ———

He who talks like a big wheel may be only a spokesman.

——— **SPORTING** ———

It was hunting season when a state trooper walked up to a man and his son, and said, "That's a nice buck you have on the top of your car." The surprised man couldn't say anything, so his son answered for him, "That's nothing! You should see the one we have in the trunk!"

———◆———

Boxer: Have I done any damage?
Trainer: No, but keep swinging. The draft might give him a cold.

———◆———

There are two kinds of hunters . . . those who hunt for sport and those who catch something.

———◆———

Golfer: Pardon me, but would you mind if I played through? I've just heard that my wife has been taken seriously ill.

————————◆————————

"When I was in India," said the club bore, "I saw a tiger come down to the water where some women were washing clothes. It was a very fierce tiger, but one woman, with great presence of mind, splashed some water in its face and it slunk away."

"Gentlemen," said a man in an armchair, "I can vouch for the truth of this story. Some minutes after this incident, I was coming down to the water. I met this tiger, and, as is my habit, stroked its whiskers. Gentlemen, those whiskers were wet."

————————◆————————

Two boxers had placed bets and each backed himself to lose the fight. During the progress of the bout, one accidently hit his opponent a light tap on the face. He immediately laid down and the referee proceeded to count him out. The other boxer was in a quandary. Just as the referee got to nine, he had a magnificent idea come to him. He rushed to the prostrate man and kicked him, and was instantly disqualified.

————————◆————————

Two hunters had been out several hours and one of them had been growing uneasy. Finally panic overtook him. "We're lost!" he cried to his companion. "What shall we do?"

"Keep your shirt on!" said his companion. "Shoot an extra deer and the game warden will be here in a minute and a half."

————————◆————————

Sportsman: Is there much good hunting in these parts?
Native: Sure, there's plenty of hunting but very little finding.

————————◆————————

Talkative hunter: Once while I was having a meal in the jungle, a lion came so close to me that I could feel his breath on the back of my neck. What did I do?
Bored listener: Turned your collar up?

————————◆————————

"I hear your husband is a linguist."

"Yes. He speaks three languages . . . golf, football, and baseball."

———— SPORTS CARS ————

One nice thing about small sport cars . . . if you flood the carburetor, you can just put the car over your shoulder and burp it.

Sports car driver: Yes, my car is air-conditioned and it gets 40 miles to an ice cube.

This afternoon I saw two little cars under a station wagon. I didn't know if they were hiding or nursing.

A man returned to his sports car to find a freshly crushed fender and this note affixed to his windshield wiper: "The people who saw me sideswipe your fender are now watching me write this note, and doubtless figure I'm telling you my name and address so you can contact me and send me the bill. Ho! Ho! You should live so long."

An old gent was passing a busy intersection when a large St. Bernard brushed against him and knocked him down. An instant later a foreign sports car skidded around the corner and inflicted more damage.

A bystander helped him up and asked him if the dog had hurt him. "Well," he answered, "the dog didn't hurt so much, but that tin can tied to his tail nearly killed me."

Small car salesman to prospect: It only seats two but can easily accommodate 14 bumper stickers.

———— SPOUTING OFF ————

Be reminded of the whale: When it's spouting off, that is when it is in the most danger of being harpooned.

——— SPRING ———

Time of year when a young man's fancy turns to what the girls have been thinking about all winter.

——— SPRINGTIME ———

On the first day of springtime my true love gave to me: five packs of seed, four sacks of fertilizer, three cans of weed killer, two bottles of insect spray, and a pruning knife for the pear tree.

——— SQUEAKS ———

Wife: George, wake up, there's a mouse in the bedroom. I can hear it squeaking.

Husband (as he rolled over): What do you want me to do? Get up and oil it?

——— SQUIRREL ———

Wife: You don't expect me to wear this old squirrel coat the rest of my life do you?

Husband: Why not? The squirrels do!

——— STALEMATE ———

A spouse who is beginning to smell musty.

——— START A RIPPLE ———

He has so many chins, he should be careful not to burp—it would start a ripple.

——— STATION ———

A janitor who worked in a railroad station decided to get married in a huge room on the upper floor of the station. So many friends and kinfolk showed up, their combined weight caused the building to collapse. Moral of the story: Never marry above your station.

——— STATIONERY STORE ———

A store that stays pretty much at the same location.

——— STATISTICIAN ———

A liar who can figure.

——— STATISTICS ———

Statistics prove that marriage is a preventive of suicide. But, on the other hand, they also prove that suicide is a preventive of marriage.

——— STEADY ———

Bill: I'm a steady worker.
Bob: Yeah, and if you were any steadier, you would be motionless.

——— STEAK ———

Customer: Your sign says you will cook any type of steak. I'll try an elephant steak.
Waiter: Will that be African or Indian?

———◆———

Waiter: And how did you find your steak, sir?
Customer: I just lifted one of the brussels sprouts and there it was!

——— STEAM ———

Too many people work up a head of steam before they find out what's cooking.

———◆———

Father: What good is the steam that comes out of the spout on the kettle when it boils?
Son: Mother can open your letter before you get home.

——— STEELWOOL ———

Ned: I am going to feed my sheep ironized yeast.

Jed: Why are you going to do that?
Ned: So I'll be able to get steel wool.

——— STEP ON IT ———

Customer: Waitress, why is my doughnut all smashed?
Waitress: You said you wanted a cup of coffee and a doughnut, and step on it.

——— STICK 'EM UP ———

A fellow walked up to me and said, "Stick 'em down."
I said, "You mean stick 'em up."
He said, "No wonder I haven't made any money."

——— STINK ———

Coach (to referee): You stink!
Referee (who picked up the football, marked off another 15-yard penalty, and turned to the coach): How do I smell from here?

——— STIRRUP ———

What you do with cake batter.

——— STOCKBROKER ———

A man who can take a bankroll and run it into a shoestring.

——— STOCKS ———

March is a very dangerous month in which to speculate in stocks. The other months are April, May, June, July, August, September, October, November, December, January, and February.

——— STONE ———

"My husband didn't leave a bit of insurance."
"Then where did you get that gorgeous diamond ring?"
"Well, he left $1,000 for his casket and $5,000 for a stone. This is the stone."

——— STONES ———

The following are famous birthstones:

> For architects, the cornerstone.
> For beauties, the peachstone.
> For borrowers, the touchstone.
> For burglars, the keystone.
> For cooks, the puddingstone.
> For editors, the grindstone.
> For laundresses, the soapstone.
> For motorists, the milestone.
> For pedestrians, the tombstone.
> For policemen, the pavingstone.
> For politicians, the blarneystone.
> For soldiers, the boldstone.
> For stockbrokers, the curbstone.
> For tourists, the Yellowstone.

——— STOP THE PRESSES ———

Newspaper misprint:
Mr. Carlson won a ten-pound turkey at Saturday's shurkey toot.

Newspaper misprint:
At the Ladies' Aid Society meeting many interesting articles were raffled off. Every member brought something she no longer needed. Many members brought their husbands.

Newspaper misprint:
First printing: Mr. Janelli was a defective in the police force.
Correction: Mr. Janelli was a detective in the police farce.

Newspaper misprint:
The wildwife league will meet tonight.

Church bulletin misprint:
Nine volunteers put in new church furnace.

Newspaper misprint:
Father of ten shot—mistaken for rabbit.

Newspaper misprint:
Dr. Jeremiah is the author of a brand-new book that is expected to outsmell the two million copies of his first book.

Newspaper misprint:
Man found dead in cemetery.

Newspaper misprint:
For sale: A full-blooded cow, giving three gallons of milk, two tons of hay, a lot of chickens, and a cookstove.

Newspaper misprint:
The general will remain unequaled in history for his accomplishment on the bottlefield.

Newspaper misprint:
Help Wanted: Adult or mature teenager to babysit. One dollar an hour, plus frige benefits.

Newspaper misprint:
Lost· Gray and white male cat. Answers to electric can opener.

Church bulletin misprint:
The church had a going-away party for Pastor Hanson. The congregation was anxious to give him a little momentum.

Newspaper misprint:
Found: False teeth, in parking lot at the Walters Department Store. Please come in and smile at the switchboard operator, and she will return them to you.

Church bulletin misprint:
Twenty-five-year friendship ends at altar.

Newspaper misprint:
Dead policeman on force 17 years.

Newspaper misprint:
The Army has tested some new explosives recently. In fact, they dropped four-ton blondes on the test site.

Newspaper misprint:
City officials talk rubbish.

Misprinted sign:
Don't kill your wife. Let our washing machine do the dirty work.

Church bulletin misprint:
Pastor Moore has spoken in the largest Baptist churches in America. To miss hearing him will be the chance of a lifetime!

Newspaper misprint:
For Sale: Two plots in lively Fairmount Cemetery.

———◆———

Church bulletin misprint:
Ushers will swat latecomers at these points in the service.

———◆———

Newspaper misprint:
Clarksville, Tennessee, which calls itself the largest outdoor mule market in the world, held a mule parade yesterday, headed by the governor.

——— STORK ———

The bird with the big bill.

——— STORY ———

We like the fellow who says he is going to make a long story short, and does.

——— STRIFE ———

If you want to avoid domestic strife, don't marry in January . . . and that goes for the other months, too.

——— STRIKE ———

One sit-down strike in a public building was ended very quickly. The official in charge of the building simply locked all the toilets.

"My uncle is still on strike."
"How long has he been on strike?"
"Fifty-two years."

——— STRIKING SERMON ———

One which hits the man who is not there.

——— **STUCCO** ———

What you get when you sit on gummo.

——— **STUDY** ———

Why study? The more we know, the more we forget. The more we forget, the less we know. The less we know, the less we forget. The less we forget, the more we know. So why study?

——— **STUPENDOUS** ———

Advanced stupidity.

——— **STUPID** ———

Are you naturally stupid or did a Cuban hijack your brain?

——— **SUBMARINE** ———

First rookie: Did you volunteer for submarine service?
Second rookie: No, sir. I don't want to get on a ship that sinks on purpose.

——— **SUBSIDY** ———

A town underneath another town.

——— **SUCCEED** ———

If at first you don't succeed, you'll have a lot more friends.

——— **SUCCESS** ———

With some people success turns their heads. With others, too bad it doesn't wring their necks.

———◆———

Needless to say, one of the most successful inventors of all time was the man who invented a hay-bailing machine. He made a bundle.

———◆———

The next most successful man was the chemist who created a lubricant for furniture wheels. He called it caster oil.

———◆———

The road to success is dotted with many tempting parking places.

——— SUCCESSFUL ———

A young man came for an interview with a bank president.
"Tell me, sir, how did you become so successful?"
"Two words."
"And what are they, sir?"
"Right decisions."
"How do you make right decisions?"
"One word—experience."
"And how do you get experience?"
"Two words."
"And what are they?"
"Wrong decisions!"

——— SUED ———

Jack and Jill
Went up the hill
To fetch a pail
Of water.
Jack fell down
And broke his crown,
And sued the farmer
And his daughter.

——— SUFFER ———

Some persons won't suffer in silence because that would take the pleasure out of it.

——— SUGAR ———

Gen: One of our little pigs was sick so I gave him some sugar.
Dan: Sugar! What for?
Ben: Haven't you ever heard of sugar-cured ham?

─── SUGAR DADDY ───

One form of crystallized sap.

─── SUGGESTION BOX ───

After examining the contents of the employees' suggestion box, the boss complained, "I wish they'd be more specific. What kind of kite? What lake?"

─── SUICIDE ───

The last thing a person should do.

───◆───

Frontier coroner's verdict: We find that the deceased came to his death by an act of suicide. At a distance of a hundred yards he opened fire with a six-shooter upon a man armed with a rifle.

─── SULTAN ───

Sultan to small boy: Go ask one of your mothers.

─── SUN ───

Did you hear about the fellow who stayed up all night wondering where the sun went? It finally dawned on him.

─── SUNBATHE ───

My wife loves to sunbathe—she's a fry in the ointment.

─── SUNBURN OIL ───

Husband: Why does this meat taste so funny?
Wife: Well, I burned it a little . . . but I put some sunburn oil on it at once.

─── SUNDAY ───

Q: What is the strongest day in the week?
A: Sunday. The rest are weekdays.

───◆───

Mother: You shouldn't be flying that model airplane in the back yard on Sunday.

Johnny: Oh, it is all right to fly this one. It isn't a pleasure plane. It's a missionary plane going to the jungle.

——— SUNDAY SCHOOL ———

Son: Dad, did you go to Sunday school when you were young?
Dad: Never missed a Sunday.
Son: Bet it won't do me any good either.

———◆———

Sunday school teacher: What must you do to receive the forgiveness of sin?
Pupil: Sin.

———◆———

Q: Who was Round John Virgin?
A: One of the twelve Opossums.

———◆———

Sunday school teacher: Now, who decreed that all the world should be taxed?
Student: The Democrats.

———◆———

Father: What did you learn in Sunday school this morning?
Son: We learned about how Moses went behind enemy lines to rescue the Jews from the Egyptians. Moses ordered the engineers to build a pontoon bridge. After the people crossed, he sent bombers back to blow up the bridge and the Egyptian tanks that were following them. And then . . .
Father: Did your teacher really tell it like that?
Son: No, but if I told you what he said you would never believe it!

———◆———

A little boy came home from Sunday school and told his mother that they had just learned a new song about a boy named Andy. His mother couldn't understand what he meant until he sang:
Andy walks with me,
Andy talks with me,
Andy tells me I am His own. . . .

———◆———

Overheard after Sunday school:
"Is it true that shepherds have dirty socks?"
"What do you mean?"
"I heard that the shepherds washed their socks by night."

Sunday school teacher: Why would it be wrong to cut off a cat's tail?
Student: The Bible says, "What God hath joined together, let no man put asunder."

Sunday school teacher: Why would it be wrong to cut off a cat's tail?
Student: The Bible says, "What God hath joined together, let no man put asunder."

A clergyman had been invited to attend a party of the Sunday school nursery department. He decided to surprise them, so getting on his hands and knees, flapping his coattails over his head like wings, he hopped in on all fours, cackling like a bird. Imagine his surprise when he learned that due to a switch in locations, he had intruded on the ladies' missionary meeting!

A Sunday school teacher asked a little girl, "What are the sins of omission?"
After some thought, she answered, "They're the sins we ought to have committed but haven't."

Little Suzie: My Sunday school teacher says we're put on earth to help others. Is that right, Mom?
Mother: Of course, dear.
Little Suzie: Then what are the others here for?

In a Sunday school class the teacher asked the students to write down the Ten Commandments. For the fifth commandment one boy put, "Humor thy father and thy mother."

A Sunday school teacher asked her students to draw a picture of the Holy Family. After the pictures were brought to her, she saw that some of the youngsters had drawn the conventional pictures—the Holy Family and the manger, the Holy Family riding on the mule, etc.

But she called up one little boy to ask him to explain his drawing, which showed an airplane with four heads sticking out of the plane windows.

She said, "I can understand you drew three of the heads to show Joseph, Mary, and Jesus. But who's the fourth head?"

"Oh," answered the boy, "that's Pontius the pilot!"

A little boy forgot his lines in a Sunday school presentation. His mother was in the front row to prompt him. She gestured and formed the words silently with her lips, but it did not help. Her son's memory was blank.

Finally she leaned forward and whispered the cue, "I am the light of the world."

The child beamed and with great feeling and a loud, clear voice said, "My mother is the light of the world."

——— SUPERIOR ———

Son: Dad, do you think that the American Indians were superior to the white men who took this land from them?

Father: You bet. When the Indians were the sole occupants of this land, they had no taxes, no national debt, no centralized government, no military draft, no foreign-aid programs, no banks, no stock markets, no nuclear weapons, and their women did all the work. What could be more superior than that?

——— SUPERIORITY ———

My kid sister has a superiority complex . . . she thinks she's almost as good as me.

——— SUPERSTITIOUS ———

Burglar: The police are coming! Quick, jump out the window!

Accomplice: But we're on the thirteenth floor!

Burglar: This is no time to be superstitious.

——— SUPPER ———

Mother (to manager of a movie theater): Did my little boy come in here at 12:00? He had on a blue sweater and a red cap. He has blond hair.

Manager: Yes, he is sitting in the fourth row.
Mother: Do you mind giving him this package? It's his supper.

——— **SURFER** ———

Man-over-board.

——— **SURLY** ———

Cheerful people, the doctors say, resist disease better than the glum ones. In other words, the surly bird catches the germ.

——— **SURRENDER** ———

Another word for engagement.

——— **SURREY MAKERS** ———

People who are always looking for fringe benefits.

——— **SUSPICIOUS CHARACTER** ———

A man who suspects everybody.

——— **SWAP** ———

Seems that a tribal chieftain's daughter was offered as a bride to the son of a neighboring potentate in exchange for two cows and four sheep. The big swap was to be effected on the shore of the stream that separated the two tribes. Pop and his daughter showed up at the appointed time only to discover that the groom and his livestock were on the other side of the stream. The father grunted, "The fool doesn't know which side his bride is bartered on."

——— **SWEATER** ———

A garment worn by a small child when his mother feels chilly.

——— **SWEET DREAMS** ———

Q: Why did Clarence sprinkle sugar all over his pillow?
A: He wanted to have sweet dreams.

—— SWEETHEART ——

Millionaire: What's your name, driver?
Driver: Alfred, sir.
Millionaire: I always call my drivers by their last names.
Driver: It's Sweetheart, sir.
Millionaire: Drive on, Alfred.

—— SWELL-HEAD ——

Nature's frantic effort to fill a vacuum.

—— SWIMMING ——

I learned how to swim the old way when I was about five years old. My dad took me out to the middle of a lake in a boat and then threw me into the water. The swim back to shore was not too bad . . . it was getting out of the gunny sack.

—— SWIMMING POOL ——

A crowd of people with water in it.

—— SYMPATHY ——

Sympathy is what one girl offers another in exchange for details.

—— SYNONYM ——

"Johnny, what is a synonym?"
"A synonym is a word you use when you can't spell the word you want."

—— SYNTAX ——

A new tax that should bring in all the money the government needs.

T

——— TACT ———

At a reception in Washington, a young man was asked by a widow to guess her age. "You must have some idea," she said, as he hesitated.

"I have several ideas," he admitted, with a smile. "The trouble is that I hesitate whether to make it ten years younger on account of your looks or ten years older on account of your intelligence."

♦

Tact is the ability to make your guests feel at home when you wish they were.

♦

What you don't say when you're angry.

♦

What you think but don't say.

♦

Thinking all you say without saying all you think.

♦

The art of saying nothing when there is nothing to say.

——— TAILOR ———

Customer: I'm sorry, but I won't be able to pay for this suit for two months.

Tailor: Oh, that's all right.

Customer: When will it be ready?

Tailor: In two months.

——— TAILOR SHOP ———

Last of the big-time menders.

—— TAKING IT EASY ——

Nothing reminds a woman of all that needs to be done around the house like a husband who is taking it easy.

—— TALK ——

Talk is cheap because the supply is greater than the demand.

"You say there was something in her speech that sounded strange. What was that?"
"A pause."

"I don't think success has gone to her head."
"No, just to her mouth."

Son: Why do the ladies always bring their knitting when they come to visit?
Father: So they will have something to think about while they talk.

———◆———

Trying to get a word in edgewise with some people is like trying to thread a sewing machine with the motor running.

———◆———

There's nothing wrong with having nothing to say—unless you insist on saying it.

———◆———

Fred: What's more clever than speaking several languages?
Sally: Keeping your mouth shut in one.

———◆———

Clara: My pastor is so good he can talk on any subject for an hour.
Sarah: That's nothing! My pastor can talk for an hour without a subject!

─── **TALKER** ───

A great talker may be no fool, but he is one that relies on him.

───◆───

Two great talkers will not travel far together.

─── **TALKING** ───

Long talking begets short hearing.

───◆───

The other day I was driving under the influence of my husband. He talks and talks. He gets two thousand words to the gallon.

───◆───

Son: What do you call it when one is talking?
Dad: Monologue.
Son: What do you call it when two women are talking?
Dad: Cat-alogue.

───◆───

Young Tom told his father that when he grew up, he wanted to drive a big army tank.

"Well, son," said his dad, "if that's what you want to do, I certainly won't stand in your way."

─── **TANTRUM** ───

Teenager: Can I call you back in around 15 minutes? I can't talk now; I'm in the middle of a tantrum.

───◆───

The orchestra leader kept throwing tempo tantrums.

─── **TAP** ───

Q: What is the best cure for water on the brain?
A: A tap on the head.

272

In explaining her tardiness to English class, a high school junior stated demurely, "The boy who was following me walked very slowly."

Some tasks have to be put off dozens of times before they will completely slip your mind.

A place with a lot of cowboys.

The income tax has made more liars out of the American people than gold has.

—*Will Rogers*

What is the difference between a taxidermist and a tax collector? The taxidermist takes only your skin.

—*Mark Twain*

The tax collector must love poor people—he's creating so many of them.

Nothing makes time pass more quickly than an income tax installment every three months.

"What would be a good way to raise revenue and still benefit the people?"
"Tax every political speech."

The reward for saving your money is being able to pay your taxes without borrowing.

An American can consider himself a success when it costs him more to support the government than to support a wife and children.

———◆———

It's awfully difficult to believe that only about 200 years ago we went to war to avoid taxation.

———◆———

I'm gonna put all my money into taxes. They're sure to go up.

———◆———

Income tax song: "Everything I Have Is Yours."

———◆———

April 15 should be called Taxgiving day.

———◆———

Taxpayer: I always pay my income taxes all at once.
Tax collector: But you are allowed to pay them in quarterly installments.
Taxpayer: I know it, but my heart can't stand it four times a year.

———◆———

Joe: Did you know that some of the presidents gave their salaries back to the government?
Moe: That idea really caught on. Now they have us all doing it.

———◆———

A man walked into the tax collector's office and sat down and smiled at everyone.
"May I help you?" said the clerk in charge.
"No," said the man. "I just wanted to meet the people I have been working for all these years."

———◆———

Tax collector: Why don't you pay your taxes with a smile?
Taxpayer: I'd love to but you insist on money!

———◆———

Conscience is that still small voice that tells you the Internal Revenue Service might check your return.

A distraught taxpayer handed in his income tax return with his check to the Internal Revenue agent.

"Boy," complained the man, "the boys in Washington are a heartless bunch. They sure cleaned out my bank account!"

"Cheer up," consoled the revenue man. "Remember what Benjamin Franklin said: 'Nothing is certain but death and taxes.' "

"Yeah," said the taxpayer. "I only wish they came in that order."

I'm a little worried about this year's income tax. I think I made it out wrong. I've got 42 cents left.

I don't know if we'll ever get a cure for poverty, but the way taxes and prices are going up, we've got a sure cure for wealth!

You should file your income tax, not chisel it.

——— TAXI ———

A man had ridden three miles in a taxi when he suddenly realized he had left his wallet at home. He leaned forward and told the driver: "Stop at the drugstore for a minute. I want to get some matches so I can look for a $20 bill I've lost back here."

When he came out of the drugstore, the taxi had disappeared.

——— TAXIDERMIST ———

Man who knows his stuff.

——— TAXPAYERS ———

People who don't have to take a civil service test to work for the government.

——— TEA ———

Three Englishmen stopped at a restaurant for a spot of tea. The waiter appeared with pad and pencil.

"I'll have a glass of weak tea," ordered the first.

"I'll have tea, too," said the second, "but very strong with two pieces of lemon."

"Tea for me, too, please," said the third. "But be sure the glass is absolutely clean."

In a short time the waiter was back with the order. "All right," he asked. "Which one gets the clean glass?"

——— TEA BAG ———

Kathy: My husband has dreadful table manners. He always holds his little pinky finger out when he holds a cup of tea.

Julie: In society it is considered polite to hold out your little pinky when drinking tea.

Kathy: With the tea bag hanging from it?

——— TEACHER ———

Teacher: What do you call a person who keeps on talking when people are no longer interested?

Student: A teacher.

———— ◆ ————

Not only is he the worst-behaved child in my class, but he also has a perfect attendance record!

——— TEAMWORK ———

Panting and perspiring, two men on a tandem bicycle at last got to the top of a steep hill.

"That was a stiff climb," said the first man.

"It certainly was," replied the second man. "And if I hadn't kept the brake on, we would have slid down backward."

——— TEARS ———

The world's greatest waterpower—women's tears.

——— TEENAGER ———

Father: Operator, I have been trying to reach my home for an hour and the line is busy. Could you please cut in on the line?
Operator: We can only cut in when it is a case of life or death.
Father: Well, I can tell you this much—if it's my teenage daughter on the phone, there's going to be a murder!

The best substitute for experience is being 16.

God is very providential. He gives us 12 years to develop a love for our children before turning them into teenagers.

Father to teenage son: Do you mind if I use the car tonight? I'm taking your mother out and I would like to impress her.

I never met a teenager who didn't get hungry from eating.

My teenager finally found his stereo headphones that he's been looking for all winter. He got a haircut.

Today's teenagers are on the phone so much, they don't even start talking until they hear a dial tone.

Girl answering telephone: Judy isn't in just now. This is her 111-pound, five-foot-three, blonde, blue-eyed sister.

Homework is something teenagers do between phone calls.

The telephone is a remarkable invention. It allows teenagers to go steady without being able to hold hands.

———————◆———————

Why can't life's problems hit us when we're 18 and know everything?

———————◆———————

My teenage daughter is at the stage where she's all skin and phones.

———————◆———————

If you want to recapture your youth, cut off his allowance.

———————◆———————

"Here is something that will make you feel really grown up," a father said to his daughter. "Your own phone bill."

———————◆———————

Teenagers are people you pay an allowance to for the privilege of living with them.

———————◆———————

A babysitter is a teenager who gets $2 an hour to eat $10 worth of food.

———————◆———————

Teenagers complain there's nothing to do, then stay out all night doing it.

———————◆———————

"What did your teenage daughter do all summer?"
"Her hair and her nails!"

———————◆———————

Oh, to be only half as wonderful as my child thought I was. And only half as stupid as my teenager thinks I am.

———————◆———————

Father to teenage daughter: "I want you home by 11:00."
"But Daddy, I'm no longer a child."
"I know, that's why I want you home by 11:00."

———————◆———————

A teenager is someone who can eat his heart out without affecting his appetite.

———◆———

Dialogue between teenager and parent:
"I'm off to the party."
"Well, have a good time."
"Look, Pop, don't tell me what to do."

———◆———

If you live in a house full of teenagers, it is not necessary to ask for whom the bell tolls. It's not for you.

———◆———

Dad: Did you use the car last night?
Son: Yes, Dad. I took some of the boys for a ride.
Dad: Well, tell them I found two of their lipsticks.

———◆———

About the time the bedtime stories are televised, many youngsters are going out for the evening.

——— TELEPATHY ———

A disease that you get from talking on the phone too much.

——— TELEPHONE ———

Mother: Is this telephone call really necessary?
Daughter: How can I tell till I've made it?

———◆———

Did you hear about the teenager who plans to run away from home just as soon as she gets a long enough telephone extension cord?

——— TEMPERAMENTAL ———

Ninety percent temper; ten percent mental.

279

——— TEMPT ———

"Keep your feet where they belong."
"Don't tempt me."

——— TEMPTATION ———

A driver tucked this note under the windshield wiper of his automobile: "I've circled the block for 20 minutes. I'm late for an appointment and if I don't park here I'll lose my job. 'Forgive us our trespasses.' "

When he came back he found a parking ticket and this note: "I've circled the block for 20 years and if I don't give you a ticket, I'll lose my job. 'Lead us not into temptation.' "

——— TEN COMMANDMENTS ———

Husband: Wouldn't it be fun to go to the Holy Land and stand on Mount Sinai and shout out the Ten Commandments?
Wife: It would be better if you stayed home and kept them.

——— TENANT ———

Tenant: I want you to get rid of the mice in my apartment.
Landlord: Not me . . . if they don't like it here, let them move.

——— TENDER ———

Q: Why did the locomotive refuse to sit?
A: Because it had a tender behind.

——— TENNIS ———

A very overweight man was discussing his tennis game with a friend.

"My brain barks out commands to my body: Run forward speedily! Start right away! Hit the ball gracefully over the net! Get back into position!"

"Then what happens?" asked the friend.

"And then, my body says, 'Who, me?' "

——— TENURE ———

The number following nineure.

——— TERMITES ———

Dan: What do termites do when they want to relax?
Stan: They take a coffee-table break.

——— TEST ———

Student: I don't think I deserve a zero on this test!
Teacher: Neither do I, but it's the lowest mark I can give you.

——— TEXAN ———

Did you hear about the Texan who was trying to make a phone call?
"Operator, how much does it cost to call New York?"
"Three dollars and seventy-five cents," replied the operator.
"Why, I can call hell and back for that much," said the Texan.
"Yes, sir," said the operator, "that's a local call!"

An ardent fisherman from Dallas made a trip to Bull Shoals Lake in Arkansas. After pulling in a 6½ pound largemouth bass, the Texan boasted to his native guide, "Why, heck, in Texas we use that size for bait."
The Arkansan smiled, nodded appreciatively—and dropped the fish back into the lake.

On a visit to tiny Israel, a Texan boasted, "Why, in Texas you can get on a train, ride for days, and still be in Texas."
His Israeli companion nodded sympathetically.
"We have the same trouble with our trains," he said.

When you find a pair of boots on the floor with a big ten-gallon hat on top of them, what have you got? A Texan with all the hot air let out of him.

——— TEXT ———

That which ministers preach from, and often vary far from.

——— THANK YOU ———

Son: Dad, guess what? I can say please and thank you in Spanish.
Father: That's more than you ever learned to say in English.

——— THE END ———

A man was walking down some stairs when all of a sudden he slipped. In the process a stout lady toppled against him and they ended up on the bottom step with the lady sitting in the man's lap. The man tapped the lady on the shoulder. "I'm sorry, lady," he rasped, "but this is as far as I go."

——— THEOLOGY ———

Division has done more to hide Christ from the view of all men than all the infidelity that has ever been spoken.

——— THIEF ———

A person who has the habit of finding things before the owner loses them.

——— THINK ———

The less a man thinks, the more he talks.

———◆———

The reason some of us find it difficult to think is that we haven't had any previous experience.

———◆———

There are two kinds of thinkers in the world. Those who think they can and those who think they can't . . . and they're both right.

———◆———

The person who thinks before he speaks is silent most of the time.

———◆———

My wife and I always think exactly alike, only she usually has the first think.

——— THIRSTY ———

Pete: I had an operation and the doctor left a sponge in me.
Bill: Got any pain?
Pete: No, but boy do I get thirsty.

——— THOR ———

The thunder god went for a ride
Upon his favorite filly.
"I'm Thor," he cried.
The horse replied,
"You forgot your thaddle, thilly."

——— THOUGHT ———

The main reason that some of us get lost in thought is that it is such unfamiliar territory.

——— THOUGHTFUL ———

A very tight man was looking for a gift for a friend. Everything was too expensive except for a glass vase that had been broken, which he could purchase for almost nothing. He asked the store to send it, hoping his friend would think it had been broken in transit.

In due time, he received an acknowledgement. "Thanks for the vase," it read. "It was so thoughtful of you to wrap each piece separately."

——— THREE FEET ———

"I've got a brother with three feet."
"What do you mean?"
"Well, my mother got a letter from my brother and he said, 'You would hardly know me—I've grown three feet.'"

——— THUMB ———

A modern means of transportation.

THUMB-SUCKER

A little boy was in the habit of sucking his thumb all the time. His mother tried everything to break him of the habit. Finally, one day she pointed to a fat man with a very large stomach and said that the man had grown his big stomach because he did not stop sucking his thumb.

The next day the child was with his mother in a supermarket, and he kept staring at a woman with a stomach that was obviously not at all normal. In fact the woman was very pregnant.

Finally the annoyed woman said to the child, "Stop staring at me like that. You don't know who I am."

"No," said the boy, "but I know what you have been doing."

TIBET

A housewife in Tibet smelled something burning in the kitchen, rushed in, and saw smoke pouring out of the oven. "Oh, my baking yak!" she said.

TIGER

He who rides a tiger is afraid to dismount.

A tiger was walking through the jungle one day and saw two men relaxing under a tree. One was reading a newspaper, and the other was working feverishly on a manual typewriter.

The tiger leapt on the man with the newspaper, and ate him up. The tiger did not bother the other man at all. That's because any predator knows that readers digest but writers cramp.

TIGHT

He's so tight he keeps five dollar bills folded so long that Lincoln gets ingrown whiskers.

TIME

The shortest known unit is the time between the change of the traffic light and the honk from the kook behind you.

Pilot: Control tower, what time is it?

Control tower: What airline is this?

Pilot: What difference does that make?

Control tower: If it is United Airlines, it is 6:00 P.M.; if it is TWA, it is 1800 hours; if it is Ozark, the big hand is on the. . . .

——— TIP ———

Customer: I am sorry, waiter, but I only have enough money for the bill. I have nothing left for a tip.

Waiter: Let me add up that bill again, sir.

I hate to always eat and run, but the way I tip, it's the only safe procedure.

——— TIRED ———

"I think I labor too hard sometimes. I'm a farmer and I work 15 hours a day, seven days a week."

"What do you grow?"

"Very tired."

I just found out why I feel tired all the time.

We made a survey and found I was doing more than my share of the world's work.

The population of the country is 160 million, but there are 62 million over 60 years of age. That leaves 98 million to do the work. People under 21 years of age total 54 million which leaves 44 million to do the work.

Then there are 21 million who are employed by the government and that leaves 23 million to do the work. Ten million are in the Armed Forces. That leaves 13 million to do the work. Now deduct 12,800,000—the number in state and city offices—and that leaves 200,000 to do the work. There are 126,000 in hospitals, insane asylums, and so forth, and that leaves 74,000 people to do the work.

But 62,000 of these refuse to work, so that leaves 12,000 to do the work. Now it may interest you to know that there are 11,998 people in jail, so that leaves just *two* people to do all the work and that's *you* and *me*, and I'm getting tired of doing everything myself.

——— **TITANIC** ———

Q: What do you get if you cross the Atlantic on the *Titanic*?
A: Very wet.

——— **TITLE** ———

In an age when everyone seems to be playing the name game of glorifying job titles, the man in charge of the meat department at a store in Wichita Falls, Texas, deserves a round of applause. On his weekly time card he describes his position as "Meat Head."

——— **TOE** ———

Nothing is harder to do secretly than stub your toe.

——— **TOLERANCE** ———

Tolerance is the uncomfortable suspicion that the person you're talking to may be right.

———◆———

Tolerance is the art of putting up with people who aren't perfect like you.

——— **TOM** ———

"My name is T-t-t-t-tom."
"I'll call you Tom for short."

——— **TONGUE** ———

The tongue is a wet place, and easily slips.

———◆———

A sharp tongue is the only edge tool that grows keener with constant use.

—Washington Irving

———◆———

Don't let your tongue say what your head may pay for.

He who has sharp tongue usually cuts his own throat.

A loose tongue often gets its owner into a tight place.

When you are in deep water, it's a good idea to keep your mouth shut.

——— TONGUE SANDWICH ———

"I seem to be a rose between two thorns," remarked Miss Prettygirl as she seated herself between two men at a football game.
"I'd say it's more like a tongue sandwich," retorted one of the men.

——— TONGUE TWISTERS ———

Six shy soldiers sold seven salted salmons.

Two tree toads tied together tried to trot to town twice.

Bisquick, kiss quick.

Six slippery, sliding snakes.

Fat friars fanning flames.

Jack Jackson Zachary.

The judge judged Judd.

Three terrible thieves.

Tim, the thin twin tinsmith.

Strange strategic statistics.

Toy boat.

Six slick saplings.

Six gray geese on green grass grazing.

Copper coffee pot.

Ziggy Jazinski.

Bill had a billboard. Bill also had a board bill. The board bill bored Bill, so that Bill sold the billboard to pay his board bill. So after Bill sold his billboard to pay his board bill, the board bill no longer bored Bill.

If a Hottentot tutor taught a Hottentot tot
To talk 'ere the tot could totter,
Ought the Hottentot be taught to say aught?
Or, what ought to be taught her?
If to hoot and toot a Hottentot tot
Be taught by a Hottentot tutor,
Should the tutor get hot if the Hottentot tot
Hoots and toots at the Hottentot tutor?

——— **TOO LONG** ———

The master of ceremonies got up to close the meeting after a very long-winded speaker. "You have just been listening to that famous Chinese statesman, On Too Long."

——— **TOOTHACHE** ———

There was never yet a philosopher
That could endure the toothache patiently.

—*Shakespeare*

——— **TOOTHPASTE** ———

Did you hear about the new toothpaste that has shoe polish in it? It is for people who put their feet in their mouths.

———◆———

Did you hear about the new toothpaste with food particles in it? It is for people who can't eat before brushing.

——— **TOTAL** ———

The sum total of our national debt is some total.

———◆———

Dad: When I was in the Army, Harvey, we had a drill sergeant who was so tough he used to wear a wig.
Harvey: What's so tough about that?
Dad: He used to keep it on with a nail.

——— **TOUGH MEAT** ———

The manager of a restaurant called his waitresses together. "Girls," he began, "I want you all to look your best today. Greet every customer with a smile, put on a little extra makeup, and see to it that your hair is in place."

"What's up?" asked one of the girls. "Bunch of big shots coming in today?"

"No, the meat's tough today."

---- **TOUGH NEIGHBORHOOD** ----

My neighborhood was so bad that even the police station had a peephole in the front door.

---◆---

My neighborhood was so bad that our school newspaper had an obituary page.

---◆---

I don't want to say that I live in a bad neighborhood, but the criminals are so tough that they attack people with chewed-off shotguns.

---- **TOURIST** ----

A person who travels 1,000 miles to get a picture of himself standing by his car.

---- **TOWER OF BABEL** ----

Q: What was the Tower of Babel?
A: Wasn't that where Solomon kept his wives?

---- **TOWN** ----

Native: What do you think of our little town?
Traveler: It's the first cemetery I've ever seen with traffic lights.

---- **TRAFFIC COURT** ----

Sign at a traffic court: **"Don't complain, think of the summonses you have deserved but didn't get!"**

---- **TRAFFIC FINE** ----

"What am I supposed to do with this?" grumbled the motorist as the police clerk handed him a receipt for his traffic fine.
"Keep it," the clerk advised. "When you get four of these, you get a bicycle."

---- **TRAFFIC JAM** ----

A substance for spreading on streets at five o'clock.

──── TRAFFIC LIGHT ────

A little green light that changes to red as your car approaches.

──── TRAIN ────

Porter: Did you miss that train, sir?
Man: No! I didn't like the looks of it, so I chased it out of the station.

──── TRAIN OF THOUGHT ────

"Be quiet. You're interrupting my train of thought."
"Let me know when it comes to a station."

──── TRAIN RIDE ────

A big executive boarded a New York to Chicago train. He explained to the porter: "I'm a heavy sleeper and I want you to be sure to wake me at 3:00 A.M. to get off in Buffalo. Regardless of what I say, get me up, for I have some important business there."

The next morning he awakened in Chicago. He found the porter and really poured it on with abusive language.

After he had left, someone said, "How could you stand there and take that kind of talk from that man?"

The porter said: "That ain't nothing. You should have heard what the man said that I put off in Buffalo."

──── TRAMP ────

Lady: You should be ashamed to ask for handouts in this neighborhood.
Tramp: Don't apologize for it, ma'am. I've seen worse.

──── TRANQUILIZER ────

Lately he's tried tranquilizers to reduce. He hasn't lost any weight, but he has stopped worrying about being beefy and paunchy.

──── TRAPEZE ARTIST ────

A guy who gets the hang of things.

——— TRAVELING SALESMAN ———

A traveling salesman was held up in the West by a storm and flood. He wired his office in New York: **"Delayed by storm. Send instructions."** His boss wired back: **"Commence vacation immediately."**

——— TREE ———

Something that will stand in the same place for 60 years and then suddenly jump in front of a car.

——— TRICKLE ———

Teacher: What does trickle mean?
Student one: To run slowly.
Teacher: Good. And what does anecdote mean?
Student two: It's a short, funny tale.
Teacher: Well done. Now, give me a sentence with both of those words in it.
Student three: Our dog trickled down the street wagging her anecdote.

——— TRICYCLE ———

A tot rod.

——— TRIUMPH ———

Triumph is just "umph" added to "try."

——— TROJAN HORSE ———

A phony pony.

——— TROUBLE ———

A few years ago a friend was in trouble and I helped him out. "I won't forget you," he vowed. And he didn't. He's in trouble again and just called me.

———◆———

Professor: Name a product in which the supply always exceeds the demand.

Student: Trouble.

──────── **TROUBLES** ────────

So you think you have troubles! When I got to the building, I found that the hurricane had knocked some bricks off the top. So I rigged up a beam with a pulley at the top of the building and hoisted up a couple of barrels full of bricks. When I had fixed the building, there were a lot of bricks left over. Then I went to the bottom of the building and cast off the line. Unfortunately, the barrel of bricks was heavier than I was, and before I knew what was happening, the barrel started down, jerking me off the ground.

I decided to hang on and halfway up I met the barrel coming down and received a hard blow on the shoulder. I then continued to the top, banging my head against the beam and getting my fingers jammed in the pulley. When the barrel hit the ground it burst its bottom, allowing all the bricks to spill out.

I was now heavier than the barrel and so started down again at high speed. Halfway down I met the barrel coming up and received more injuries to my shins.

When I hit the ground, I landed on the bricks, getting several painful cuts. At this point I must have lost my presence of mind because I let go the line. The barrel came down, giving me another heavy blow on the head and putting me in the hospital.

I respectfully request sick leave.

───────◆───────

Remember this before you burden other people with your troubles. Half of them aren't the least bit interested, and the rest are delighted that you're getting what they think is coming to you.

──────── **TRUCK DRIVING** ────────

Two truck drivers applied for a job. One said, "I'm Pete and this is my partner, Mike. When I drive at night, he sleeps."

The man said, "All right, I'll give you an oral test. It's three o'clock in the morning. You're on a little bridge and your truck is loaded with nitroglycerin. All of a sudden a truck comes toward you at about 80 miles per hour. What's the first thing you do?"

"I wake up my partner Mike—he never saw a wreck like this before."

——— TRUMPET ———

A man mentioned to his landlord about the tenants in the apartment over his. "Many a night they stamp on the floor and shout till midnight."

When the landlord asked if it bothered him, he replied, "Not really, for I usually stay up and practice my trumpet till about that time most every night anyway."

——— TRUST ———

In God we trust—all others pay cash.

♦

I would trust other people more if I knew myself less.

♦

Judge: How could you swindle these good people who trusted you so?
Con man: Your Honor, you can't swindle people who don't trust you.

——— TRUTH ———

Wife to husband: I don't mind your little half-truths, but you keep telling me the wrong half.

♦

Pompous politician: I was never whipped but once in my life, and that was for telling the truth.
Heckler: It sure cured you, didn't it?

——— TRUTHFULNESS ———

There's no limit to the height a man can attain by remaining on the level.

——— TRY AGAIN ———

Off the coast of Oregon, a ship collided with a fishing boat in heavy fog. No real damage was done, but as the offending ship tried to back off, it banged into the boat again. The captain was afraid he might have done some damage with the second blow. "Can you stay afloat?" he shouted through a megaphone to the floundering victim.

"I guess so," called back the skipper of the boat. "Do you want to try again?"

——— TRYING ———

Mother: Johnny, this isn't a very good report card. Are you trying?
Johnny: Yes, my teacher said I am the most trying boy in the class.

———◆———

Mother, having finally tucked a small boy into bed after an unusually trying day: Well, I've worked today from son-up to son-down!

——— TULIPS ———

The standard number of lips assigned to each person.

——— TURKEY ———

"I'd let those doctors experiment on me for the sake of science. I'm not afraid. I've gone through the war. Why once I even volunteered to let them put a new heart into my chest if one was available which suited my character."
"What was the matter? Couldn't they find a chicken big enough?"

——— TURN OFF THE GAS ———

Right in the middle of the service, and just before the sermon, one of the congregation remembered she had forgotten to turn off the gas under the roast. Hurriedly she scribbled a note and passed it to the usher to give to her husband. Unfortunately, the usher misunderstood her intention and took it to the pulpit. Unfolding the note, the preacher read aloud, "Please go home and turn off the gas."

——— TURN SIGN ———

A lady made a right-hand turn from the left-hand lane and promptly collided with another car. The driver got out and accosted her.
"Lady, why didn't you signal?"
"Mister, I always turn here."

——— TURTLE ———

A reptile who lives in a mobile home.

––––––– **TV DINNER** –––––––

"One more TV dinner and you'll be looking for a new sponsor."

–––––◆–––––

I know a woman who has cooked so many TV dinners she thinks she's in show business.

––––––– **TWENTY-THIRD PSALM** –––––––

A small boy was reciting Psalm 23 for his parents . . . "Surely good Mrs. Murphy shall follow me all the days of my life."

––––––– **TWIN BELLIES** –––––––

He has T.B.—Twin Bellies.

––––––– **TWINS** –––––––

Instant replay.

–––––◆–––––

Insult added to injury.

–––––◆–––––

Melba: I guess your husband was pleased when he found himself the father of twin boys.
Pam: Was he! He went around grinning from heir to heir.

–––––◆–––––

Jill: Are you an only child?
Bill: No, used to be twins.
Jill: When were you twins?
Bill: My father has a picture of me when I was two.

––––––– **TWO-FACED** –––––––

Once during a debate Lincoln was accused by Douglas of being two-faced. Without hesitation, Lincoln calmly replied, "I leave it to my audience . . . if I had two faces, would I be wearing this one?"

——— TYPEWRITER ———

"I operate a typewriter by the biblical system."
"What is that?"
"The 'seek-and-ye-shall-find' system."

——— TYPING ———

"Miss Hatfield, I was just reading over this letter you did. Your typing is really improving. I see there are only seven mistakes here."
"Thank you, sir."
"Now, let's take a look at the second line."

——— UGLY AND OLD ———

Wife: Are you positive you'll love me after I get ugly and old?
Husband: Who says I don't?

——— UGLY FAT ———

His wife got rid of 235 pounds of ugly fat—she divorced him.

——— ULCER ———

An ulcer is what you get mountain-climbing over molehills.

——— UMBRELLA ———

The man of the house finally took all the disabled umbrellas to the repairer's. Two days later, on his way to his office, he got up to leave the streetcar and absentmindedly laid hold of the umbrella belonging to a woman beside him. The woman cried, "Stop, thief!" rescued her umbrella, and covered the man with shame and confusion.

The same day, he stopped at the repairer's and received all eight of his umbrellas duly repaired. As he entered a streetcar, with the unwrapped umbrellas tucked under his arm, he was horrified to behold glaring at him the lady of his morning adventure. Her voice came to him charged with withering scorn: "Huh! Had a good day, didn't you!"

——— UMPIRE ———

Wife: John, what becomes of a ball player when his eyesight starts to fail?
John: They make an umpire of him.

——— UNABATED ———

A mousetrap without any cheese or a fishhook without a worm.

——— UNABRIDGED ———

A river you have to wade across.

——— UNAWARE ———

Q: What is the meaning of the word "unaware"?
A: Unaware is what you put on first and take off last.

——— UNBALANCED ———

They say that one in every four Americans is unbalanced. Think of your three closest friends. If they seem okay, then you're in trouble.

——— UNCLE SAM ———

The one who wears a tall hat so he can pass it around.

——— UNDERTAKER ———

"Do you believe in the survival of the fittest?"
"I don't believe in the survival of anybody. I am the undertaker."

———◆———

"I just found out your uncle's an undertaker. I thought you told me he was a doctor."

"Nope, I just said he followed the medical profession."

Pat: I never have any trouble with backseat drivers. I never hear a word from behind.

Mike: What do you drive?

Pat: A hearse.

——— **UNDERWEAR** ———

Something that creeps up on you.

——— **UNION** ———

Man filling out an application for union membership: "Does this union have any death benefits?"

"Sure does," replied the union representative. "When you die you don't have to pay any more dues."

Unions are getting such a bad name, it's no wonder they're called Brother Hoods.

——— **UNISON** ———

An only male child.

——— **UNITED STATES** ———

A Russian was about to be sentenced to Siberia and said to his captors, "If the United States is such a terrible place, why not send me there instead?"

——— **UNIVERSITY** ———

Universities are full of knowledge; the freshmen bring a little in and the seniors take none away, and knowledge accumulates.

An institution for the postponement of experience.

——— UNKEMPT ———

A guy goes to the doctor and the doctor says, "You have the dirtiest, most unkempt, uncivilized body I have ever seen." The patient says, "That's funny, that's what the other doctor told me yesterday." "Then," asks the doctor, "why did you come to see me?" The patient answers, "I wanted a second opinion."

——— UNLUCKY ———

Kenny: I think we had better get going Friday.
Lenny: Not Friday. That's an unlucky day.
Kenny: I was born on Friday, and I don't think it's unlucky.
Lenny: Yeah, but what do your parents think?

——— UNTOLD WEALTH ———

That which does not appear on the income tax returns.

——— UNTOUCHABLES ———

People as broke as we are.

——— UPPER CRUST ———

A lot of crumbs held together by dough.

——— VACATION ———

A period of travel and relaxation when you take twice the clothes and half the money you need.

No man needs a vacation so much as the man who has just had one.

A vacation resort is where you go when you are worn out and where you come back from a complete wreck.

A vacation resort is where you go when you are worn out and where you come back from a complete wreck.

The bigger the summer vacation the harder the fall.

Husband to wife: Well, in a way it's a two-week vacation . . . I take a week and then the boss takes a week.

Jack: You didn't take a vacation this year, did you?
Mack: No, I thought I needed a rest.

—— VALUABLE SENSE OF HUMOR ——

One that enables a person to see instantly what isn't safe to laugh at.

—— VALUE ——

If a man empties his purse into his head, no one can take it from him.
—*Benjamin Franklin*

—— VANGUARD ——

A person who protects trucks.

—— VASE ——

Benjie: Mom, do you remember that vase you always worried I would break?
Mom: Yes, what about it?
Benjie: Your worries are over.

—— VEIL ——

A minister married a couple. The woman had on a veil and he could not see her face. After the ceremony, the man asked the minister, "How much do I owe you?"

"No charge," replied the minister.

"But I want to show my appreciation." So the man gave him fifty cents.

About that time the bride pulled off her veil, and the minister, looking at the bride, gave the man twenty-five cents change.

—— VENETIAN BLIND ——

Sign on car of a venetian-blind salesman: WATCH OUT! BLIND MAN DRIVING!

—— VENTRILOQUIST ——

A person who talks to himself for a living.

—— VERBOSITY ——

Inebriated with the exuberance of his own verbosity.

—*Benjamin Disraeli*

—— VETERINARIAN ——

A rancher asked a veterinarian for some free advice. "I have a horse that walks normally sometimes, and sometimes he limps. What shall I do?"

The veterinarian replied, "The next time he walks normally, sell him."

—— VICE PRESIDENT ——

A man who had just been promoted to vice president boasted of it so much to his wife that she finally said, "Vice presidents are a dime a dozen. Why, in the supermarket they even have a vice president of prunes!"

Furious, the husband phoned the supermarket with the expectation of refuting his wife. He asked to speak to the vice president in charge of prunes.

"Which one?" was the reply. "Packaged or bulk prunes?"

——— VICIOUS CIRCLE ———

Bad company.

——— VINEGAR ———

A Boy Scout was out trying to raise funds for his troop by collecting bottles and cans. He went to one house and asked the lady if she had any old beer bottles.

The self-righteous woman retorted, "Do I look like the kind of person who would drink beer?"

"Pardon me," apologized the Boy Scout. "Do you have any old vinegar bottles?"

——— VIRUS ———

Virus is a Latin word used by doctors to mean "your guess is as good as mine."

——— VISION ———

One may have good eyes, and see nothing.

———◆———

Don't call the world dirty because you have forgotten to clean your glasses.

——— VOICE ———

Pretty young student: Professor Boschovich, do you think I will ever be able to do anything with my voice?

Weary teacher: Well, it might come in handy in case of fire or ship-wreck.

——— VOTING ———

A man walked up to a farmer as he came out of a voting booth, "I'm from the FBI."

"What seems to be the trouble?"

"We happen to know that you accepted a bribe and sold your vote."

"That's not true. I voted for the candidate because I like him."

"Well, that's where we've got you. We have concrete evidence you accepted $50 from him."

"Well, it's plain common sense. If someone gives you $50, you're going to like him."

——— WAITER, OH, WAITER! ———

Diner: Is it customary to tip the waiter in this restaurant?
Waiter: Why...ah...yes, sir.
Diner: Then hand me a tip. I've waited almost an hour for that steak I ordered.

A waiter is one that believes that money grows on trays.

Waiter: May I help you with that soup, sir?
Sailor: What do you mean, help me? I don't need any help.
Waiter: Sorry. From the sound I thought you might wish to be dragged ashore.

Diner: Waiter, please close the window.
Waiter: Is there a draft, sir?
Diner: Yes, it's the third time my steak has blown off the plate!

Customer: I'll have some raw oysters, not too large nor too small, not too salty nor too fat. They must be cold and I want them quickly!
Waiter: Yes, sir! With or without pearls?

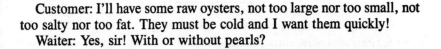

Customer: Would you mind taking the fly out of my soup?
Waiter: Do it yourself. I'm no lifeguard.

———◆———

Customer: This coffee tastes like mud.
Waiter: Well, it was ground this morning.

———◆———

Man: There's a splinter in my cottage cheese!
Waiter: What do you expect for 55 cents... the whole cottage?

———◆———

Customer: Waiter! There's a fly in my soup!
Waiter: Don't worry sir, the spider in the bread will get it.

———◆———

Customer: Waiter! There's a fly in my soup!
Waiter: Don't worry! The frog will surface any moment now.

———◆———

Customer: Waiter! There's a fly in my soup!
Waiter: Okay, here's a flyswatter.

———◆———

Customer: Waiter! There's a fly in my soup!
Waiter: Just a moment, sir—I'll get some fly spray.

———◆———

Customer: Waiter! There's a fly in my soup!
Waiter: Now there's a fly that knows good soup.

———◆———

Customer: Waiter! There's a fly in my soup!
Waiter: Go ahead and eat him; there's more where he came from.

———◆———

Customer: Waiter! There's a fly in my soup!
Waiter: Just wait until you see the main course.

———◆———

Customer: Waiter! There's a fly in my soup!
Waiter: Yes, sir, better sip it with care.

Customer: Waiter! There's a fly in my soup!
Waiter: Serves the chef right. I told him not to strain the broth through the flyswatter.

Customer: Waiter! There's a fly in my soup!
Waiter: That's funny. There were two of them when I left the kitchen.

Customer: Waiter! There's a fly in my soup!
Waiter: Half a fly would be worse.

Customer: Waiter! There's a fly in my soup!
Waiter: Shhhhhhh! Everyone will want one.

Customer: Waiter! What's this fly doing in my soup?
Waiter: Dunno, sir. It looks like the backstroke to me.

Customer: Waiter! There's a dead fly swimming in my soup!
Waiter: Nonsense, sir. Dead flies can't swim.

Customer: Waiter! There's a fly in my applesauce!
Waiter: Of course, sir. It's a fruit fly.

Customer: Waiter! What's this cockroach doing in my soup?
Waiter: We ran out of flies.

Customer: Waiter! There's a twig in my soup!
Waiter: Sorry, sir. I'll go get the branch manager.

Customer: Waiter! I can't seem to find any oysters in this oyster soup.
Waiter: Would you expect to find angels in angel food cake?

Customer: Waiter! I'm so hungry I could eat a horse!
Waiter: You certainly came to the right place.

Customer: Waiter! I'll have some kidleys.
Waiter: Do you mean kidneys, sir?
Customer: That's what I said, didle I?

Customer: Waiter! This sausage has meat at one end and bread at the other.
Waiter: Well, sir, you know how hard it is to make both ends meet these days.

Customer: No, I won't have any mushrooms, waiter. I was nearly poisoned by them last week.
Waiter: Is that so? Then I've won my bet with the cook!

Customer: Waiter! This food is terrible. I won't eat it! You had better get the manager.
Waiter: Won't do any good, mister. The manager wouldn't eat it either.

Waiter: Would you like your coffee black?
Customer: What other colors do you have?

Customer: Is your water supply healthy?
Waiter: Yes, sir. We only use well water.

———————◆———————

Customer: Waiter! There's no chicken in my chicken soup!
Waiter: There's no horse in the horseradish either.

——————— **WALKIE-TALKIE** ———————

The opposite of sittie-stillie.

——————— **WALLSTREET** ———————

"I hear that your uncle lost his wealth on Wall Street."
"Yes, that is true. He was standing on the corner and dropped his last quarter into the sewer."

——————— **WAR** ———————

Another thing against war is that it seldom if ever kills off the right people.

——————— **WARGAMES** ———————

An Army base staff that was planning war games did not want to use live ammunition. Instead they informed the men: "In place of a rifle, you go, 'Bang, bang.' In place of a knife, you go, 'Stab, stab.' In place of a hand grenade, you go, 'Lob, lob.'"

The game was in progress when one of the soldiers saw one of the enemy. He went, "Bang, bang," but nothing happened. He ran forward and went, "Stab, stab," but nothing happened. He ran back and went, "Lob, lob," but nothing happened. Finally he walked up to the enemy and said, "You are not playing fair. I went, 'Bang, bang,' and, 'Stab, stab' and, 'Lob, lob,' and you haven't fallen dead yet!"

The enemy responded, "Rumble, rumble. I'm a tank."

——————— **WARDROBE** ———————

The Law of the Wardrobe:
    Daring .... 1 year before its time
    Chic .... in its time

308

Dowdy	3 years after its time
Hideous	20 years after its time
Amusing	30 years after its time
Romantic	100 years after its time
Beautiful	150 years after its time

——— WART ———

Willy: They tell me that the way to get rid of a wart is to bury a cat. Do you think that will work?

Billy: Yes, if the wart is on the cat.

———◆———

A man walked into a doctor's office with a frog growing out of his ear.

Doctor: When did you first notice it?

Frog: It started with a wart.

——— WASHINGTON ———

Washington, D.C.: Fund city.

——— WATCH ———

First man: I got my wife a lady's wristwatch.

Second man: Did she like it?

First man: Yes, but the lady came and took it back.

——— WATERMELONS ———

Fruit and vegetable market: Best watermelons you ever seed.

———◆———

Two watermelons cannot be held under one arm.

——— WAVELENGTH ———

The distance from the scalp to the end of the curl.

——— WEAKNESS ———

Don't judge your wife too harshly for her weaknesses. If she didn't have them, chances are she would never have married you.

——— WEALTHY ———

Most of us have two chances of becoming wealthy . . . slim and none.

——— WEATHER ———

Don't knock the weather; nine-tenths of the people couldn't start a conversation if it didn't change once in a while.

———◆———

Everybody talks about the weather but nobody does anything about it.

———◆———

Probably the last completely accurate weather forecast was when God told Noah there was a 100 percent chance of precipitation.

———◆———

Postcard to Weather Bureau: "Sirs: I thought you would be interested in knowing that I have just shoveled three feet of partly cloudy from my front steps."

——— WEATHER GAUGE ———

A tourist stopped at a country gas station. While his car was being serviced, he noticed an old-timer basking in the sun with a piece of rope in his hand. The tourist walked up to the old-timer and asked, "What do you have there?"

"That's a weather gauge, sonny," the old-timer replied.

"How can you possibly tell the weather with a piece of rope?"

"It's simple," said the old-timer. "When it swings back and forth, it's windy. And when it gets wet, it's raining."

——— WEDDING ———

Did you hear about the married man who ran his wedding movies backward . . . he wanted to remember what it was like to be a free man.

———◆———

"I hear the groom ran away from the altar."
"Lost his nerve, I suppose?"
"No, found it again."

Christy: Do you think it's unlucky to postpone a wedding?
Lisa: Not if you keep on doing it.

"It's a dollar and sense wedding."
"What do you mean?"
"He hasn't a dollar and she hasn't any sense."

——— WEDDING RING ———

A one-man band.

——— WEEVILS ———

Two boll weevils came from the country to the city. One became rich and famous. The other remained the lesser of the two weevils.

——— WEIGHT ———

Some women would be more spic if they had less span.

Wife: Honey, will you still love me after I put on a few pounds?
Husband: Yes, I do.

Doctors tell us there are over 7 million people who are overweight. These, of course, are only round figures.

It's not the minutes you spend at the table that make you fat—it's the seconds.

There's a reducing salon in Wall Street for stocky brokers.

I fell asleep on a beach and burned my stomach. You should see my pot roast!

You can't reduce by talking about reducing. It's better to keep your mouth shut.

The best way to look thin without dieting is to hang around with people who are fatter than you.

Wife: I've lost quite a lot of weight.
Husband: I don't see it.
Wife: Sure you don't. I've lost it.

Wife to husband as tailor measures his waist: It's quite amazing when you realize it takes an oak tree 200 years to attain that girth!

"I just lost ten pounds!"
"Turn around; I think I found them!"

Wife to husband (who just got off the scale): Your fortune says that you are handsome, debonair, and wealthy. It even has your weight wrong!

She weighs 100 and plenty.

"You ran me down! Why couldn't you have driven around me?"
"I didn't think I had enough gas."

312

He's living way beyond his seams.

———————◆———————

He can sit around a table all by himself.

———————◆———————

My girlfriend weighs 500 pounds. She isn't fat but, boy, is she ever tall!

———————◆———————

For the past two weeks she's been doing a lot of horseback riding, and she's taken off ten pounds . . . from the horse.

——— WELFARE ———

Protester to his girlfriend: I'm on my way to pick up my unemployment check. Then I'll go over to the university office to see what's holding up this month's Federal Education Grant. Then I'll go and get this week's food stamps. Meanwhile you can go over to the Free Health Clinic and check up on your tests. I've got to drop around at the Welfare Department and demand our eligibility limit again. Then at 4:00 P.M. we'll meet at the Federal Building for another mass demonstration against this stinking, rotten establishment.

——— WELL-DEVELOPED ———

Lucy: What well-developed arms you have.
Betty: Yes, I play a lot of tennis.
Lucy: You ride horseback, too, don't you?

——— WELL-DRESSED ———

General Custer was a well-dressed man. When they found him he was wearing an Arrow shirt.

——— WHALE SANDWICH ———

Customer: Your sign says, "Any sandwich you can name." I would like a whale sandwich.
Waiter: Okay. (Disappears into kitchen and shortly returns.) I'm afraid I can't get you a whale sandwich.
Customer: Why not? Your sign says "any sandwich."
Waiter: The cook says he doesn't want to start a new whale for one lousy sandwich.

—— WHAT A TAIL ——

A man walked by a table in a hotel and noticed three men and a dog playing cards. The dog was playing with extraordinary performance.

"This is a very smart dog," the man commented.

"Not so smart," said one of the players. "Every time he gets a good hand he wags his tail."

—— WHAT DO YOU WANT? ——

A blowhard Air Force major was promoted to colonel and received a brand new office. His first morning behind the desk, an airman knocked on the door and asked to speak to him. The colonel, feeling the urge to impress the young airman, picked up his phone and said:

"Yes, General, thank you. Yes, I will pass that along to the president this afternoon. Yes, good-bye, sir."

Then, turning to the airman he barked, "And what do you want?"

"Nothing important, sir," said the airman. "I just came to install your telephone."

—— WHAT'S FUNNY? ——

Two men went to the train station with a friend. The train was late so they sat down for a cup of coffee. They talked and drank and forgot about the train. Suddenly they heard the last announcement about the departing train. They all got up and started running. They ran down the tracks as the train was pulling out of the station. Two of the men made it to the last car and the third man was just not fast enough. The third man slowed to a stop and started laughing. An onlooker went up to the laughing man and said, "What are you laughing for? You just missed your train."

"You're right," was the reply. "I did miss my train. What's funny is those two men came to see me off."

—— WHEELBARROWS ——

One day a fellow started through the gate of a large factory wheeling a wheelbarrow full of sawdust and was stopped by the guard. He told the guard he had permission to take the sawdust out of the factory.

The guard checked and found out that this was correct, and so he let the fellow go on his way. This same thing continued for many days thereafter.

Finally, a fellow worker asked the sawdust collector what he was up to. "Are you stealing all this sawdust, or what?"

"No," was the reply, "Not sawdust—I'm stealing wheelbarrows."

——— WHIM ———

The plural of whim is women.

——— WHISKERS ———

"He spilled rum on his whiskers and when lighting his cigarette his whiskers caught on fire."

"What did he do then?"

"Oh, he just fiddled with his whiskers while rum burned."

———◆———

Q: Why are there so few men with whiskers in heaven?

A: Because most men get in by a close shave.

——— WHISPER ———

Some people believe everything you tell them—especially if you whisper it.

——— WHISTLE ———

Mark: I'll bet you're one of those people who drop their work and beat it as soon as the 5:00 P.M. whistle blows.

Clark: Not me. After I quit work I usually wait about ten minutes for the whistle to blow.

——— WHITEHOUSE ———

Honorable mansion.

——— WHO PAYS THE BILL? ———

In reply to your request to send a check, I wish to inform you that the present condition of my bank account makes it almost impossible.

My shattered financial conditions are due to federal laws, corporation laws, mother-in-law, brother-in-law, sisters-in-law, and outlaws.

Through these taxes I am compelled to pay a business tax, assessment tax, head tax, school tax, income tax, casket tax, food tax, furniture tax, sales tax, and excise tax. Even my brain is taxed.

I am required to get a business license, car license, hunting license, fishing license, truck and auto license, not to mention marriage and dog license. I am also required to contribute to every society and organization which the genius of man is capable of bringing into life; to women's relief, unemployed relief, and gold digger's relief. Also to every hospital and charitable institution in the city, including the Red Cross, the Black Cross, the Purple Cross, and the Double Cross.

For my own safety, I am compelled to carry life insurance, liability insurance, burglary insurance, accident insurance, property insurance, business insurance, earthquake insurance, tornado insurance, unemployment insurance, old age insurance, and fire insurance.

My own business is so governed that it is no easy matter for me to find out who owns it. I am inspected, suspected, disrespected, rejected, dejected, and compelled until I prove an inexhaustible supply of money for every known need of the human race.

Simply because I refuse to donate something or another I am boycotted, talked about, lied about, held up, held down, and robbed until I am almost ruined. I can tell you honestly that except for a miracle that happened I could not enclose this check. The wolf that comes to my door nowadays just had pups in my kitchen. I sold them and here's the money.

Would like more business to pay more taxes.

Sincerely yours,

——— **WHO'S THERE?** ———

Knock, knock.
Who's there?
Duane.
Duane who?
Duane the tub—I'm drowning!

———◆———

Knock, knock.
Who's there?
Freeze.

Freeze who?
Freeze a jolly good fellow.

Knock, knock.
Who's there?
Olive.
Olive who?
Olive you.

Knock, knock.
Who's there?
Mayonnaise.
Mayonnaise who?
Mayonnaise have seen the glory of. . . .

Knock, knock.
Who's there?
Della.
Della who?
Della Katessen.

Knock, knock.
Who's there?
Amos.
Amos who?
A mosquito bit me.
Knock, knock.
Who's there?
Andy.
Andy who?
And he bit me again.

Knock, knock.
Who's there?

Banana.
Banana who?
Knock, knock.
Who's there?
Banana.
Banana who?
Knock, knock.
Who's there?
Orange.
Orange who?
Orange you glad I didn't say "banana" again?

———————◆———————

Knock, knock.
Who's there?
Gorilla.
Gorilla who?
Gorilla my dreams, I love you.

——— **WHOLE LOAD** ———

One Sunday a farmer went to church. When he entered he saw that he and the preacher were the only ones present. The preacher asked the farmer if he wanted him to go ahead and preach. The farmer said, "I'm not too smart, but if I went to feed my cattle and only one showed up, I'd feed him." So the minister began his sermon.

One hour passed, then two hours, then two-and-a-half hours. The preacher finally finished and came down to ask the farmer how he had liked the sermon.

The farmer answered slowly, "Well, I'm not very smart, but if I went to feed my cattle and only one showed up, I sure wouldn't feed him all the hay."

——— **WIFE** ———

Any wife with an inferiority complex can cure it by being sick in bed for a day while her husband manages the household and the children.

———————◆———————

Nobody can cook like my wife, Joan, but they came pretty close to it when I was in the Army.

———————◆———————

First husband: Last night my wife dreamed she was married to a millionaire.
Second husband: You're lucky. My wife thinks that in the daytime.

———————◆———————

My wife is just as beautiful today as when I married her 20 years ago. Of course, it takes her longer.

———————◆———————

First husband: I think my wife is getting tired of me.
Second husband: What makes you feel that way?
First husband: She keeps wrapping my lunches in road maps.

———————◆———————

If your wife wants to learn to drive, don't stand in her way.

———————◆———————

My wife is such a bad driver—she got three tickets on her written test.

———————◆———————

A husband was reading a newspaper when he came across the following advertisement:

"What we want is a night watchman who will be alert and ready for the slightest noise or indication of a burglar. Somebody who can sleep with one eye and both ears open and is not afraid to tackle anything."

Husband: Honey, I think I have found the job you are looking for.

——————— WIFE BEATING ———————

Wife: Why do you go out on the balcony when I sing? Don't you like to hear me?
Husband: I want the neighbors to see I'm not beating my wife.

———————◆———————

"Do you know that Joe beats his wife up every morning?"
"Really?"
"Yes, he gets up at 6:00 A.M. and she gets up at 7:30 A.M."

——— **WIG** ———

Now there's a wig to wear to the supermarket. It has curlers in it.

——— **WILL** ———

A dead giveaway.

———◆———

Lawyer, reading a wise old man's will to the relatives: And being of sound mind, I spent every dollar I had.

———◆———

A rich uncle died and a line in his will read as follows: I leave to my beloved nephew all the money he owes me.

———◆———

Lawyer: What's so different about your will?
Man: I want to leave everything to my wife only if she marries again. I want to be sure someone is sorry when I'm gone.

———◆———

"My uncle changed his will six times in three years."
"Aha! A fresh heir fiend!"

———◆———

Do you want to know a way to drive people crazy? Walk up to a complete stranger and say, "It's good to see you again, you lucky dog. So you finally struck it rich! Well, see you at the reading of the will."
Then rush away before that person can say anything.

——— **WIND** ———

No wind is a good wind if you don't know where the harbor is.

———◆———

A tourist traveling through western Kansas saw a man sitting by the ruins of a house that had been blown away.

"Was this your house, my friend?" he asked sympathetically.

"Yep."

"Any of your family blown away with the house?"

"Yep, wife and four kids."

"Great Scot, man, why aren't you hunting for them?"

"Well, stranger, I've been in this country quite a spell. The wind's due to change this afternoon. So I figure I might as well wait here till it brings 'em back."

—— WINDJAMMER ——

A person who spreads jelly on bread during a hurricane.

—— WINDMILL ——

The new preacher, at his first service, had a pitcher of water and a glass on the pulpit. As he preached, he drank until the pitcher of water was completely gone.

After the service someone asked an old woman of the church, "How did you like the new pastor?"

"Fine," she said, "but he's the first windmill I ever saw that was run by water."

—— WINDOW ——

"Did you hear the story about the window you couldn't see through?"

"No."

"Well, that's okay ... it's too dirty to tell anyway!"

—— WINDOW-SHOPPER ——

A store gazer.

—— WINDY ——

Two farmers were boasting about the strongest wind they'd seen.

"In California," said one, "I've seen the fiercest wind in my life. You know those giant redwood trees? Well, the wind once got so strong that it bent them right over."

"That's nothing," said the other. "Back on my farm in Iowa, we had a terrible wind one day that blew a hundred miles per hour. It was so bad, one of my hens had her back turned to the wind and she laid the same egg six times."

——— **WINE-AGE** ———

People are like wine—age sours the bad and improves the good.

——— **WISDOM** ———

The older I grow the more I distrust the familiar doctrine that age brings wisdom.

———◆———

He that gets money before he gets wit,
Will be but a short while master of it.

———◆———

It is wit to pick a lock and steal a horse, but wisdom to let them alone.

——— **WISE WIFE** ———

A wise wife is one who asks for something she knows her husband can't afford so that she can compromise on what she really wants.

——— **WISH** ———

Husband: Why do you always wish for something you haven't got?
Wife: What else could one wish for?

——— **WISHY-WASHY** ———

"I hate vague, noncommittal, middle-of-the-road people, don't you?"
"Mmmmmmm!"

——— **WIT** ———

A fellow who thinks he's a wit is usually half-right.

———◆———

Wit is the salt of the conversation, not the food.

The next best thing to being witty oneself is to be able to quote another's wit.

He who has provoked the shaft of wit, cannot complain that he smarts from it.

—*Samuel Johnson*

To be witty is not enough. One must possess sufficient wit to avoid having too much of it.

Wit is not always grinning.

Wit without wisdom is salt without meat.

All wit is not wisdom.

Wit without discretion is a sword in the hand of a fool.

Use your wit as a buckler, not as a sword.

Wit is a good servant but a bad master.

—*Talleyrand*

The wittiest man laughs least.

A fool attempting to be witty
Is an object of profoundest pity.

——— WITS ———

Bill: I have had to make a living by my wits.
Gill: Well, half a living is better than none.

——— WIVES ———

Men do not know their wives well; but wives know their husbands perfectly.

——— WOLF ———

A girl can be scared to death by a mouse or a spider, but she's often too willing to take her chances with a wolf.

A sailor has been called a wolf in ship's clothing.

——— WOMAN ———

Creature whom God made beautiful that man might love her, and unreasonable that she might love man.

Woman was created after man and has been after him ever since.

Any man who thinks he's more intelligent than his wife is married to a smart woman.

A fallen woman is a mother whose children didn't pick up their toys.

You see, dear, it is not true that woman was made from man's rib; she was really made from his funny bone.

The way to fight a woman is with your hat. Grab it and run.

—*John Barrymore*

Being a woman is a terribly difficult task since it consists principally in dealing with men.

On one issue, at least, men and women agree; they both distrust women.

Woman begins resisting man's advances and ends by blocking his retreat.

A good woman inspires a man, a brilliant woman interests him, a beautiful woman fascinates him—but a sympathetic woman gets him.

A woman without religion is as a flower without scent.

The reason women live longer than men is because paint is a great preservative.

The seven ages of a woman are baby, child, girl, young woman, young woman, young woman, and poised social leader.

Women like the simpler things of life—men.

 **WOMEN'S LIB**

Adam-smasher.

Women's libber: The time will come when women will get men's wages.

Husband in audience: So true, next payday.

———◆———

"For months," said a women's libber, "I couldn't imagine where my husband spent his evenings."

"And then what happened?" breathlessly asked her friend.

"Well," she said, "one evening I went home and there he was."

———◆———

With the Women's Lib movement coming in so strong, one cereal company had to change their advertisement to "*snap, crackle, mom.*"

———◆———

A Ms. is as good as a male.

——— WONDERFUL ———

"Has anyone ever told you how wonderful you are?

"Nope."

"Well, then, where did you get the idea?"

——— WOODEN LEG ———

Fred: There is a man outside with a wooden leg named Martin.

Jed: What is the name of his other leg?

Fred: I think it's Peg.

———◆———

Timmy: My grandfather has a wooden leg.

Jimmy: Well, my grandmother has a cedar chest.

——— WOOL ———

There was a man who owned a lot of sheep and wanted to take them over a river that was all ice, but the woman who owned the river said, "No." So he promised to marry her and that's how he pulled the wool over her ice.

326

———— WORK ————

Don't bother to boast of your work to others; the work itself has a much better voice.

———◆———

No bees, no honey;
No work; no money.

———◆———

Pursue thy work without delay,
For the short hours run fast away.

———◆———

Modern-day teenager to millionaire: "What's the first secret of your success?"
"Hard work."
"What's the second one?"

———◆———

God gives every bird its food, but does not throw it into the nest.

———◆———

Half the people like to work and the other half don't, or maybe it's the other way 'round.

———◆———

Jim: It's no disgrace to work.
Tim: That's what I tell my wife.

———◆———

Lady: Why don't you work? Hard work never killed anyone.
Bum: You're wrong, lady. I lost both of my wives that way.

———◆———

Work is the yeast that raises the dough.

———◆———

It's probably true that hard work is a tonic, but many people never get sick enough to try the remedy.

Father: Why don't you get yourself a job?
Son: Why?
Father: So you could earn some money.
Son: Why?
Father: So you could put some money in a bank account and earn interest.
Son: Why?
Father: So that when you're old you can use the money in your bank account... and you would never have to work again.
Son: I'm not working now.

Boss: Jones, how long have you been working here?
Jones: Ever since I heard you coming down the hall.

Boss: I notice you go out and get your hair cut during business hours.
Employee: My hair grows during business hours.
Boss: But it doesn't all grow during business hours.
Employee: I didn't get it all cut.

First employee: How long have you been working here?
Second employee: Ever since the day the foreman threatened to fire me.

By working faithfully eight hours a day, you may eventually get to be a boss and work 12 hours a day.

Some people are like blisters. They don't show up until the work is finished.

328

Visitor: How many people work here in your plant?
Manager: Oh, about one out of ten!

———◆———

Politician: What we need is a working majority.
Merchant: What we really need is a majority working.

———◆———

"Here's one name on the committee that I never heard of."
"Oh, that's probably the person who actually does the work."

———◆———

Boss to new employee: Most amazing; you've been with us two weeks and already you're a month behind in your work.

———◆———

A sportsman went to a hunting lodge and bagged a record number of birds, aided by a dog named Salesman. Next year he returned and asked for Salesman again. "The hound ain't no durn good now," the handler said.
"What happened!" cried the sportsman. "Was he injured?"
"No. Some fool came down here and called him 'Sales Manager' all week instead of Salesman. Now all he does is sit on his tail and bark."

———◆———

Boss: You should have been here at eight o'clock this morning.
Secretary: Why? What happened?

———◆———

Teach your son to cut his own wood. It will warm him twice.

———◆———

Boss: Have you anything to say before I fire you?
Employee: Yes. How about a raise?

———◆———

"I'm not really late, boss. I just took my coffee break before coming in."

———◆———

Employer: Why do you ask me for a raise?

Employee: Sir, I wouldn't ask you for a raise, but somehow my kids found out that other families eat three times a day.

———————◆———————

Salesman to customer: This is actually a fire sale. The boss said that if I don't make a sale, I'm fired.

———————◆———————

One unemployed man to another: What hurts was that I wasn't replaced by a whole computer—just a transistor.

———————◆———————

First girl: I lost my job because of illness and fatigue.

Second girl: That's too bad.

First girl: Yeah, my boss got sick and tired of me.

———————◆———————

Personnel man to trainee: Or if you prefer, you may elect to skip coffee breaks entirely and retire three years early.

———————◆———————

Employee: Sir, I've been with you for 27 years, and I've never before asked for a raise.

Boss: That's why you've been with me for 27 years.

———————◆———————

One employee to another employee: "And when the boss' son starts working here tomorrow he'll have no special privileges or authority. Treat him just as you would anyone else who was due to take over the whole business in a year or two."

———————◆———————

The only man who ever got all his work done by Friday was Robinson Crusoe.

———————◆———————

If lawyers are disbarred and ministers unfrocked, perhaps electricians get delighted . . . Far Eastern diplomats disoriented . . . cashiers distilled . . .

alpine climbers dismounted...piano tuners unstrung...orchestra leaders disbanded...artists' models deposed...cooks deranged...nudists redressed...office clerks defiled...mediums dispirited...dressmakers unbiased.

Work—an unpopular way of earning money.

The following announcement was placed on the bulletin board of a large company:

To all employees: Because of increased competition and a keen desire to remain in business, we find it necessary to institute a new policy. Effective immediately, we are asking that somewhere between starting and quitting time—without infringing too much on the time devoted to lunch period, coffee breaks, rest periods, storytelling, ticket-selling, golfing, auto racing, vacation planning, and rehashing of yesterday's TV programs—that each employee try to find some time that can be set aside and be known as The Work Break.

The only time people work like a horse is when the boss rides them.

First man: Why do you wear dark glasses?
Second man: Because I can't bear to see my wife work so hard.

—— WORLD ——

A big ball that revolves on its taxes.

—— WORLD'S CHAMPIONSHIP ——

"I remember my wedding day very distinctly," said the elderly gentleman. "I carried my new bride across the threshold of our little house and said, 'Honey, this is your and my little world.'"
"And I suppose you've lived happily every after?"
"We've been fighting for the world's championship ever since."

—— WORRY ——

Worry is interest paid on trouble before it is due.

———◆———

Don't tell me that worry doesn't do any good. I know better. The things I worry about don't happen.

———◆———

Worry gives a small thing a big shadow.

———◆———

The reason why worry kills more people than work is that more people worry than work.

—*Robert Frost*

———◆———

I am an old man and have known a great many troubles, but most of them never happened.

—*Mark Twain*

———◆———

To worry about tomorrow is to be unhappy today.

———◆———

To carry care to bed is to sleep with a pack on your back.

———◆———

There are two days about which nobody should ever worry, and these are yesterday and tomorrow.

———◆———

Worry grows lushly in the soil of its sorrow; it only saps today of its joy.

———◆———

We probably wouldn't worry about what people think of us if we could know how seldom they do.

The greatest fool is he who worries about what he cannot help.

"You sure look worried."
"Man, I've got so many troubles that if anything happens to me today, it'll be at least two weeks before I can worry about it."

Red: I'd give a thousand dollars to anyone who would do my worrying for me.
Ted: You're on. Where's the thousand?
Red: That's your first worry.

———◆———

Three out of four things you worry about happening don't happen; and three out of four things you don't worry about happening do. Which all goes to prove that even if you're worrying about the wrong things, you're doing just about the right amount of worrying!

——— WORSE ———

I took her for better or worse—but she's much worse than I took her for.

——— WORTH ———

It's not what you pay a man, but what he costs you that counts.

—*Will Rogers*

——— WRECKED ———

Pretty young girl to friend: Not only has Jack broken my heart and wrecked my whole life, but he has spoiled my entire evening!

——— WRINKLE ———

Show me a wrinkle, and I'll show you the nick of time.

——— WRINKLE-PROOF ———

An affidavit stating that you have wrinkles.

——— WRINKLES ———

If you would keep the wrinkles out of your face, keep sunshine in your heart.

——— WRITER ———

Writer: Have you read my latest joke book?
Friend: No, I only read for pleasure or profit.

Writer: Have you read my latest joke book?
Friend: Not yet. But I shall lose no time reading it.

Writer: Have you read my latest joke book?
Friend: No. But I have no doubt that your joke book will fill a much-needed void.

Writer: Just think ... my parents didn't want me to become a well-known author.
Friend: I guess they got their wish.

——— WRITER'S CRAMP ———

Authoritis.

——— WRONG AGAIN ———

Husband: We have been married five years and haven't agreed on a thing.
Wife: You're wrong again—it has been six years.

——— WRONG WAY ———

A policeman stopped a man driving the wrong way on a one-way street. "Didn't you see the arrow?" he demanded.
"Arrow? Honest, officer, I didn't even see the Indians."

X

──── **X-RAY** ────

Belly vision.

Y

──── **YOU ASKED FOR IT** ────

"Doctor," she said loudly, bouncing into the room, "I want you to say frankly what's wrong with me."

He surveyed her from head to foot. "Madam," he said at length, "I've just three things to tell you."

"First, your weight needs to be reduced by nearly 60 pounds.

"Second, your beauty would be improved if you used one-tenth as much rouge and lipstick.

"And, third, I'm an artist—the doctor lives on the next floor."

──── **YOU SURE TOLD THEM** ────

There was a certain energetic young preacher who had a thriving country church. He was always prodding his people to do greater things for God. He spent much time in preparation of his sermons. There was a deacon in his congregation who did little and seemed to care less. It caused the young preacher much concern. On several occasions the preacher would tell him exactly what he thought. The old deacon never caught the point. The old deacon always thought he was referring to someone else. One Sunday, the preacher made it plainer as to whom he was talking. Following the service the deacon said, "Preacher, you sure told them today."

The next sermon was still more pointed than ever. Again the deacon said, "Preacher, you sure told them today."

The next Sunday it rained so hard that no one was at the church except this one deacon. The preacher thought that he would now know about whom he was talking. The sermon went straight to the deacon who was the only one in the congregation. Following the service, the deacon walked up to the preacher and said, "Preacher, you sure told them if they had been here."

—— YOUNG PEOPLE ——

Young people are often bad because their parents did not burn their britches behind them.

Z

—— ZOO ——

A place devised for animals to study the strange habits of human beings.

Other Books by Bob Phillips

For information on how to purchase any of the above books,
contact your local bookstore or send a self-addressed stamped envelope to:

**Family Services
P.O.Box 9363
Fresno, CA 93702**